AN ANTHROPOLOGICAL TROMPE L'OEIL FOR A COMMON WORLD:
AN ESSAY ON THE ECONOMY OF KNOWLEDGE

Ethnography, Theory, Experiment

Series Editors:
Martin Holbraad, Department of Anthropology, University College London
Morten Axel Pedersen, Department of Anthropology, University of Copenhagen
Rane Willerslev, Museum of Cultural History, University of Oslo

In recent years, ethnography has been increasingly recognized as a core method for generating qualitative data within the social sciences and humanities. This series explores a more radical, methodological potential of ethnography: its role as an arena of theoretical experimentation. It includes volumes that call for a rethinking of the relationship between ethnography and theory in order to question, and experimentally transform, existing understandings of the contemporary world.

Volume 1
AN ANTHROPOLOGICAL TROMPE L'OEIL FOR A COMMON WORLD
AN ESSAY ON THE ECONOMY OF KNOWLEDGE
By Alberto Corsín Jiménez

Titles in preparation:

Figurations of the Future
Forms and Temporality of Left Radical Politics in Northern Europe
Krøijer, Stine

AN ANTHROPOLOGICAL TROMPE L'OEIL FOR A COMMON WORLD: An Essay on the Economy of Knowledge

By Alberto Corsín Jiménez

berghahn
NEW YORK · OXFORD
www.berghahnbooks.com

Published in 2013 by

Berghahn Books

www.berghahnbooks.com

© 2013 Alberto Corsín Jiménez

Library of Congress Cataloging-in-Publication Data

Corsín Jiménez, Alberto.
  An anthropological trompe l'oeil for a common world / by Alberto Corsín
Jiménez.
        p. cm. — (Ethnography, theory, experiment ; v.1)
  Includes bibliographical references.
  ISBN 978-0-85745-911-4 (hardback) — ISBN 978-0-85745-912-1 (ebook)
  1. Anthropology—Philosophy. 2. Political anthropology—Philosophy. I. Title.
  GN33.J53 2013
  301.01—dc23

                                                                        2012037870

British Library Cataloguing in Publication Data

A catalogue record for this book is available from the British Library.

ISBN 978-0-85745-911-4 (hardback)
ISBN 978-0-85745-912-1 (institutional ebook)

To my parents, María Luisa and Gerardo

Anthropologists have no need to aggrandise their own accounts; in any case, to do so runs the risk of failing to see the work that aggrandisement does in human affairs.

—Marilyn Strathern, *Shifting Contexts*

CONTENTS

ILLUSTRATIONS

Figures

PREFACE

This book has been a long time in the making. In a sense, it charts and reproduces its own subject matter: my itinerary and rambles in trying to find a form of description suitable to the topic at hand. The languages of description I have felt comfortable with over the past ten years have shifted. Sometimes gaining a deeper understanding of a problem – reading new authors, encountering new evidence – led me to drop or change my vocabulary. Sometimes I was taken aback by new theoretical developments. It was not simply that I felt I had to catch up with new authors and ideas. Rather, I remained fascinated at the ways in which 'theory' reconfigured internally as a descriptive form. So when anthropology and social theory began to work with the theoretical equipment of, say, 'networks' or 'scale' or 'ontology', I wanted to know a little bit more, not only about where these concepts came from, or what differences they allegedly made to our sociological traditions, but also about how they were organized as theoretical effects to start with. I wanted to understand how a network cleared the conceptual space for its own 'networking' effects to be seen as doing any work. This book could be said to be 'an anthropology of theory', insofar as the history of its writing is really the history of my struggle to understand how the theories I have had to live through as an academic over the past fifteen years get to do the kind of descriptive work they say they do.

Although I did not quite know it at the time, I began writing this book roughly at the time of my appointment to a university lectureship at the University of Manchester in 2003. The year I joined Manchester, the university had only just merged with the University of Manchester Institute of Science and Technology (UMIST). The merger was hailed in various contexts as a harbinger of the changes to come in UK higher education. A strategic plan was drafted that aimed to place Manchester amidst the best twenty universities in the world. Nobel Prize winners were recruited; a new campus with flagship new buildings was built; additional layers of audit paperwork were introduced. What really caught my attention, however, was the sudden appearance of a language of 'ethics', 'trust' and 'public goodness' in describing the university's institutional agenda. This was not something peculiar to Manchester. In June 2005 the Council of Industry and Higher Education (CIHE) organized a conference on 'Ethics and Higher Education' where the neo-liberalization of higher education was presented as indispensable for the fine-tuning of its moral equipment. In this spirit CIHE itself had published an 'ethical toolkit' and 'user's guide' aimed at establishing good practices and benchmarks for institutionally ethical behaviour in universities. Ethics was therefore the rubric under which a model of stakeholder management was being introduced to the university environment.

When my first sabbatical at Manchester came up in 2006, I made plans to explore the ethical turn in higher education and research by carrying out an ethnography of academic work at the Spanish National Research Council (CSIC). I was interested in the terms through which humanities and social scientists conceived of their own work as a 'public good'. I was also intrigued by the fact that most descriptions of scientific work until that point had been of laboratory science. Few ethnographic studies addressed the labour of scholarship in the humanities. And yet I had the suspicion that the 'public value' of science might take a different shape in a laboratory than in a library or archive. I carried out fieldwork at CSIC between July 2006 and August 2007, spending six months working with Biblical and Hebrew philologists, and an additional six months with historians of science.

My time at CSIC, and in particular at the History of Science department, had an enormous impact on my theoretical outlook and preoccupations. It soon became obvious to me that neither ethics, nor indeed the public value of academic labour, was of immediate concern to my fellow colleagues and informants. Of course they were keenly concerned with the craft of their labours, and of course they worried about the exigencies of proof of 'public engagement' in the humanities. But they remained highly sceptical about the terms (journal impact factors, international collaborations, research grants, etc.) in which the worth of their work was being caricatured for measurement. Their scepticism, however, was not simply a reaction to managerial encroachment or to the epistemological grossness of audit cultures. Or rather, they did in fact react to such encroachment, but they did so by doing things to 'the ethical' that I for one found utterly wondrous.

For example, while talking over CSIC's new strategic plan for inter-disciplinary research, someone would recall the colours or forms of a seventeenth-century lamina drawn by a Jesuit scholar. The question of interdisciplinarity would subtly disappear from the conversation, which then turned instead to the granularity of the lamina, its tactility, the details of its reproduction, the Jesuits' scholarship and archiving prac-tices, or the circuits of trade wherein they provisioned themselves with exotica and paraphernalia and enriched their curiosity cabinets, for ex-ample. Scholarship had forms and colours and textures and journeys, they seemed to be insinuating, that escaped the hubris of audit. Perhaps because of my ignorance of the history of science I found such disquisi-tions absolutely fascinating. But it soon occurred to me that the images and stories evoked by the historians were not simply analogies; they actually re-inscribed and modulated the forms of knowledge available to us in the present.

The historians' stories and similes and excursions did more than set up a semiotic landscape of comparison. They enabled comparison itself to be rendered visible as an epistemic form through the work of certain scopic images and trajectories. Comparison 'ascended' as the very effect of moving between epochs, scales, details, artefacts: it was the produce of zooming in and out of particulars and global accounts. I was particu-larly struck – and this book is the obvious outcome of my captivation – by the role of optics in the internal configuration of such ascensions, and in particular by the use of visual affect. My historian of science friends employed visual tactility as an epistemic engine that amazed me not so much in its historicity as in its role as an anthropological form. Certain optical effects rendered certain forms of description more effec-tive than others by making things big or small, material or immaterial, visible or invisible, significant or insignificant. There seemed to be an anthropology 'captured' in the internal self-presentations through which historians of science made sense of their academic predicament, and indeed on their subsequent judgments over matters of science policy or the politics of knowledge at large.

This book, then, could have been an ethnography of the labour of scholarship in the humanities at the turn of the twenty-first century. I failed to write such a book, however, because somewhere along the way I got trapped in the internal anthropology of theorizing as a form of description itself. That trap is this book's trompe l'oeil: an account of how science studies, the knowledge economy and ethnography perpendicularize each other as descriptive forms. Thus, although this book is nothing quite what I expected it to be when I first set out to study the rise of ethics in the university environment, I still think of it as making an argument about the contemporary political economy of knowledge.

Sections of this book have appeared in print before. Portions of Chapter 2 appeared in 2011 in 'Daribi Kinship at Perpendicular Angles: A Trompe l'Oeil Anthropology', *HAU. Journal of Ethnographic Theory* 1(1): 141–157; some passages of Chapter 4 have been reproduced from the 2008 article 'Relations and Disproportions: The Labor of Scholarship in the Knowledge Economy', *American Ethnologist* 35(2): 229–242; and sections of Chapter 5 appeared in 2010 in 'The Political Proportions of Public Knowledge', *Journal of Cultural Economy* 3(1): 69–84. I am grateful to the publishers for permission to use this material.

Despite the larger institutional changes going on at the time, or perhaps because of them, joining the immensely vibrant academic community at the University of Manchester's Social Anthropology Department in 2003 was a blessing and a life-changing windfall. Penny Harvey, Sarah Green, Peter Wade, Stef Jansen, John Gledhill, Soumhya Venkatesan, Cathrine Degnen, Dick Werbner, Rupert Cox, Ian Fairweather, Tony Simpson, Andrew Irving, Paul Henley, Sharon Macdonald, Karen Sykes and Jeanette Edwards have all shaped my habits of mind and anthropological sensibility for the better, and they showed me the possibilities of academic collegiality. Lynn Dignan was an absolutely brilliant organizer of our Roscoe-floor logistics.

On my first day at Manchester I met Rane Willerslev, who had likewise been appointed to a social anthropology lectureship that year. We got along from the very first moment and spent one too many nights at Big Hands, and I am grateful to count him as one of my best friends today. He is also, quite simply, one of the most truly original minds I have ever met. Through Rane I was lucky enough to meet a cohort of Cambridge-trained or based anthropologists whose work has been a continuous reminder of the purchase of ethnography as a source of theory: Martin Holbraad, James Leach, James Laidlaw, Rebecca Empson, Adam Reed, Matei Candea, Giovanni da Col and Morten Pedersen, as well as Morten Nielsen at Aarhus University.

I am also deeply indebted to Marilyn Strathern, who, ever since I sent her a manuscript ('The Form of the Relation, or Anthropology's Enchantment with the Algebraic Imagination') back in 2004, has been a steadfast supporter and most generous commentator on my work. The profound influence of her writings on my thinking will be evident in the pages that follow, but it is the generosity of her interlocution that has been a continuous source of inspiration.

I am also very grateful to Berghahn's two anonymous peer reviewers for the care and insight with which they read the manuscript, and for the quality of their comments and suggestions, which have greatly improved the final text. At Berghahn I would also like to thank Ann Przyzycki de Vita, Lauren Weiss and Melissa Spinelli for their advice and guidance in bringing the book to fruition. Thanks also to Jamie Taber for copyediting the book with expert care. The book's final title owes more than a little to Ann Przyzycki and Giovanni da Col's suggestions.

When I first moved to Spain to carry out fieldwork at CSIC, I could have hardly imagined that my informants would in time become my colleagues. It is indeed a measure of my profound admiration for their work that I found the prospect of joining CSIC's history of science department attractive. I do not think I will ever have the courage to think of my work as coming anywhere close to the history of science, but not a day goes by without my feeling graced and lucky to enjoy the company and erudition of Juan Pimentel, Leoncio López-Ocón, Adolfo Estalella and, most especially, Antonio Lafuente. I am also indebted to Felipe Criado, who cleared access to and endorsed my research project within the Centre of Humanities at CSIC in Madrid and supported my research there throughout my stay.

In Buenos Aires and Madrid, Pablo Katchadjian listened patiently to most of the arguments I make in the book, and in the calmness of his unparalleled wit simply encouraged me to radicalize them further. Paulo Drinot, Jelke Boesten, Jacqueline Behrend and Goran Janev may or may not recognize themselves in the text, but they should know that it is all to be found there, in the beginning, in Abbey Road. To my doctoral supervisor at Oxford, Peter Rivière, I owe my being taught the difference between ethnography, theory, and clear writing, although it is my failing that I have not yet quite resolved how to keep from mixing them up.

But really, the whole book is what it is because roughly eight years ago, my very good friend Luis Garcillán, who at the time was bartending at a nightclub, introduced me to someone who was visiting him in Manchester and asked me to take care of this friend over the weekend. Thus I met Laura. I followed her to Madrid (my interest in the history of science notwithstanding), only to be followed by her to Buenos Aires, Manchester, Sheffield and Derby, and Madrid again. Halfway through, in Buenos Aires, our beautiful son Alejo was born. Laura and Alejo are my trompe l'oeil. The world is truly a different place in their company.

I dedicate the book to my parents. I cannot think of anything quite as brilliantly baroque as supporting a son's transformation from financial economist to anthropologist. I am forever grateful.

Zoom In

What Kind of Object Is Knowledge?

When Robert Hooke in 1665 famously used his microscope to observe the detailed qualities of a fly's eye or a plant cell, he also noted how the optical mediation of lenses 'might be of very good use to convey secret *Intelligence* without any danger of *Discovery*' (Hooke 1665: 3). One could trade in state secrets, he insinuated, by exchanging miniaturized diplomatic correspondence. One could make knowledge disappear in *size* (disappear from view) and yet retain the full *scale* of its power. Knowledge could travel without leaving visible traces behind.

Hooke's wonder at the consequences of optical miniaturization captures well the impressions made on the modern consciousness by experimenting with that thing called 'knowledge', an object whose epistemic qualities (liable to aggrandizement and miniaturization) rendered it useful in politics, diplomacy or government. Hooke's insight gave birth to what may be called the *political optics of modernity*: the idea that the effects of information may leave and travel beyond its scale of representation, and that some objects of governance are therefore politically larger than others. It is this quality of knowledge that Foucault stressed when he noted that the seventeenth century marked the reorganization of governance around the rise of 'political economy as its major form of knowledge' (Foucault 2007: 108). Governmentality, in other words, is what knowledge looks like when seen through the optics of modernity.

The political optics of modernity foiled the world into a baroque aesthetic and sensibility: a political epistemology organized around notions of scale and size, the mediation of instruments and the illusions of representation, and the aristocratic governance of knowledge. The baroque polity described a world whose objects of knowledge were constantly, some would say hopelessly, resizing themselves to fit and suit a nascent global order – a world zooming in and out of its own sense of dimension, where polity, economy and society suddenly became subject to dis/proportionate description with respect to each other.

Hooke's revelation anticipated a project of baroque governance where information travelled effortlessly inside, outside and across different scales of representation: a world governed by spheres of influence invisible to modern eyes, a world shaped by the apparent intangibility of form. Thanks to instrumentation, secret, undetectable information thus was suddenly accorded global political status, and the capacity to zoom in on an infinitesimal object now signalled its capacity to zoom out into much wider territories.

Importantly, such intangible forms were rendered intelligible through particular sets of epistemological engines, including the optical work of aggrandizement and miniaturization, the oscillation and reversibility enabled by scoping in and out of objects and their representations, or indeed the imaginary purchase of scientific paraphernalia at large.

Today, zooming in and out of the world and its objects of knowledge places ontology and epistemology in a fraught relationship. What appears to be a description of an object is, on closer inspection, turned inside out into a description of epistemic awareness. Describe again, however, and we may find the epistemic reverting back into a world-constituent object. The world appears and disappears as an effect of this sizing up and down of descriptions. Sometimes *description itself* is caught up in between: a trompe l'oeil effect of its own internal organization as a descriptive form.

To the question 'What kind of object is knowledge?' then, perhaps we can essay an anthropological trompe l'oeil, whose aim would be to find novel forms of description for our contemporary political economy.

Introduction

On 12 May 2010, an exhibition titled *The Potosí Principle: How Shall We Sing the Lord's Song in a Strange Land?* opened at the Museo Nacional Centro de Arte Reina Sofía in Madrid, Spain's national museum for contemporary art, home to artworks such as Picasso's *Guernica* or Dalí's *Girl in the Window*. The exhibition was curated by international contemporary artists Alice Creischer and Andreas Siekmann, and the art and cultural critic Max Hinderer (Creischer, Hinderer and Siekmann 2010). In the words of the curators, *Potosí principle* aimed at offering 'a critical re-reading of the dynamics of global capitalism from the oblique viewpoint of the Spanish colonial empire and its imagery':

> What would happen if we substituted for Descartes' 'ego cogito' Hernán Cortés' 'ego conquiro', or Kant's concept of pure reason for what Marx termed the principle of primitive accumulation? What if, instead of starting our account of the modern age in the England of the Industrial Revolution or the France of Napoleon III, we started it in vice-royal South America? (Borja-Villel 2010: 2)

The exhibition worked as a meeting and dialogical space for two main curatorial projects that were intended to work simultaneously and cross-fertilize each other. On the one hand, Creischer, Siekmann and Hinderer had put together a number of colonial Baroque paintings belonging to the current loosely known as the Potosí School: works that emanated from the seventeenth-century silver capital at a time when, according to some accounts, the city was an art factory producing at least 200,000 paintings a year. On the other hand, the curators invited a number of international artists, variously resident in so-called contemporary centres of accumulation (Dubai, London, Moscow, Shanghai, Berlin), to produce artwork that would speak to and/or interpellate the original Potosí pieces.

The exhibition set up a number of relations between the Potosí and the contemporary artworks. Upon arriving, visitors were handed a thirty-five-page exhibition guide presenting four different itineraries around the exhibition: four ways of moving through the space, four exhibition narratives. Each route developed a language and made a visual and imaginary proposition that offered not so much an alternative imagination of modernity as a critical implosion from within. The different itineraries across and around the space 'activated' up to four different narratives – about primitive accumulation, human rights, the place and role of religion in empire, and a call to see the 'world upside down' – to make manifest and visible the inversions hidden by mainstream political economy. The pieces of contemporary art were deliberately invested with Potosí Baroque efficacy to make explicit their own creative intricacies and institutional location.

For instance, some artworks that the Bolivian and Spanish states had not agreed to loan were made present by their absence: the letters of rejection were printed and posted, or calligraphic reproductions were commissioned on translucent paper, generating fragile silhouettes of the in/visible. Other pieces demanded sudden alterations of visitors' body emplacement and viewpoint, requiring them to climb a staircase to level the perspective on a painting that had been elevated, or use binoculars to look more closely at photographs or vignettes that had deliberately been pinned high up on the walls or ceilings. Some pieces further called out other pieces from across the room, acting out a globalization effect in miniature. There were also temporal implosions: a copy of Guamán Poma de Ayala's *La primera nueva corónica y buen gobierno* (*The first new chronicle and good government*) was placed for visitors to read at the beginning of the second spatial itinerary. Literary theorists and historians have hailed this text, an illustrated chronicle of colonial government published in 1615 by an indigenous Peruvian noble as a letter to King Philip III (Adorno 2001), as an astonishing and prescient piece of postcolonial exegesis (Pratt 1994). The exhibition also effected some institutional inversions, such as a contemporary metropolitan art museum's displaying of historical ethnological collections.

Such optical tricks and playful operations with scopic regimes are well-known Baroque interventions. Baroque aesthetics was obsessed with the phantasmagorical, allegory and what Christine Buci-Glucksmann has called our 'unconscious optics'. The Baroque also articulated a deep concern for the exuberance, excess and 'deformalization' of forms: for holding or containing things within, and thus for expressing the inside/outside of bodies and emanations (Buci-Glucksmann 1994 [1984]: 48, 140).[1]

Certainly, the exhibition was exuberant in more ways than one: most visitors saw the thirty-five-page guide as 'overwhelming'. Likewise, they judged the four genealogical routes and narratives 'excessive' but at the same time 'insufficient' context: visitors left feeling overburdened with information they could not make much sense of because it was insufficiently backgrounded. As it turns out, this, too, is a baroque experience: a 'double vision' of ambiguity (too much / too little) leading to spleen. That it referred to that most adequate of neo-liberal forms, information, was surely not coincidental.

This book is about our neo-baroque political economy. *Principio Potosí* offers in this respect a useful point of entry into our subject matter: a visual and critical exploration of the forms of modern capitalism that finds a contemporary aesthetic and imaginary in the Baroque. That the vanguard of contemporary art sees in the visual and provocative language of the Baroque a vehicle for awakening and electrifying the political consciousness of liberal Euro-American subjects is certainly worthy of attention. The Baroque is here unleashed as a new space of political hope and critique: an alter to the modern, as the curators saw it. But a second noteworthy moment in this Baroque awakening is its very self-perception as critique: the Baroque is here deliberately and strategically mobilized as an organon of cultural and political shock. Carefully and creatively manufactured as shock, the neo-baroque emerges in this context as the atmospheric foil of its own source of production: the neo-baroque as political economy.

That our age is characterized by a baroque aesthetic is of course not a new claim. Walter Benjamin's whole oeuvre is very much dedicated to fleshing out the tragic and phantasmagorical drama of capitalism, as intuited in the works of Baudelaire, Nietzsche or Blanqui (Buci-Glucksmann 1994 [1984]). Gilles Deleuze went further, describing our age as indeed being characteristic of 'a new Baroque and a neo-Leibnizianism' (Deleuze 1993: 136). More recently, Bryan Turner has drawn out an analogy between modern cultural industry and the baroque culture of spectacle: 'The culture industry of modern society is ... a new version of the culture industry of the baroque in which absolutism in government and the superficialities of everyday consumption are perfectly combined to produce a passive mass audience' (Turner 1994: 25). Furthermore, to the question 'What indeed might a critical theory look like in today's informationalized, yet more than ever capitalist, world order?' Scott Lash has propounded an answer that radicalizes the notion of 'reflexive modernization' to incorporate its 'doubles': its 'unarticulated other' and 'unspoken assumptions' (Lash 1994: 110) – a superlative baroque image, if there ever was one.

A few pages ahead I will look a little more closely at what this turn to the neo-baroque consists of, borrowing in particular from recent work in Spanish and Latin American cultural and literary studies, where the neo-baroque label has been deployed most consistently (Egginton 2010; Kaup 2006; Zamora 2009). Against the background of this literature, the allusion and intuitions of *Principio Potosí* doubtless carry some seductive promise of an argument about the Baroque aftermath and contemporary legacy of Iberian imperial reason in the wider development of capitalism (see, e.g., Moreiras 2005, 2008). However, notwithstanding the cultural landscape that this literature hints at, whether we are indeed living through a neo-baroque period is not a claim I can make, let alone prove. I have no particular interest in pegging the neo-baroque label to our political contemporary. But I do think that the fact that the vocabulary of the Baroque offers a suitable toolbox for thinking through some of the manifestations of contemporary political economy is an observation worthy of attention. The baroque I am after is therefore less a cultural style, sociological template or aesthetic register than an anthropological epistemology. As the curators of *Principio Potosí* made clear, a baroque imagination offers promising points of entry for destabilizing and gaining hold over the dynamics of modern-day capitalism. A baroque epistemology can aid in the critical understanding of the present. It can help radicalize the present from within. This is what this book aims to radiograph.

In this vein, in *An Anthropological Trompe l'Oeil* I attempt to outline what a radical anthropology of our modern political economy might look like. I use the word 'radical' here with intent, in a sense that hopes to retain both its critical and historical edge (etym. *radice*, roots). For Christine Buci-Glucksmann, the intricate displacements of baroque reason afford a journey into the interiorities of modernity. If we ever hoped for effecting an 'inside-out' of modernity, it would require a familiarity with or a fidelity to the language and imagination of the Baroque (Buci-Glucksmann 1994 [1984]). Following this path, in *An Anthropological Trompe l'Oeil* I delve deep into the interiority of the neo-liberal economy in an attempt to extract its 'inside-outs'. To put it bluntly, I want to explore what happens if we place the descriptive forms of late liberalism *at perpendicular angles* within themselves – what would happen, say, if the 'public' or 'knowledge' were seen as effects of an anamorphic projection? Such radicalization of the political economy of modernity summons an anthropological project that this book aims to map out.

Today some prominent baroque themes, such as preoccupations with the effects of shifting scales, optics, or the ontological materiality of social process, have become central motifs of social and cultural theory: for example, the way in which the rise of information and communication technologies is said to have created context- and scale-free circuits of exchange, enabling information and knowledge to become 'global public goods' (Kaul, Grunberg and Stern 1999) or old political tropes to acquire new sociological and cross-cultural valence, as is the case with the 'commons' (Bardhan and Ray 2008); the mode in which 'networks' have become repositories and idioms for both social and techno-economic knowledge, thus setting in motion new experiences of 'double vision' (Law and Mol 2002; Riles 2001); or the so-called 'ontological turn' in social theory, which signals a shift towards an object-oriented ontology that grants new analytical and explanatory powers to objects and the materiality of social life (Henare, Holbraad and Wastell 2007; Latour 2005). All these phenomena resonate with the exaggerated and ambiguous rhetoric of the baroque, as well as with its obsession with the residual forms and marginal instrumentalia of knowledge. If there has ever been a time when the peripheral, the corporeal, the artefactual and the uncanny in knowledge undergirded epistemic productivity, that time was surely the Baroque.

The Neo-baroque

In a deservedly famous essay, Spanish historian José Antonio Maravall argued that seventeenth-century Baroque culture articulated the first large-scale media and propaganda industry through which political elites held an emerging urban populace in awe and wonder (Maravall 1986). Baroque society was the first media society. The first articulated expression of a theory of media was therefore produced in the context of Baroque political work, and every theory of media since has been in effect a theory about the pervasiveness and reach of baroque effects.

An aspect of the historic Baroque that Maravall insists on, and one I believe is worth keeping in sight, is the relation he draws between the political sovereignty of the landed classes and the rise of a culture of the sublime. The experience of the sublime, for Maravall, captures the historical experience of the terribleness of the instability and crisis that characterized the seventeenth century. The century of the Baroque, lest we forget, was a time of extraordinary economic crisis and ensuing political outrage and upheaval, when 'the world was turned upside down', in a well-known period idiom – a time of commotion and yet of subterranean aspirations.[2] 'The baroque lived this contradiction', as Maravall put it, 'in the form of an extreme polarization of laughter and crying'

(Maravall 1986: 156). The world was felt in all its 'disproportion' and 'extremeness', provoking reactions and experiences of 'astonishment' and 'wonder', and a general sentiment of 'terribleness' (Maravall 1986: 212). Perhaps unsurprisingly, in this context the sublime worked as a cipher of the political economy of the Baroque's psyche. The sublime captured the wounded pathos of an incipient modern consciousness. Indeed, Maravall further re-describes the culture of the Baroque as a 'culture of alienation' and 'solitude', thus gesturing towards later developments in the history of capitalism (Maravall 1986: 122, 213).[3] 'If the Baroque has often been associated with capitalism', Deleuze further ventured, 'it is because the Baroque is linked to a crisis of property, a crisis that appears at once with the growth of new machines in the social field and the discovery of new living beings in the organism' (Deleuze 1993: 110). According to this embryonic interpretation, Baroque culture would have therefore contributed fundamentally to placing the body and its world of affects and prosthetic extensions at the very centre of the political economy of modernity.

It follows that a number of assumptions about the work that media does on the body- and *cogito* polity have their origin in the material culture and practices of the Baroque. One example is the sixteenth-century dramaturgical technique known as 'the theatre in the theatre'. The technique dwelled on the then emerging distinction between the world on and off the stage, between performance and audience. It was an elaboration of the literary device known as *mise en abyme*: the miniature replication of an art object within itself, which found inspiration in the optical illusionism of the sixteenth century (Dällenbach 1989). An instance is Shakespeare's writing of a play into a scene in *Hamlet,* or Velazquez's famous reproduction of his own artistic stance in *Las Meninas.* The audience is split into interior and exterior manifestations of itself, sometimes to infinite regress.[4] The staging of the world as a place capable of holding internal replications within opened up a rich cultural epistemology founded on the recursive play of insides and outsides. As William Egginton has noted, even Descartes's distinction between an inner residency of human cognition and an outer space of extended reality responded already to such a theatrical division of the world (Egginton 2010: 14). Other typically Baroque techniques included anamorphosis and trompe l'oeil effects in painting and architecture, where the division between spectator and spectacle is blurred, interpenetrated and mutually reabsorbed. On the whole, then, a concern with illusionism, wonderment, and the recursive and unstable relations between the real and the unreal in a now-theatricalized lifeworld characterized the Baroque.

Against this background, the return of the baroque, as Gregg Lambert has called it (2008), may be explained simply as an expression of the overdetermination of media in the shaping of contemporary economy and governance. '[W]e are perhaps living in a new seventeenth century', writes Paolo Virno, 'or in an age in which the old categories are falling apart and we need to coin new ones' (Virno 2004: 24). Today this is best illustrated by the role of new media relations, namely social networks and peer-to-peer communities, in the reconfiguration of economy as a sphere of productive sociality and commensality. In an intriguing sense, the age of new media is throwing into relief questions about the ongoing epistemic sustainability and stability of emerging social and political projects – that is, how traditional centres for the production of knowledge (and I use the word 'centre' here to designate both an institutional and an epistemic location) are being destabilized and reconfigured by the appearance of such new actors as the free and open source software movements, urban hacktivists, do-it-yourself science, and a newly empowered citizenry of scientific non-experts at large. Thus, classic baroque tropes, such as 'the world as a confused labyrinth', 'the world as hostelry' or the 'large plaza, where everybody assembles pell-mell' (Maravall 1986: 153–154) find resonance in today's Internet-mediated cacophony of information exchanges. The analogy with the knowledge economy of the global hostelry is particularly poignant:

> In the goings and comings of people who gather in an inn, in the brief time they spend there, in the variety and confusion of however many people there are in it, in the lies and deceptions it is full of, and in its disorder, the image turns out to be extremely adequate as a version of the world comprising our existence: 'Human existence is a hostelry where the wise is a lingering pilgrim,' … Fernandez de Ribera called it the 'university of students passing through this life'. (Maravall 1986: 154)

This explosion of confused and creative intermingling is, according to Lambert, what has historically characterized the return of the baroque:

> the Baroque … [occupies] the exact *middle* of modernity, in the sense that it can be understood to recur historically precisely in the moment when one tradition of modernity exhausts its own possibilities and transitions into another, and even as the symptomatic principle of this exhaustion. It is important to note, however, that the signs of exhaustion and decay … are not marked by attrition and lethargy, but rather by the sudden bursts of frenetic and frenzied creativity. (Lambert 2008: 170)

The Baroque's 'middleness' – its occupying the exact middle of modernity, in Lambert's turn of phrase – may be read as both a historical and a cultural trait. The Baroque is of course that period in history that was caught up between the Renaissance and the Enlightenment. It was a historical time of profound economic and social crisis that upended narratives and visions of progress. Somewhat less prosaically, however, Baroque culture was also obsessively concerned with the production of aesthetic, political and material devices aimed at opening up middle spaces for themselves. Baroque art and literature, for example, rejoice in the production of gaps that interrupt the flow of narrative or visual integration. Cervantes' Quixote is of course the archetype in literature, whilst trompe l'oeil techniques provided a model for the experience of suspended and enfolded wonderment in art. It is this conceptual function that Deleuze beautifully termed 'the fold', and that generally points to the image of something being held in suspension, forever 'stuck' or in the 'middle' of things. An argument I will be making at greater length in later chapters is that today the experience of entrapment and enfoldment is nowhere more evident than in the heightened consciousness of (being trapped in) media relations.

Perhaps unsurprisingly, this 'middleness' of social relations is also what some commentators have singled out as characteristic of the knowledge society. Thus, Thomas Osborne has described the rise of a new style of intellectual practice or 'epistemic form', that of 'mediation', and a new type of knowledge worker, the 'mediator', for whom 'an idea is seized or appropriated as much as it is created out of nothing (in Deleuze's language, the mediator is a bit like an empiricist – always "in the middle of things")' (Osborne 2004: 437, 440) The centrality of the middle, or rather, of middleness as an epistemic orientation, lends knowledge a certain elusive quality, where knowledge is deemed productive if it is seen to be moving. In this economy of knowledge, 'ideas', writes Osborne, 'are meant to get us from one place to another, to move things along; they are propellants' (Osborne 2004: 441). It is the overdetermined nature of media as an epistemic form, then, that lends them their sociologically salient qualities: 'It is not simply that we are all necessarily mediators now but that the world itself is imaged through various media, and not least by mediator intellectuals, *as* a mediated one' (Osborne 2004: 445). The world, then, is doubled back upon itself in an over-mediation that is characteristically baroque.

Also, it should not be forgotten that the apparatus of persuasion that Baroque absolutist power set in motion in the seventeenth century encountered, for the first time, a predisposed and 'active public participation in support of the guiding actions of baroque culture' (Maravall 1986: 75) – admittedly not an emancipated and self-fashioned public, but a public nonetheless conversant with the complex subtleties and modulations of political rhetoric. Thus, if the historical Baroque came up with techniques for decentring the state's political stage vis-à-vis an emerging urban mass culture, ours might be a neo-baroque age insofar as the notion of an *episteme* is itself being repopulated, intermediated and decentred in novel ways. My interest in this context is what I take as an emerging paradigm of global commensality and common knowledge: a new ontological transparency between knowledge / economy / the social, as characterized for example in parlance about the network and social economies, new digital and knowledge commons, or open science movements. The open, the public and the commons are tropes of extreme baroque self-consciousness: social forms on social forms, representations on representations.

Despite the promising analogies between the political economy of historical Baroque society and our late liberal predicament, no analyses in social theory to date have attempted to extricate the baroque qualities of contemporary liberal economy. Thus, the rest of the Introduction offers an elaboration and preliminary route-guide to this connection. First, I shall outline recent developments in social and critical theory whose interest in the vitalistic and affective dimensions of economic relations stage a return of baroque aesthetics and epistemology. Next, I shall sketch out the recent revival of interest in the baroque, which has been most prominent in Spanish and Latin American literary and cultural studies. In the final section I introduce the concepts of 'strabismus', 'proportionality' and 'reversibility'. Their work as epistemic engines, I suggest, plays a central part in the epistemological organization of modernity as a neo-baroque political economy.

Political Ethics

In *The Human Condition*, Hannah Arendt famously described the constitution of modernity as 'the rise of the social': the historical moment when social life abandoned the realm of the household (*oikonomía*) and moved into the *polis* or public sphere; that is, the moment when the *oikonomía*, the economy, went public (Arendt 1998 [1958]: 45). Modernity, in other words, came into being with the advent of political economy. This volume moves in the wake of Arendt's original analysis by offering a map of a new historical episteme: the rise of political ethics. The book uses the analytical sensibility of contemporary anthropology to interrogate central epistemic assumptions about the political ontology of modern society: for example, about the rise of a liberal philosophy of public choice, the immanence of the new networked economy of information, the commons as a novel expression and configuration of global commensality and political hope, or the reach of the economics of public goods into the productive realms of knowledge and intellectual capital.

In light of these developments, this volume takes as its central object of study the theoretical status of the Public as a political and economic epistemic object in modernity. I take the Public as an epitome of our baroque present: a social form tripled back upon itself as economy, polity and society.[5] We may say that it is an over-socialized form, or an over-formalization, an indication of the baroque epistemology that is a sign of our times.

I should say from the outset, however, that I am addressing a multi-faceted and multi-theoretical public. What follows is no historical sociology of the public sphere or of the category of publicness. I do not set out to correct, revisit or re-theorize Hannah Arendt, Jürgen Habermas or Michael Warner, to cite but three well-known public theory scholars. My interest in the public, rather, is in its epistemic productivity, especially in the context of modern political economy. Certain ways of talking about the public mobilise ethno-possibilities proper to those who do the talking. As Alastair Hannay has observed, that 'the public figures quite naturally in our thoughts of our society, that it is a kind of public figure, is a fact that conceals many less immediately accessible facts about society, its distinctiveness, its possibilities and also its alternatives' (2005: 3). In this sense I am interested in the cultural epistemology through which the public's polysemy is deployed as an argumentative logic in contexts of political economy – not what the public is, nor where it comes from, but how the mechanics of its invocation work. All publics perform a 'routine form of self-abstraction', an abstraction of anonymity where we each de-individuate into a mass public. If print was the 'rhetoric of disincorporation' used by the eighteenth-century literary bourgeois public sphere (Warner 2005: 164, 165), today these effects are rendered visible by devices such as 'global networks', 'intellectual property rights' or 'economic externalities'. These artefacts all cohere into a Public or common society whose membership is defined by participation, stakeholdership and commitment. Successful invocations of the Public 'trap' us as political and ethical subjects. What is remarkable about our present age, then, is the extent to which such moments and artefacts of public self-abstraction are endowed with an ethic of global commensality. Ethics is popular because it is a way of making our common or public subjectivity available. It is a trap (a trompe l'oeil trick) for the modern consciousness.

Certainly, the public has long had an iconic status in political and economic theory as a symbol at once of political will, economic welfare and sociological representativeness. Discourses about the public have traditionally had to perform exceedingly exigent functions. In fifteenth-century political theology, for instance, the king's body was an exegetical corpus for both divine and corporational versions of social reproduction: a body for a god and a body for a *populus* (Kantorowicz 1997 [1957]). Habermas, in turn, famously found in the constitution of the eighteenth-century public sphere the epitome of modern communicative rationality, since corrupted by the exaggerated mediations of (post-) industrial capitalism (Habermas 1989). In nineteenth-century marginal economic theory, on the other hand, public welfare became a proxy for collective preferences: a trick through which the aggregate individuality of consumers cohered into a social whole (Musgrave 1985). Plural and self-identical at once, the Public is therefore a classic figure of anthropological ambiguity: a patent symbol of the spectral or ghostly character of modern political ontology.

Today, the Public has assumed new figurations. There is the immanent networked economy of information, where users are producers and everything is editable (Benkler 2006; Lessig 2008). There is the new commons, an emerging public domain of collaborative, cooperative, sharing, and distributed gift-givers (Benkler 2003b; David 2000). There is so-called Mode 2 Knowledge: a neo-republican paradigm for explaining the dialogical co-production of knowledge by science and society – robust science, that is, as Public knowledge (Nowotny, Scott and Gibbons 2001). There is an emerging definition of knowledge as an economic global public good (Stiglitz 1999), a good forever spilling over itself, always accessible, inexhaustible and 'infinitely expansible', as economist Paul David describes it (1993: 28).

Of course the new Public is no singular object to which all these very different parties and traditions can lay claims to. There are indeed many different publics. It is, rather, the pervasive 'public philosophy' spirit undergirding this sociological current that deserves commentary and analysis. Cori Hayden has appositely described it as a neo-liberal fascination with the production of 'public-ization' (2003: 47). I shall give it a name of my own by calling the public philosophy of the Public an *anthropology of political ethics*.

The anthropology of political ethics signals a time when neo-liberal economy explicates itself through the language of a global *ecumene* and ethical commons. 'Democracy is embalmed in public rhetoric', says Sheldon Wolin, 'precisely in order to memorialize its loss of substance' (2000: 20). The view here is that the social is inherently self-eliciting, robust and virtuous; that because there is an internal commensurability to all social forms, all social exchanges are carriers of commensality;

and finally, that insofar as we remain globally 'public', we must therefore remain naturally good.

The virtuosity and self-eliciting features of contemporary public economy have prompted some to describe a turn towards a new 'vitalist capitalism' (Thrift 2008: 30): a vibrant, sentient, self-generative cultural economy that feeds on the distributive emergence of affect, mimesis and sympathy (Lepinay 2007). The following description is exemplary:

> If a public involves self-organizing open communication amongst strang-
> ers, then there may be many emergent forms of public life. Rather than the
> model of the global public sphere, it can be argued that it would be more
> appropriate to think of 'global public life', with the displacement of the term
> 'sphere' by the term 'life' suggesting the difficulty of separating politics and
> aesthetics, and cognition and affect. The accent on life, furthermore, points
> to the potential for information to be conceived as *alive*, as an autopoietic
> system, or as a complex multiplicity which does not necessarily behave and
> act as a docile tool but rather is worldling, inventive and generative. (Feath-
> erstone and Venn 2006: 11)

The shift towards the attentive and post-phenomenological dimen-sions of economy has demanded from social theorists the development of a new vocabulary, a language modulated to, and capable of capturing, the excitations of ever more elusive consumer impulses. Michel Callon et al. have called this economy of nervous signals an 'economy of qualities' (Callon, Meadal and Rabeharisoa 2002). The economy figures thence as a nervous body or a nervous system (Taussig 1992), proactively engag-ing the inherent re-activity of consumers' being-in-the-world. As Paul Virno puts it, when 'thought becomes the primary source of the produc-tion of wealth', it 'ceases to be an invisible activity and becomes some-thing exterior, "public", as it breaks into the productive process' (Virno 2004: 64).[6]

The publicness of thought production, as Virno puts it, opens up novel genealogical possibilities for the extension of the Arendtian *oikonomia*. The image recalls a *locus classicus* of anthropological economy: the changing spatial relations between household production (the domestic sphere) and wilderness transactions (the political sphere, the realm of stranger-cum-mercantile relations). Thus, whereas for Arendt the rise of the social marked the migration of household life to the political wilder-ness, what Virno and others are pointing to is a new migratory process whereby political economy itself is transformed wholesale into a super-social and therefore ethical object. The household's threshold (which in Arendt's account once separated social reproduction from political and economic production) has shifted and taken residence now within the ethical. We designate as strangers today not those who stand outside our *oikonomía*, but those whose ethical knowledge makes them stand apart from us. It is ethics that makes us different, signalling what is inside and what remains outside the economy – an anthropology of political ethics.

The transformation of political economy into an ethical space may be read inversely, as a transformation of ethics into a repertoire of political economy objects. Thus, parlance of 'cognitive capital', 'social innovation' or 'immaterial labour' – of capitalism as productive of vitality, conviviality and sociality – points in this context to a regime of production where knowledge (as embodied, for example, in novel technological devices and digital media) allegedly becomes radically sociologically transparent: where knowledge is public because its production is social. In effect this amounts to the mutual reabsorption of all sociological domains thereafter: knowledge, sociality and the economy collapsing into a self-similar Public. The question we must now ask ourselves, then, is: Who plays host and who plays guest – knowledge or society – in the house of the global economy?

An argument I shall put forward is that parlance of 'public knowledge', 'trust', 'global networks' and other such idioms of political ethics work in this context as thresholds of our new global household, of our emerging *oikonomía*. Such objects stand at the doorstep as prophylactic or hospitable devices – as 'mediators', in Osborne's poignant imagery, of novel economic exchanges in which a little 'knowledge-management' or 'collaboration' can help transform strangers into 'users' (-friendly). They are devices with one foot in and another foot outside the economy, inclined towards the productive and the convivial but also towards the predatory and the vitalistic. Intellectual property rights, for instance, are seen as the effect of relational productivity *and* their own stoppage. They internalize and externalize social relations in a complex double move: the patent internalizes the virtues of information disclosure and yet externalizes the compulsion of appropriation (Strathern 2002a). They operate a sort of trompe l'oeil anthropology, where one perspective is brought into focus as the perpendicular effect of another, and therefore where a double or 'strabismic' vision is required to grant epistemic status to an object.

Anthropological Baroques

The baroque has undergone a number of revisitations in the humanities over the past half-century. Although it is not my intention to provide a history of the term's use, I must note that it has indeed been widely employed as a currency of explanation and analysis in literary studies, and Spanish and Latin American literature in particular, for the past thirty or forty years. Not being a scholar-in-residence in the field, I shall next attempt a quite improbable sketch of such periodical turns (for a comprehensive and insightful review of baroque returns, see Zamora and Kaup 2010).[7]

The baroque makes a central appearance in the 1970s and 1980s as an analytical descriptor of the early postmodern turn. Around this time we encounter reappraisals of Benjamin's baroque lucidity by Buci-Glucksmann (1994 [1984]) or of the baroque's purchase as a trans-historical category by Omar Calabrese (1992). In this context, the baroque provides 1980s postmodernism with plausibility and genealogical depth. An earlier, and in my view more intriguing use of the baroque as a provocative device (in its original context, now called *neobarroco*) made its appearance in the 1950s and 1960s among a group of Cuban writers (Alejo Carpentier, José Lezama Lima, Severo Sarduy) and Latin American novelists (including such noted figures as Jorge Luis Borges or Octavio Paz). The baroque qualities of Borges' literature in particular have had a major influence on late twentieth-century social theory, as reflected in famous citations of his Chinese encyclopaedia in Foucault's *The Order of Things* (Foucault 1970: 17) or the Chinese 'garden with bifurcating paths' that appears in Deleuze's *The Fold* (Deleuze 1993: 62). This *neobarroco* moment has in turn spawned a modern-day 'New World Baroque' literature among Spanish and Latin American cultural and literary theorists interested in exploring the purchase of the baroque as a figure of alter-modernity for the Latin American experience (Kaup 2006; Zamora 2009; Zamora and Kaup 2010).

Perhaps the most cited of all recent baroque recuperations is to be found in Deleuze's chiaroscuro philosophy of curvature and sinuosity (Deleuze 1993). Deleuze's take on the baroque is interesting because of his open disregard for the concept's historicity or sociology. For Deleuze, the baroque remains of interest because of its qualities as an 'operative function', namely the function of producing and conceptualizing folds – the baroque, then, as concept (Deleuze 1993: 3, 33). There are no distinct insides and outsides in this operative and conceptual functioning of the baroque – the baroque, remember, is always 'in the middle'. Objects do not so much occupy unique and distinct parcels of geometrical space in the world as they exude the world in their material and proliferative intensiveness. They spill over the world as its shadows. World and objects display changing figurations with respect to each other through the simplest and most infinitesimal of variances. Indeed, according to Deleuze, one would do better without a world/object distinction and speak of a calculus of folding moments instead, of the unfolding and infolding luxuriance of material variance.

I find Deleuze's baroque of great appeal because his emphasis on functionality makes the baroque into an engine for producing epistemic operations – not historical or sociological explanation, but epistemological productivity. At this point I should explain why I insist on stressing my interest in the neo-baroque as anthropological epistemology rather than cultural style or historical formation. Simply put, I am interested not in what a baroque moment looks like, nor in what it effects are, but in how these effects are organized to be rendered 'effective' to start with. The internal organization of such effects, I shall argue, responds to the work of particular 'epistemic engines' – to an anthropological epistemology.

Thus, the recovery of the baroque in literary and cultural studies tends, on the whole, to see in the baroque an alternative or counter current to the Enlightenment project. The baroque stands in this light as a historical marginalized or alternative form of rationality, one whose recuperation today, it is argued, has valuable lessons for critical theory. Monika Kaup, for example, applies Deleuze and Guattari's theories of morphogenesis (where structures are seen to develop as strata or as rhizomes) in her description of 'two types of Baroque: on the one hand, the homogenizing and hierarchical official European Baroque of Absolutism and Counter Reformation, and on the other, the decolonizing and racially, culturally heterogeneous New World Baroque … that … was generated from the European Baroque by a destratifying process that deterritorialized its colonizing hierarchical order' (Kaup 2005: 112). The subaltern traditions of Latin America mestizo populations, for example, are re-described in this context as experiences of 'becoming-minor', in Deleuze and Guattari's usage (Deleuze and Guattari 1987 [1980]: 116–117): processes of identity formation that operate as 'transcreations' through the displacement, dilation or decentring of received forms (Kaup 2005: 125).

Although I think there are indeed some elements of interest in these readings, this is not the project or stance I want to recuperate here. If I retain an interest in the baroque it is rather in the contemporary manifestation and purchase of its epistemology, that is, in the modes through which its sensibilities and aesthetics deploy epistemic effects. What singles out the baroque in this context is its investment in the production of *effects* – where the 'effect' itself becomes a novel *form*. Thus, José Antonio Maravall reminds us for example that the first beheading of a king took place in England in Baroque times, or that the seventeenth century witnessed a heightened consciousness of the cultural forms of sorcery and witchcraft (Maravall 1986: 51, 230). Baroque times celebrated novelty and invention, and thus rejoiced in the splendour of effects as forms. We may describe the baroque, then, as an 'age of form' whose very own form is to effect a moment of suspension for new forms/effects to appear.[8] The baroque inaugurates the conditions for an *epistemological recursion* between form and effect.

In this sense, baroque work is indeed transformative, in that it stretches or works across forms to novel effects. Importantly, however, this may be – but often is not – put to critical use in the contexts in which it appears. In fact, nowadays when a baroque image or intervention crops up, we may well be looking at a gesture or expression of neo-liberal politics. The economic theory of externalities, for example, which we shall be looking at in greater detail in Chapter 5, is built using a powerful baroque epistemology: economic markets are here oriented to the process of becoming their outsides, a 'becoming', however, that retains very little of the revolutionary newness that Deleuze and Guattari originally intended the term to carry. The novelty, if there is any, is that the orientation towards 'becoming' has assumed a metrological-cum-technical form in late liberal economies. Thus, there is nothing inherently critical or radically creative in the new baroque except its very surfacing or emergence, and its formalization as such. Whether it is employed for critical or conservative purposes remains in the last instance a matter of the political vanguard one chooses to observe or side with. An anthropological epistemology, on the other hand, aims instead to grasp the tensions and pulsations of the recent interest in processes of emergence and formalization. Hence in this book I extend this interest to contemporary processes and theories of political economy – to the study of the forms and effects of new economic epistemic objects: global public goods, knowledge or the commons.

Of course no epistemology can be said to be historically uprooted. Historical and sociological reasons may be mobilized to help contextualize why we may be living through a third wave of baroque aesthetics and cultural logics. Angela Ndalianis, for instance, has produced an exhaustive inventory of cultural forms of the entertainment industry in high liberal capitalism and shown it to have many traits in common with the sensorium of seventeenth-century Baroque spectacle culture (Ndalianis 2004). But as William Egginton has noted, it is important to keep the work of the epistemological in view, because if the adoption of baroque styles is an expression of the contemporary, then the baroque *itself* affords no critical purchase. Beyond the 'mere excitement of affect' delivered by baroque mass spectacle capitalism, an epistemologically critical baroque aims instead 'to affect the core of our being, since it leaves us with the uncanny sense' that there is 'no other world to buttress our fragile selves against the tumult of signs and senses in which we find ourselves immersed' (Egginton 2010: 84). Take away epistemological finesse, and it may turn out that critical and capital baroque all look the same.[9]

Strabismus

To help us understand some of the epistemological effects through which modern knowledge has assumed a sociological form, a baroque toolbox can outline the conditions that have enabled knowledge to become an enabler itself, letting us see what the growth of knowledge – or its rise as an expression of enablement – looks like. What does knowledge need to grow 'out of' for such an escalation to become meaningful or, simply, visible?

The making visible of knowledge as an object of growth in modernity has its own anthropology. In this book I suggest that this anthropology involves playful operations with social ideas of size and vision, and is materialized in a practical epistemology where the optical plays an intriguing culturally salient role. Optics makes size an effect of exploration. It makes things big and small in different proportions, intensities and shapes. It provides a form or carrier for the expansions and contractions in and of knowledge.

The playful experimentations with optics in the seventeenth century, of which Robert Hooke's microscopic investigations were exemplary, awakened the epistemology of the moderns to what I shall call here its *strabismus*. The strabismus of knowledge practices hinted at the realization that the new epistemic objects of modernity – the objects made visible by new instruments, such as telescopes, air pumps or microscopes – remained nevertheless unstable and impure, insofar as one could rarely stabilize them along a singular scale of representation. The scale of an observation made inside a microscope had to be 'translated' back into the scale of a drawing or a technical description. Performing the translation – moving in and out of the various scales – lent the object epistemic stability. These objects therefore were squinted at in various directions and recursions, moving in and out of a variety of lines of flight.

In the first part of this book I explore some of the artefacts and artifices through which sixteenth- and seventeenth-century artistic and scientific exploration hinted at the role of strabismus in the shaping of the cultural epistemology of the moderns. My main proposition here is that the political ontology of modernity has been historically configured under the long shadow of such a strabismic or baroque epistemology. In

Chapters 1–3 I take a closer look at the characteristic hallmarks of such a baroque political. For the sake of illustration, however, let me offer a quick sketch of its two central features. I borrow from Don Ihde's description of the camera obscura as an 'epistemological engine' involved in the Renaissance configuration of knowledge as something instrumentally generated. For Ihde, the camera obscura operates two optical transformations with epistemic effects:

> The first is one of escalation – from Alhazen's observation of an optical effect; to da Vinci's camera as analogue for the eye; to Locke's and Descartes' analogue of camera to eye to mind – by which the camera is made into a full epistemology engine. The second is the inward progression of the location where 'external' reality, itself an artefact of the geometry of the imaging phenomenon, interfaces with the 'inner' representation. For da Vinci, the interface of external/internal occurs 'in the pupil'; for Descartes, it is the retina; and, still continuing the camera epistemology, contemporary neuroscience locates it in the brain. (Ihde 2000: 21)

The hypothesis of *An Anthropological Trompe l'Oeil* is that the political ontology of modernity is conjured into existence through the compound work of these two epistemic engines. What Ihde calls 'escalation' is an instance of the larger relation of magnitude that I shall call 'proportionality'; the movement between internal and external domains corresponds to the function that I call 'reversibility'.

Bruno Latour has famously suggested that the functioning of modernity as a wholesale epistemic regime rests on two intertwined processes: 'The first set of practices, by "translation", creates mixtures between entirely new types of beings, hybrids of nature and culture. The second, by "purification", creates two entirely distinct ontological zones: that of human beings on the one hand; that of nonhumans on the other'. (Latour 1993: 10–11) My suggestion here, however, is that further epistemological finesse is required to fully appreciate how the modern accomplishes its tricks.

First, following a suggestion by historian of art Martin Jay, I propose we distinguish between styles, or what Jay calls 'scopic regimes of modernity': Cartesian, baroque and descriptive modernity (Jay 1988). Second, we must distinguish between types of epistemological engines. Purification and translation may indeed be two, to which I would like to add proportionality and reversibility. The compound work of proportionality and reversibility gives form to the strabismus of modern knowledge.

Proportionality refers to the preoccupations with 'size' and 'scale' that have historically characterized Euro-American social and philosophical theory, for example, in the geometrical fascination with telescopes or microscopes throughout the Renaissance and the Enlightenment, or in the more recent disquisitions about the global scale of new economic, scientific or political ventures. This has created the fantasy of modern knowledge as growing through a play of aggrandizements and miniaturizations, therefore endowing all epistemic objects with expectations about their size and scale. The comment by Robert Hooke with which I opened the book is exemplary: information becomes more powerful by virtue of a newly acquired capacity to optically transform its scales of representation. Somewhat remarkably, in the *longue durée* of these traditions, explanations of nature and/or the social world have retained the use of idioms of size and magnitude to 'net out' their political-cum-ontological accounts, for instance in the fitness with which two otherwise disparate meta-sociological distributions such as 'public' and 'global' are put to work together in parlance of 'global public goods' or 'global public sphere'. In these contexts the world has been rendered 'proportionate' to the forms of description that summoned it in the first place. Proportionality, then, is a descriptive-cum-analytical means to hold the world to account.

The strabismic operates a second effect on the workings of knowledge, giving shape to the second element of the baroque political, which I call *reversibility*. Reversibility points to the recurrent motif of movements between the visible and the invisible, the inside and the outside, through which modern knowledge has provided explanations about its internal functioning. 'Such is the Baroque trait', writes Deleuze, 'an exterior always on the outside, an interior always on the inside' (1993: 35). The recent turn, in social theory, to the use of analytical terms such as 'oscillation' or 'depth-surface' and 'figure-ground' reversals exemplify this trend (Law and Mol 2002). Reversibility thus describes the double vision required to grant theoretical status to an object. The optical simultaneity through which Robert Hooke acknowledged the properties of 'discovery' and 'intelligence' in knowledge serves likewise as an example. What Hooke discovered *inside* the microscope (miniaturized writing) was promptly equated by him to knowledge *outside* the microscope (political intelligence). The instrument's optical lens performed the trick of reversible understanding. The Public is also an exemplar of this strabismic aesthetic, because it functions as a placeholder for both political and economic aspirations; in the liberal philosophy of public choice theory, for instance, the Public stands as an idiom of both political representation and an objective of economic distribution.

Take for example Cori Hayden's study of bioprospecting programmes in Mexico. The 1992 UN Convention on Biological Diversity introduced a mandate on benefit-sharing into bioprospecting projects: extractive companies are required to compensate or share benefits with source communities. A bioprospecting contract, then, recruits and temporarily stabilizes a number of diverse interests. An important point, Hayden stresses, is the way in which in this context the practice of field science becomes suddenly loaded with social obligations – as she puts it, 'to collect not just plants but the benefit-recipients that "come with" these plants' (Hayden 2003: 29). Compensation frameworks demand therefore an additional explicitation of social relationships. We might say that in this context bioprospecting is thrice social: three times objectified into a social affair as scientific life, as social life, and as self-explicitated ethical exchange. Thus, bioprospecting poses interesting challenges to ethnographic description. Moving in and out of all these social formats is no easy task. Indeed, it is perhaps no coincidence that 'moving in and out' becomes a preferred idiom for describing the complex super-position of all such social moments. Hence, in Hayden's account, her own project is 'to track the ways in which a host of political liabilities and property claims, accountabilities and social relationships are being actively written *into routine scientific practices, tools, and objects of inter-vention and back out of them again,* in ways not quite anticipated by a traditional science studies approach' (Hayden 2003: 29, emphasis in the original). Ethnography amounts to an incursion *into and out of the social* in order to de-stick it from its own internal recursions. It is the revers-ibility – the inside-out – that accomplishes the analysis.

The idiom of a 'world within' and the use of a variety of techniques to turn its 'insides out' are of course classic Baroque tropes (Maravall 1986: 197). Nowhere has the analytics of the inside-out been put to work as clearly and eloquently as in Annelise Riles's study of the duality of net-working as a bureaucratic and sociological form. For Riles, the network refers 'to a set of institutions, knowledge practices, and artifacts thereof that internally generate the effects of their own reality by reflecting on themselves' (Riles 2001: 3). Her ethnography of Fijian bureaucrats and activists preparing for the United Nations Fourth World Conference on Women clearly shows the efficacy of the network as a sociological form used by her informants for their own analytical-cum-practical purposes. As she puts it, 'networkers deploy the *optical effect* of Network form as a "fulcrum or lever" that generates *alternative inverted forms* of sociality by projecting an image of each – Network and "personal relations" – *from the point of view of the other*' (Riles 2001: 115–116, emphasis added). The network thus functions as a commentary on one's capacity to at once hold a commentator's perspective and displace or invert this per-spective. In this form it echoes Hooke's microscope by leveraging alter-nating configurations of knowledge depending on whether the viewer's perspective is internal or external to the domain of representation. The network, then, is a strabismic and neo-baroque device.

Optics, scale and reversibility are also put to analytical effect in Marilyn Strathern's interesting essay on the epistemic character of Euro-American 'interpretative' practices (Strathern 2002b). In this piece Strathern offers an interpretation of four visual images: a photograph of two women carrying *bilums* (net bags) up a stream, an ultrasound scan, a photograph of two prospective parents looking at the enlarged image of their own fertilized ovum on a TV screen, and a photograph of a man's painted face. For each image, Strathern mobilizes a number of possible interpretative perspectives. Each perspective holds its own order of reality but could eventually be 'dwarfed' by phenomena of a different order, thus pointing to the effects that scale can have. Interpretation is therefore seen to work by scaling the items that are being interpreted, aggrandizing or diminishing them in a manner akin to what the technique of figure-ground reversal does:

> Figure-ground reversal involves an alternation of viewpoints. Now although ground by definition encompasses figure, what is to count as figure and what is to count as ground is not a definitive matter at all ... Figure and ground promote, we might say, unstable relationships. I further speak of oscillation, a tied divergence, when what are summoned are worlds or value systems at once seemingly different from yet also comparable to each other. Here the freight of 'quantity' introduces an asymmetry. When there can be too much or too little of something, when vastness appears to overwhelm, or when a single perspective appears to miss so much, then scale can give a particular impetus to the very decision of what is to be rendered as figure and what as ground. Ground acquires the value of an unmarked category. So when the greater (unmarked) value can be expressed in terms of an appropriateness of quantity – neither too much nor too little – then *that* is what locates the entity in question as ground ... Quantity thus turns out to have a (re)stabilizing effect. (Strathern 2002b: 92–93)

Scale appears as an explanatory and hermeneutic framework for the work of interpretation through the operations of oscillation (i.e., reversibility) and optics (i.e., perspectives). This is not an axiomatic or 'philosophical endgame', as Strathern puts it, but 'of a piece ... with certain modernist and Western (Euro-American) projections at large' (Strathern 2002b: 109). This is certainly true, but as I will attempt to show throughout this book, the format of this Euro-American projection is by no means generic but rather presumes a productivity whose epistemic engines find their source of power in a baroque epistemology.

An important mediator in the configuration of present-day anthropological baroques is the figure of complexity. As William Egginton has observed, in the historical Baroque a complexity-affect surfaced when further complexity took the place of hitherto expected simplicity (Egginton 2010: 97): the complex surfaced in the aftermath of *failed* simplicity. An example provided by Egginton is Gongora's pastoral poetry. Gongora is known as an exemplary Baroque poet for the opacity of his language and his intentional effacement of transparency. Commenting on the couplet, 'the hypocrite apple, which fools, not in its pallor, in its redness', Egginton notes how the text's deliberate deceptiveness enables the verses to 'double back on themselves, revealing only further folds of complexity where the simple is expected' (Egginton 2010: 63). A baroque effect dwells, then, not in the complex qua complex, but in the expectations of its non/appearance.

Expectations of the appearance of complex forms have also become a matter of interest for the social sciences today, for example in the study of failure and its modes of emergence (Miyazaki and Riles 2005). Here the form of the complex is often related to another form, that of information, and to its own internal economy of signals and references: complexity is said to emerge as a function of the extent of relations set up within an informational data set. Marilyn Strathern's well-known observation about the fatuous conflation of questions of complexity with 'amounts' of informational context puts the question of in-formation thus:

> the question of complexity seems from one point of view a simple matter of scale. The more closely you look, the more detailed things are bound to become. Increase in one dimension (focus) increases the other (detail of data) ... Complexity thus also comes to be perceived as an artefact of questions asked, and by the same token of boundaries drawn: more complex questions produce more complex answers ... at every level complexity replicates itself in scale of detail. 'The same' order of information is repeated, eliciting equivalently complex conceptualization ... We are dealing with a self-perpetuating imagery of complexity. (Strathern 2004 [1991]: xiii, xvi)

The 'self-perpetuating imagery of complexity' rehearses in this context a classical baroque aesthetic, one that Chunglin Kwa distinguishes from a Romantic mode of looking – whilst '[t]he romantics look up' in a 'process of abstraction' that 'recognize[s] collections of individuals as higher-order individuals', the 'baroque looks down and ... observes the mundane crawling and swarming of matter' (Kwa 2002: 26) – appositely citing Leibniz on the self-perpetuating complexity of matter: 'Every bit of matter can be conceived as a garden full of plants or a pond full of fish. But each branch of the plant, each drop of its bodily fluids, is also such a garden or such a pond' (Leibniz 1991: 228, cited in Kwa 2002: 26). The zooming in and out of the real and the complex, the direction and intensity of looking, thus capture the artistry at play in the epistemology of strabismus, where the objects held in view by one eye are playfully deformed by the other eye, and where the different things seen by one and the other eye elicit 'knowledge' as, precisely, a relation of difference between differential orders.

Inspired by Hayden's, Riles's and Strathern's approaches to the analytical sensibilities of anthropology, this volume affords what may be glossed a genealogy of our baroque political: a radical anthropology of the present, which aims to silhouette and contrast the nerve-forms of the modern polis, and to operate a radiographic inversion, a black-and-white reversal, of our sociological consciousness. The book may be read as an inquiry into the forms and proportions of our modern political economy, where the latter is contrasted and placed against the light of its own anthropological epistemology.

The book advances its argument in two parts: a first part concerned with the genealogical anthropology of the neo-baroque, and in particular its expression in the categories of strabismus, proportionality and reversibility; and a second part identifying and outlining their contemporary manifestation in political economy. The first part 'zooms in' to the interiorities of our epistemic imagination; the second part 'zooms out' to see how such imagination organizes our political world. Of course the work of zooming in and out instantiates its own cultural epistemology, and I end the book with an attempt at relocating myself, not quite by effecting yet another 'inside-out' but by moving, let us say, at perpendicular angles – anamorphically.[10]

As for the book's general structure, Part I opens with a myth of origins that sets the stage for the rest of the book: a historical vignette of the alleged origins of *Leviathan's* famous title page in Hobbes's encounter and fascination with an anamorphic (dioptric) device. The myth, then, is about the political optics and ontological politics of modernity.

In Chapter 1 I offer some examples of the centrality of scale and size in the work of contemporary social theory. I attempt here a first exercise in clearing the ground for a better appreciation of the historical and analytical relationship between optics, scale and social theory. I suggest that much social theory today works as a sort of 'architectural optics of volumes', where epistemic knowledge is marginally netted out from exercises in surviving comparison.

In Chapter 2 I develop the notion of the *strabismic eye* as an imago or figure for modern knowledge. I trace the importance of size and proportionality in sixteenth- and seventeenth-century pictorial and optical practice, and use the discovery of linear perspective as an inaugural case study. The epistemological foundations of perspectivalism have long functioned as a classic straw man for critiques of Cartesian modernity. A closer inspection of the pictorial and diagrammatic practice of perspectivalism, however, shows that the craft of perspective-making often mobilized far more complex and suggestive epistemological functions. The viewing eye was often seconded, if not haunted, by a variety of adjacent, hidden, distorted or mobile eyes: the engine of strabismus. The chapter further ventures an argument about the potential function of strabismus in the internal organization of anthropological critique at large.

In Chapter 3 I develop an analytical context for identifying the work of proportionality and reversibility at play in modern political knowledge. Both reversibility and proportionality have a distinguished genealogy in philosophy. In *The Order of Things,* Foucault famously described the 'resemblance' episteme that preceded Descartes's representational inauguration (Foucault 1970): an episteme where the qualities of knowledge could be transported between non-identical objects and forms, so long as one could identify 'resemblances', symmetries or mimetic equivalences between them. Although Enlightenment philosophy claimed to have put the spectral qualities of resemblance-reversibility to rest, today social theory is finding fertile insights into the dynamics of contemporary sociality by (often unknowingly) drawing upon the classical episteme of reversibility.

Classical antiquity can likewise lay claim to proportionality. The proportion is indeed a majestic philosophical category: it plays a central role in ancient Greek cosmology – including, of course, thinking on the structural make-up of the polis – and pervades aesthetic and political reasoning throughout the Middle Ages right up to Renaissance times (Corsín Jiménez 2008b). However, one of its most important functions, which is not always acknowledged, has been its role in configuring the political ontology of modernity from within. The work of Giordano Bruno is particularly interesting in this respect because it provides an intriguing antecedent to the vitalistic, corpuscular and monadological theories of later thinkers such as Leibniz or Tarde, and it did so at a time when the very 'proportions' of the world were being reshaped from Ptolemaic to Copernican cosmological scales. In this light, Chapter 3 offers some insights into how contemporary social theory may productively read these various analytical lineages.

Part II focuses on the characteristics of the modern *oikonomía* and attempts a tentative 'double view' of their status as epistemic objects in Euro-American discourse. The exercise may be read as offering a strabismic spin on the Public as a figure of our times.

Chapter 4 takes a look at the rise of the Public as an object of political economy. The history of this development is necessarily complex and intricate, and I come nowhere close to retracing it. My interest, rather, is in the analytical interiorities of certain classic public theory categories, such as political theology, public welfare, public choice and knowledge commons. How have these categories been deployed in social thought, and what consequences does their analytical seductiveness carry for social theory? A curious and common characteristic is that they often work as reconciliatory functions: they pose themselves as *balances* or thresholds to external and outside forces. They are therefore hollowed out from within, permanently shadowed by a sense of incompleteness, of out-of-jointness. The Public thus fares always as a ghost to its own modes of self-abstraction.

Chapter 5 explores the frail and stressful relation between production and (social) reproduction in capitalist economies. In particular, it examines what the production of knowledge and other 'public goods' entails. In the new so-called knowledge economy, where intellectual property and immaterial labour have become central productive assets, the relation between sociality and production is complex and fraught. For example, if the new network capitalism casts social relations as forces of production, the question of the ownership of capital turns out to be a question about the ownership of social relationality. Against this background, the economics of public knowledge confronts the sociology of knowledge with a complex problem of political epistemology: if knowledge can today be said to embody a pure public good (that is, a sociologically transparent commodity), what critical role is left for social theory to play? Does not the economic theory of public goods, in this context, cannibalize and prey on social theory's critical capacities – and indeed, on sociality itself as a mode of critical engagement with the world?

When the language of ethics and commensality becomes the mode of explication of an (neo-liberal) economic regime, the purview of the critical is seriously diminished. It becomes ever more difficult to find a place from which to produce critique. This cancellation of a place for society's 'critical outsidership' (Hannay 2005: 100) has its own sociological corollaries. The economic theory of externalities is a prominent example: it defines 'public goods' as an index of the market being out of proportion and therefore of the need to rebalance its forces, or to internalize its externalities.

The final chapter, Chapter 6, examines the wider political and anthropological presuppositions of the theory of externalities, that is, the forms of exteriority and interiority through which the neo-liberal economy stabilizes its sociological arithmetic. Here I explore in some detail the form of equation or equilibrium (between the inside and the outside) where the contemporary notion of public knowledge, and public science in particular, is said to obtain today.

Together, the chapters in Part II may be read as an attempt to construct a strabismic perspective on our baroque globality. To the concept of the liberal public, I offer the phantasm; to the notion of social or commensal productivity, I offer predation; to the concept of an externality, I oppose that of reversibility. These conceptual interventions should be read as an attempt to sketch a trompe l'oeil anthropology: an effort at 'trapping' the descriptive forms of late liberalism within their own culture of description, and an attempt to place description at perpendicular angles vis-à-vis emerging forms of global public knowledge. Only knowledge that has been trapped can later be properly 'released'.

As I have pointed out, I offer here an analysis of an anthropological epistemology – an epistemology that, I contend, may be described as neo-baroque. Its neo-baroque engines, moreover, fuel certain modes of presentation of the political ontology of modernity. Some of the ways through which we have come to make sense of our global condition are pumped up by such a baroque ascension. In this latter sense, too, we may further speak of an anthropological baroque: a social epistemology that shapes from within certain conceptions about the modern economy, polity and society.

The neo-baroque polis, I have intimated here and shall argue throughout, is self-enchanted by its powers of growth and economy: more knowledge, so the spell goes, equals better politics and economy. That size matters is a baroque trick, however. *An Anthropological Trompe l'Oeil for a Common World* offers, if I may put it this way, a guide to the cultural epistemology behind this enchantment. Yet the enchantment applies to critique as well. It is the book's final aspiration, then, to extricate, or complicate in a new way, the historical and theoretical relation that the economy of knowledge has had to critique as a form of analysis. By unbundling the epistemological compound of critique into a number of 'epistemic engines', and showing the different types of sociological effects that these produce, I hope somewhat to skew the perspective of critique on the social – or, in proper baroque language, to effect a shift from an anthropological perspective on to an anthropological anamorphosis of critique.

Notes

1. I shall use the term Baroque (capitalized) to refer to the historical period. I will leave 'baroque' (uncapitalized) to refer to a politico-epistemological order whose traits are defined below.

2. According to Maravall, the Baroque signalled the sociological awakening of 'aspirations' as a self-conscious modality of agency. People first became conscious of their capacity to aspire during the Baroque. Although Maravall does not provide a full-blown articulation of such a sociology, he offers a superb literary and empirical survey of where to look for it. The 'sociology of aspirations' is finally coming home today in the work of, for example, Arjun Appadurai (2004) or Hirokazu Miyazaki (2004).

3. Commenting on a passage in *Cisne de Apolo,* a text by the Baroque preceptist Carballo, Maravall notes: 'Thus we have once again come across this alienating state, which extends from the ecstasy of the mystic to the exploitation of the worker in the capitalist order' (Maravall 1986: 214).

4. The 'split between interior and exterior audience, and the concomitant negotiation and play between those levels, is perhaps the single most powerful marker of baroque aesthetics' (Egginton 2010: 42–43).

5. I shall hereafter capitalize the word 'Public' when signalling its epistemic use as an index of baroque globality.

6. As interesting and insightful as these developments certainly are, focusing on the infinitesimal, inflexional and extrovert (in the sense of overtly 'public', in Virno's use of the term above) qualities of social life has nevertheless a reputed and long tradition in social and philosophical thinking. Bruno Latour (2002), Andrew Barry and Nigel Thrift (2007) and Maurizio Lazzarato (2002) have in this respect recognized the important and yet forgotten legacy of Gabriel Tarde (see also the contributions in Candea 2010). Today Tarde's appeal for social theory lies in his explicit and eloquent opposition to the Durkheimian collective consciousness. If Durkheim saw in Society the ultimate ontic reality, for Tarde 'every thing is a society' (Tarde 2006: 55) and therefore sociologically ontological. Tarde's attention to detail and the slow motion of social life (repetition, opposition and imitation) has excited an interest in the political possibilities of affect, empathy and open-ended association.

   However, of the 'efficacy in affecting, in awakening and moving the affections', José Antonio Maravall already noted in his classic period study that it constituted 'the great motive of the baroque' (Maravall 1986: 74). And indeed Tarde is in many respects merely rehearsing classical themes in baroque epistemology, his neo-monadological project, for instance, being an obvious extension of Leibniz's philosophical calculus. Furthermore, his social theory is profoundly dimensional (Corsín Jiménez 2010), as it pertains to someone witnessing the natural sciences' uneasy confrontation with the abysses opening at the very heart of nineteenth-century ontological categories. Somewhat surprisingly, in this context, Peter Sloterdijk has observed how Tarde's monadology brings to the fore the extent to which 'societies' are 'magnitudes calling for space' that can only be described 'thanks to an analysis of extension, a topology, a dimensional theory and a "network" analysis' (Sloterdijk 2006: 227, my translation). Such sensibility towards space and form is, once again, expressive of a baroque aesthetic.

7. And taking advice from Gregg Lambert's comments apropos of the history of academic debate on the Baroque, I should probably rejoice in the implausibility of my account:

   the criticism that surrounds the Baroque reveals something like a kernel of madness in the form of Western critical reason that once again challenges its power to name, to call into existence, and to describe nominative reality … a form of madness without the style of madness—lucid, reasonable, clear, and logical to a nearly hyperbolic degree. (Lambert 2008: xxxii)

8. 'Age of form' is the phrase used by Pierre Auger to describe the revolution cybernetics brought about in systemic thought: 'Now, after the age of materials and stuff,

after the age of energy, we have begun to live the age of form'. Geof Bowker referred to Auger's statement to note how the processes of 'form' here singled out by cybernetic strategies built on a vision for the 'synchronic structure of information' (Bowker 1993: 111). The internal circulation of information in a looped economy of knowledge—the self-imaging of information as a structural form (of knowledge)—is cyberneticians' claim to universality. The Public is a universal form in this cybernetic sense too: an internally self-referred system of knowledge / economy / the social. For an account of the making of the Internet as a networked public economy building on cybernetic strategies, see Turner (2006).

9. Thus Egginton distinguishes between a 'major' and a 'minor' baroque strategy: the former is deployed as a representational strategy, a theatrical fiction that, as such, ultimately calls out and legitimates a reality 'out there'; the latter, on the other hand, is inherently unstable and takes the irony of the major strategy as 'presencing' (as opposed to representing) reality itself (Egginton 2010: 5–9). Whilst I can see how a baroque sensibility can follow both major and minor agendas, I want to insist that my interest is rather in the epistemological engines that fuel such a sensibility from within.

10. An anamorphic projection need not, of course, require an exact 90° (perpendicular) adjustment of point of view to bring the image into its proper shape.

Part I

Trompe l'Oeil

1

Surviving Comparison

> the most admirable operations
> derive from very weak means
> —Galileo Galilei, *Opere*, vol. 11

A Myth of Origins

All political thought evinces an aesthetic of sorts. Dioptric anamorphosis, for instance, was the 'science of miracles' through which Hobbes imagined his Leviathan. Exemplifying the optical wizardry of seventeenth-century clerical mathematicians, a dioptric anamorphic device used a mirror or lens to refract an image that had deliberately been distorted and exaggerated back into what a human eye would consider a natural or normal perspective. Many such artefacts played with pictures of the faces of monarchs or aristocrats. Here the viewer would be presented with a panel made up of a multiplicity of images, often emblems representing the patriarch's genealogical ancestors or the landmarks of his estate. A second look at the panel through the optical glass, however, would recompose the various icons, as if by magical transubstantiation, into the master's face.

Noel Malcolm has exposed the place that the optical trickery of anamorphosis played in Hobbes's political theory of the state (Malcolm 2002). According to Malcolm, the famous image of the Leviathan colossus that dominates the title page of Hobbes's book came as an inspiration to Hobbes following his encounter with a dioptrical device designed by the Minim friar Jean-François Nicéron. Nicéron's design (see Figures 1a and 1b) involved a picture of the faces of twelve Ottoman sultans that, when seen through the viewing-glass tube, converged into a portrait of Louis XIII (Malcolm 2002: 213).

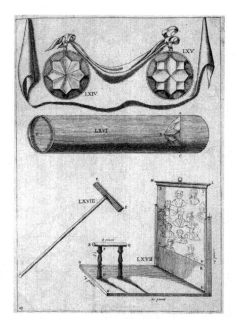 

Figures 1a, 1b. Jean François Nicéron. 1638.
La perspective curieuse, Paris, Plates 23 & 24

Seduced by the structural symbolism through which such optical illusions could be used to represent *relations* between political persons (e.g., between the state and its subjects) (Malcolm 2002: 223), Hobbes commissioned an iconographic representation of similar effects for the title page of his book. Here the image of the colossal Leviathan rises over a landscape energized by a mass of small figures. These morph by congregation into the body of the monarch, which hence takes on a life of its own. A projection of the dioptric trick onto a one-dimensional surface, the figure of the Leviathan aimed to capture the political innovation of Hobbes's theory of representational personification. For Hobbes, the aggregation of the political will of multiple individuals into an overarching sovereign person brought about a political transubstantiation: the Many became the One, which contained but also transcended the Many. This is why, for Hobbes, the theory of (political) representation is a theory of duplicity and duplication: it calls for the critical capacity to see oneself as both the creator of a political object (the body politic) and its subdued servant, both a distant outsider to the body and in partial identity with it. This entails, as Malcolm puts it, 'a curious structure of argument that requires two different ways of seeing the relation between the individual and the state to be entertained at one and the same time' (Malcolm 2002: 228).

Building on the implications of Malcolm's analysis for our theories of the state, Simon Schaffer has recently offered a phantasmagorical re-interpretation of the place of optical illusionism in political perspectivism (Schaffer 2005). For Schaffer, the dioptric capacity to 'see double' is in fact but a first step towards the cancelling of all visions but the sovereign vision. According to Schaffer, dioptrics enables this parallax shift because it rationalizes as illusory all political perspectives that do not conform with the One: outside the body politic, all visions are but the visions of political phantoms (Schaffer 2005: 202, on parallax shifts see Žižek 2006). In seventeenth-century politics this was easily accomplished, according to Schaffer, because outside the rule of sovereign law—as Hobbes noted—lay only a chaotic state of nature, shaped by mistrust, fear, witchcraft accusations and the mischievous play of invisible phantoms. The rise of the Leviathan exterminated the invisible, neatly aligning the planes of the natural and the phantasmagorical in a supreme gesture of political illusionism.

Knowledge and Politics, From the Lens's Point of View

How does social life become visible as a knowledge effect? Where and when is one to describe the beginning and end of a social moment?

In the preface to the revised edition of *Partial Connections*, Marilyn Strathern describes some of her motivations for experimenting with narrative and analytic strategies in that book. The imagery of the fractal (Cantor dust), for example, was employed as 'an artificial device' that allowed her to 'experiment with the apportioning of "size" in a deliberate manner' (Strathern 2004 [1991]: xxix). A fractal aesthetic should disavow any expectation that, say, lengthier descriptions amount to more complex analyses. More words, larger size, does not mean better understanding: 'Add or subtract, one never reduces complexity. So the size had to be an effect of perception, not of word count' (Strathern 2004 [1991]: xxix). If size had become a concern of the 1980s literary turn – the play of the fragmentary postmodern against the global hegemon, the microsociology of the situated against the transcultural economy – what forms of description should anthropology develop that could mobilize 'size' as, indeed, an adequate description of itself?

But why 'size'? What is it about Euro-American knowledge that takes size as self-evidently knowledgeable – as a vehicle of knowledge? Why and how has size become an idiom for what theory does?

A rather obvious and yet rarely acknowledged route through which the imagination of 'size' has made its way into the sociological canon is the descriptive and analytical purchase afforded by relations of magnitude known as 'proportions'. An important current in Euro-American social theory and philosophy refracts the work of knowledge through the operations of a proportional imagination. Proportionality becomes the enabling mechanism of knowledge: it is how knowledge escalates out of itself.

Take the Leviathan. Hobbes's iconographic choice makes the Leviathan appear a supreme trickster figure, at once enabling and concealing its own source of agency. The state's power figures as an aesthetic effect: the effect of a parallax shift, the alignment of two perspectives in one optical illusion. Importantly, the illusion is held in place through the work of a proportional imagination: 'the relation between the individual and the state', as Malcolm puts it, is tricked into view and held stable as a proportional artifice. The One and the Many stand in a political relation to each other *because* of their proportional relationship. As a symbolic form, not only the meaningfulness but also the 'comparability of phenomena rests on preserving proportion or scale' (Strathern 1990: 211). Nicéron's dioptric lens generates the perspective from which knowledge of the political surfaces. The lens helps scale the political *out* from the proportional relationship between the sultans and the king. 'The political' emerges as a modern theoretical object thanks to the effect of the anamorphic artifice: it is what the world looks like from the lens's point of view. Anamorphosis situates and aligns the world of political theory for us.

The anamorphic works a second effect on the constitution of the political as an epistemic object. I call it reversibility. Commenting on the illusionary character of Hobbes's Leviathan, Malcolm described it as 'the curious structure of argument that requires two different ways of seeing the relation between the individual and the state to be entertained at one and the same time' (2002: 228). The *relational* character of sovereign power thus emerges as another effect of the anamorphic artifice. It is a produce of having to hold *simultaneously* an internal and an external vision of the images of the twelve sultans and Louis XIII's emblem. Not without reason, Simon Schaffer described the methodological exigency underpinning our encounter with the phantom qualities of the Hobbesian body politic as 'seeing double' (Schaffer 2005). Moving in and out of the dioptric lens – holding a strabismic view – lends political theory its relational purchase.

The rest of this chapter explores the hold that proportionality and reversibility have over the make-up of social theory. For example, in the tricking-into-view of the Leviathan as political ontology, the compound work of proportionality and reversibility may be seen to perform the epistemological ploy of 'more than one but less than many' that Anne-marie Mol and John Law have posited as characteristic of social theory's contemporary narration of complexity (Mol and Law 2002: 17). The modern complex, according to Mol and Law, looks something like a fractal. And yet the epistemological seductiveness of the fractal, I suggest, rehearses in essence a baroque aesthetics: 'more than one but less than many' could well be the epigram employed to describe what the dioptric lens does to Louis XIII and the twelve sultans. In this light, the chapter may be read as an exploratory foray into the cultural epistemology of some aspects of Euro-American knowledge – in particular, certain received assumptions about the interrelations between complexity and magnitude, scale and size.

Scale

I start with sociologist Albena Yaneva's rich and evocative account of how architects visualize their building projects. Her field site is the Office for Metropolitan Architecture (OMA), the workplace of the famous Dutch architect Rem Koolhaas, and her focus is the work carried out by architects at OMA during the design and development of a number of models for the new exhibition hall at the Whitney Museum of American Art in New York (Yaneva 2005). Yaneva writes from a self-confessed social studies of technology perspective, and indeed declares that in her account, 'the architectural office will be studied in the same way that STS has approached the laboratory' (Yaneva 2005: 869).

The ethnography starts from the premise that 'knowing through scaling is an integral aspect of architectural practice', and the author sets herself the task of ethnographically describing the so-called enigma of the 'rhythm of scaling' (Yaneva 2005: 870, 868). The scales that inform Yaneva's task are differently sized models of the Whitney building project. Architects in OMA work with two scale models of the projected building: a small-scale model, which architects assemble quickly to provide a sketchy and abstract materialization of the basic concept guiding the project, and which includes a number of site constraints, such as urban and local zoning regulations or client requirements; and a much larger scale model, which is used to fine-tune the small model by fleshing out its concrete details.

The small and large models are set up on two adjacent tables, and architects spend a good amount of time moving from one table to the next, '"scaling up", "jumping the scale", "rescaling" and "going down in scale"', in the vernacular terminology used by Yaneva's informants (2005:

870). In moving between tables and models, architects work with an instrument known as a 'modelscope', which is used to explore the inside of the small model. By inserting a miniature periscope into the model, architects redeploy themselves as human users of the building. 'The modelscope', an architect tells Yaneva, 'gives you a view that is like the scale of that model. So, you get to express the space at that scale. It gives you the opportunity to move around spaces you ordinarily can't get into and to see how they look … We are able to see how space is inside.' Yaneva further notes that 'minimized to the scale of the tiny model, [the architect] is exploring these microscopic spaces like in Gulliver's travels, he "enters" the spaces and experiences them' (Yaneva 2005: 876). Having cruised the inside of the small model, architects then meet to discuss possible changes in the architectural layout of the building, which are later given concrete expression in changes made to the large model.

The scoping in and out of the small and large models is a recursive process: 'Scaling up', writes Yaneva, 'is immediately and reversibly followed by scaling down' (Yaneva 2005: 883). However, as times goes by, the larger model inevitably amasses more information and detail than the smaller one, for the insights gained from exploring the small model eventually get transported to the larger model, where they are reflected. Thus, the larger model grows in power and information by gathering the produce of the recursion. But importantly, Yaneva insists, this does not mean that the design involves a linear or evolutionary movement from the small model to the large model. The small model is not a precondition, or an evolutionary antecedent, for the revelation of proper and useful knowledge at the level of the large-scale model. Rather, the design is simultaneously present in the small and the large, the before and after of every recursion, the scoping in and out through which architects multiply the versions and the trajectories of the design. According to Yaneva, the shape the project finally takes emerges gradually as a form of extended and ubiquitous co-presence in the time and space of all such scalar operations. As 'it passes through these trials', she says, 'it becomes more and more visible, more present, more material, real. "Scaling" is not a way to fit into reality; rather, it is a conduit for its extraction' (Yaneva 2005: 887).

I would like to remark on two aspects of the architects' use of scaling as a method of knowledge and design. One is the extraordinary ease with which it sits next to *Gulliver's Travels*. The other is what this figure of scale takes for granted.

It is certainly worth noting that Jonathan Swift and Yaneva resort to a similar imagination of size to give their arguments force. Size is important for both, helping to render certain insights valuable and visible. In fact, literary theorist Douglas Lane Patey's description of *Gulliver's Travels* as 'laboratory experiments based on difference of size' (Patey 1991: 827) is much like Yaneva's description of her ethnography of architecture as a laboratory study in the 'rhythm of scaling'.

Of course, Swift's use of size has long attracted the attention of literary theorists for its satirical effects. It is satire that size aims for. I suggest, however, that one may explore the use of size in Swift not for its effects on something else, but for its effect on itself, that is, on its own self-apprehension as a body of knowledge – size, then, as a vehicle for making knowledge an adequate expression of itself.

A wonderful episode in *Gulliver's Travels* captures something of what I am hoping to convey here, namely, the extent to which knowledge comes in different sizes. At Brobdingnag, the land of the giants, Gulliver is taken to court for the diversion of the queen and her ladies. Impressed by Gulliver's demeanour, the king, 'who had been educated in the Study of Philosophy, and particularly Mathematicks', suspects of Gulliver being 'a piece of Clock-work ... contrived by some ingenious Artist'. He therefore sends for three great scholars to examine Gulliver's shape and make-up. The scientists all agree that Gulliver 'could not be produced according to the regular Laws of Nature'. However, an opinion that he was an 'embrio' is rejected, as is his characterization as an 'abortive Birth'; nor can he be a dwarf, because his 'Littleness was beyond all degree of comparison; for, the Queen's favourite Dwarf, the smallest ever known in that Kingdom, was near thirty Foot high' (Swift 2002 [1726]: 86–87). Thus, '[a]fter much debate', the scholars finally determined that Gulliver

> was only *Relplum Scalcath*, which is interpreted literally, *Lusus Naturae* [a freak of nature]; a Determination exactly agreeable to the Modern Philosophy of *Europe*, whose Professors, disdaining the old Evasion of *occult Causes,* whereby the Followers of *Aristotle* endeavour in vain to disguise their Ignorance, have invented this wonderful Solution of all Difficulties to the unspeakable Advancement of human knowledge. (Swift 2002 [1726]: 87)

The episode is emblematic of Swift's mordancy, and in particular his dislike of the new, modern science of the Royal Society, epitomized here in the figure of the three scholars. For Swift, modern science falls into the trap of tautology (circular and self-explanatory arguments, such as something being a 'freak of nature') as much as ancient science did. But the episode is further remarkable for its defence of size as comparative epistemology. Gulliver does not survive comparison against dwarves, embryos or abortive births, so in the end he is catalogued as a freak of nature. Not even the use of a 'Magnifying-Glass' helps the scholars reach agreement on what Gulliver may be. They size him up and size him down, only to conclude that he is not a product of nature. Thus, for Lane Patey, 'Swift's play with perspective (relative size and its implications)' ultimately enacts the question 'what is there in us that survives comparison – what that cannot be rendered ludicrous, shameful, or disgusting when magnified to Brobdingnagian proportions or shrunk to Lilliputian?' (Patey 1991: 826). Said differently, in Brobdingnag country, Gulliver lacks ontology because he is out of proportion with the world.

My second remark on architects' use of scaling as a method of knowledge builds on this question of size and the proportionality of the world. In Yaneva's account, what is at stake is how the project grows and consolidates its own size, or how it finds in the small and large models different capacities to deploy different aspects of the design. The qualities of the design are therefore allowed to emerge through recursive travelling between models of different scale. Thus, the dominant episteme is that of scale. I suggest, however, that Yaneva's ethnography provides some room to speculate about an alternative episteme by imagining the architects looking into the models for certain qualities other than those of *adjustment to scale*. For example, when a giant red escalator's effect on the interior of the exhibition hall is examined through the modelscope, the architects agree that the escalator needs to be moved to a different spot within the hall. What exactly motivates the relocation remains in the shadows, although Yaneva intimates that the 'scaling team engages in a dialogue … [about] dispositions, objects they see inside the model, spatial transitions, material properties of the foam [used to build the model], proportions and shapes' (Yaneva 2005: 875). The escalator is not quite the right fit for the architects, but it is no longer clear that this fit is a question of scale. Thus, the adjustment the architects now appear to seek seems to aim for a different kind of harmony, or an equilibrium of different proportions.[1]

Adjustments to Scale

In an age of computer technology, the way OMA's architects use scale models may appear a little surprising to those of us who are new to the field of architecture. But in fact, as historian of architecture Paul Emmons has shown, the use of scale and scalar drawings has been fundamental to architectural practice throughout history (Emmons 2005). For example, from 'the middle of the second millennium BCE', writes Emmons, 'a statue of Gudea, leader of the City State of Lagash in present day Iraq, is seated with a building floor plan resting on his lap. Also on the tablet are a stylus and a scale rule, showing fine divisions of the finger measure' (Emmons 2005: 227). Like Yaneva, in his historical survey Emmons too draws an analogy between the use of scale in architecture and Swift's *Gulliver's Travels,* and the seventeenth-century scalar imagination at large. He compares Swift's use of scale with Voltaire's in *Micromégas,* and further identifies in Robert Hooke's *Micrographia* a locus of general influence for the period. Hooke, a surveyor for the City of London who himself designed a number of buildings along with his friend Christopher Wren, 'transferred his familiarity with scale from architectural drawing to the microscope' (Emmons 2005: 231). Published in 1665, *Micrographia* described Hooke's use of a microscope to observe miniature aspects of the natural world, such as a fly's eye or a plant cell. The book became an immediate bestseller of its day.

Of interest for our purposes here is Hooke's mode of use and relationship to the microscope. Emmons cites a passage in the *Micrographia* that echoes in fascinating ways how Yaneva's architects scooped in and out of the small- and the large-scale models. 'Hooke organised his microscopic observations', writes Emmons, 'progressively from simple to complex, like a geometer ascending from point, line, plane to volume and the chain of being from mineral to vegetable and animal. He began with observing the point of a pin under the microscope … He next analysed a dot made by a pen, and in a scalar reverie imagined this dot as the earth in space.' (Emmons 2005: 231) However, Hooke was also aware that this amassment of detail – from the simple to the complex – required a second operation to remain epistemologically productive. He went to quite some effort to keep the observations made *inside* the scale of the microscope on a par with those made *outside* the microscope. As Emmons puts it, 'Hooke explained his method determining the microscope's scale of magnification by looking with one eye through the microscope as the other naked eye examines a ruler, *simultaneously engaging both scales*' (Emmons 2005: 231, emphasis added). This simultaneous engagement of both scales echoes the parallax shift of Hobbes's Leviathan as an illusion of epistemological and political efficacy enabled by some sort of 'double vision'.

Emmons concludes his observations on the historical importance of scale for architecture by commenting on contemporary architects' use of computer software to generate 1:1 or full-scale computer-assisted design (CAD) projections of architectural designs. For Emmons, the use of CAD technology emulates a Cartesian approach to the generation of objects, where things can be described or plotted through systems of notational or algebraic relations. Thus, the use of CAD-enabled full-scale drawing 'makes it more likely that the designer looks at the image as an object rather than projecting oneself into the image through an imaginative in-habitation. Scale sight is not an abstraction; it is achieved through judg-ing the size of things in relation to ourselves' (Emmons 2005: 232). His 'handbook advice', then, is to 'learn to think within a scale rather than translate from actual measure' (Emmons 2005: 232). Against Cartesian-ism, for Emmons, the 'empathetic bodily projection' of scale is 'critical to imagining a future edifice' (Emmons 2005: 232). The development of a human sense of habitation, Emmons is therefore insinuating, re-quires distinguishing between human encounters with size and human projections of scale – a point recently rehearsed by Richard Sennett in his treatise on craftsmanship when observing how '[c]omputer-assisted design also impedes the designer in thinking about scale, as opposed to sheer size. Scale involves judgments of proportion' (Sennett 2008: 41). The distinction between size and scale, then, involves an appraisal of proportionality. This moment of *reconnaissance* demarcates in turn the impression of largeness as an epistemic effect:

> Size and scale provide two measurements of how large is 'enlarged'. In archi-tecture, very large buildings can seem on an intimate human scale, whereas some small-sized structures feel very big … vast Baroque churches seem inti-mate in scale because their undulating walls and decor mimic the motions the human body makes, whereas Bramante's motionless little Tempietto feels as big, as enlarged, as the Pantheon on which it is modeled. (Sennett 2008: 85)

Knowledge, we might say, pops up as an after-effect – an enlargement – of a proportional recognition. Thus, not surprisingly, Robert Hooke realized the full epistemic power of the microscope when noting how one might compress secret knowledge into a miniature text. Such small writing, he argued, 'might be of very good use to convey secret *Intel-ligence* without any danger of *Discovery*' (Hooke 1665: 3). One could make knowledge disappear in *size* (disappear from view) and yet retain the full *scale* of its power.

Emmons's description of the history of architectural practice features two aspects that I would like to hold in view. The first deals with the proportionality of architecture as a skill and trade; the second, to which I shall return later, with the deployment of the 'double vision' entailed in the practice of scoping in and out of scale.

Emmons's concern is with current architectural practice, where scale fares as a context-free metric, and advocates instead a return to 'judg-ing the size of things in relation to ourselves'. This form of empirical judgment echoes what Yaneva called a 'rhythm of scaling': an iterative re-proportional exercise through which the world sizes its ontology (its human and non-human landscape) to a proper shape and form.

In fact, in this context architectural practice provides an interesting place for seeing not only the work of proportionality at play, but also its recurrent entanglement in larger debates about the epistemic structure of scientific knowledge. David Turnbull, for example, has described how, in the absence of knowledge about structural mechanics, the use of proportionality in medieval times enabled the construction of imposing and majestic Gothic cathedrals such as Chartres. According to Turnbull,

> In the absence of rules for construction derived from structural laws problems could be resolved by practical geometry, using compasses, a straightedge, ruler, and string. The kind of structural knowledge which was passed on from master to apprentice related sizes to spaces and heights by ratios, such as half the number of feet in a span expressed in inches plus one inch will give the depth of a hardwood joist ... This sort of geometry is extremely powerful; it enables the transportation and transmission of structural experience, makes possible the successful replication of a specific arrangement in different places and different circumstances, reduces a wide variety of problems to a comparatively compact series of solutions, and allows for a flexible rather than rigid rule-bound response to differing problems ... Essentially it enables a dimensionless analysis precluding the need for a common measure. Geometrical techniques in this case provide a powerful mode of communication that dissolve problems of incommensurability that the use of individual measurement systems might otherwise have. (Turnbull 2000: 69)

Turnbull is interested in the constitution of what he calls 'knowledge spaces'. These are the 'kinds of spaces that we construct in the process of assembling, standardising, transmitting and utilising knowledge' (Turnbull 2000: 12). In this respect Western science is no different from other knowledge systems, such as indigenous or amateur knowledge systems. What distinguishes the epistemic robustness of techno-science, rather, is its development of a corpus of techniques and protocols that enable knowledge to move and travel beyond localized sites of production. The further knowledge can travel, the more coherent and robust its epistemic make-up. This is why, for Turnbull, the architectural site of a cathedral can be imagined in terms no different from those of a laboratory (Turnbull 2000: 66–67). All it takes is identifying an analogical 'scalar' denominator: something that can operate the changes in scale required for knowledge to cohere and travel. For Turnbull, in the context of medieval cathedral building, this task was performed by the 'template':

> Three major 'reversals of forces' are achieved with this one small piece of representational technology; one person can get large numbers of others to work in concert; large numbers of stones can be erected without the ben-

efit of a fully articulated theory of structural mechanics or a detailed plan; and incommensurable pieces of work can be made accumulative. (Turnbull 2000: 68)

Turnbull's focus on proportionality as a tool for sense-making provides a vivid example of the terms through which knowledge is said to 'grow' as an epistemic object. The work of proportionality suffuses knowledge with an ontological structure. In Turnbull's account this is actually so in two senses. On the one hand, proportionality is what masons used to calculate the fit between spaces and heights. The proportion is the vehicle for lending the world a certain height, length and width (Corsín Jiménez 2010). But the imagery of proportionality is also what underpins Turnbull's own analytical explanations. Thus, in an echo of the Galilean epigram that heads this chapter – 'the most admirable operations derive from very weak means' – Turnbull writes of how the use of the template by masons enabled 'one person ... [to] get large numbers of others to work in concert'. This is a truly Archimedean metaphor, where a sociological effect is made visible by imagining agency as a leverage of sorts.

Architectural Optics of Volumes

The movements in size – the dynamics of aggrandizement and miniaturization that Turnbull describes as characteristic of the epistemic work of science – are nowhere rendered in so vivid a style as in Bruno Latour's historical ethnography of Pasteur's microbiology. According to Latour, amongst Pasteur's greatest achievements is his *translation* of nineteenth-century farmers' and veterinarians' interest in the anthrax bacillus into the discourse and practices of bacteriologists. This Pasteur accomplished by becoming a 'microbe farmer' himself, removing a cultivated bacillus from the 'outside' real world of farming and veterinary science and isolating and culturing it 'inside' a sanitized laboratory space. Whereas in the former the 'anthrax bacilli are mixed with millions of other organisms' and therefore practically invisible to the scientific gaze, in the latter 'it is freed from all competitors and so grows exponentially', 'growing so much' that it 'ends up ... in such large colonies that a clear-cut pattern is made visible to the watchful eye of the scientist' (Latour 1983: 146). The inside:outside::visible:invisible equation creates and enables different zones of empowerment and agency for different actors. Thus,

the asymmetry in the scale of several phenomena is modified: a micro-organism can kill vastly larger cattle, one small laboratory can learn more about pure anthrax cultures than anyone before; the invisible micro-organism is made visible; the until now uninteresting scientist in his lab can talk with more authority about the anthrax bacillus than veterinarians ever have before. (Latour 1983: 146)

Translation works therefore as a sort of rebalancing mechanism, where Pasteur stands as fulcrum: the messy and cloudy world of outside farming and veterinary diseases is funnelled through the inside of Pasteur's laboratory to crystallize and make visible a new balance of powers. Pasteur's laboratory becomes a lever for a new distribution of power. In Latour's succinct formulation:

> The change of scale makes possible a reversal of the actors' strengths; 'outside' animals, farmers and veterinarians were *weaker* than the invisible anthrax bacillus; inside Pasteur's lab, man becomes stronger than the bacillus, and as a corollary, the scientist in his lab gets the edge over the local, devoted, experienced veterinarian. (Latour 1983: 147, emphasis in the original)

In these and other accounts Latour uses the imagery of scale to produce sociological explanations. He sizes objects and agencies up and down vis-à-vis each other to make certain sociological effects visible. A similar appraisal of the Latourian project has been offered by Simon Schaffer, who has remarked on the extent to which '[t]he model of the lever plays a fundamental role throughout Latour's *oeuvre*: scientists achieve astonishing reversals of force by rendering lab objects commensurable with the forces of the world, then manipulating the former to shift the latter.' Schaffer notes how in his descriptions Latour chooses an 'Archimedean point' around which he then proceeds to effect an 'inversion of scale', letting certain beings (human or non-human) 'move forces apparently more powerful than' them (Schaffer 1991: 184).

Latour is certainly aware of the choice of imagery through which he fleshes out his epistemology. Of his Pasteur article, 'Give Me a Laboratory and I Will Raise the World', he writes that 'I used in the title a parody of Archimedes's famous motto' because '[t]his metaphor of the lever to move something else is much more in keeping with observation than any dichotomy between a science and a society' (Latour 1983: 154). His point, quite rightly, is that French society's reception and endorsement of Pasteur's scientific advances cannot be explained by a simple dichotomic framework of encounters between science and society. Rather, one needs to attend to the different strategies and practices through which a variety of partisan interests are recruited and converted into laboratory skills and techniques, and vice versa, the way in which the laboratory and its infrastructural equipment get deployed and travel outside the laboratory walls sensu stricto – in other words, the way in which Pasteur becomes a farmer and farmers becomes Pasteurians.

Notwithstanding this declaration of epistemological self-awareness, what remains intriguing is the long lineage of proportional epistemologies to which this style of sociological reasoning and argumentation belongs. In *We Have Never Been Modern,* Latour comments on the Hobbes-Boyle controversy by observing that Hobbes insisted on denying what was 'to become the essential characteristic of modern power: the change in scale and the displacements that are presupposed by laboratory work' (Latour 1993: 22). For Latour, the laboratory performs for modernity the role of a 'theatre of measurement', or an instrument for size-making, and indeed it is the self-explicitation of size that in his own work becomes his analytic trademark. His sociology fares as a sociology of size, or rather, of the fluctuations of size.

Michel Serres (1982) used the term 'theatre of measurement' to describe 'the scene of representation established for Western thought [by ancient Greeks] for the next millennium'. It marks the 'instauration of the moment of representation' by philosophy, an instauration brought about through the use of 'a perspectival geometry, of an architectural optics of volumes' (Serres 1982: 92). This wonderful phrase captures much of what I have been dwelling on up to this point. Serres's argument builds on the tale of Thales's measurement of the height of the great pyramid. Thales accomplishes this feat by placing a post in the sand. As the sun sets, the triangular shadows cast by the pyramid and post are then compared. Thales thereby invents 'the notion of a model' (Serres 1982: 86):

> By comparing the shadow of the pyramid with that of a reference post and his own shadow, Thales expressed the invariance of similar forms over changes of scale. His theorem therefore consists of the infinite progression or reduction of size while preserving the same ratio. From the colossal, the pyramid, to the small, a post or body, decreasing in size *ad infinitum,* the theorem states a logos or identical relation, the invariance of the same form, be it on a giant or a small scale, and vice versa. Height and strength are suddenly scorned, smallness demands respect, all scales and hierarchies are demolished, now derisory since each step repeats the same logos or relation without any changes! (Serres 1995: 78)

Steven Brown, who has commented on the originality of Serres's oeuvre for social theory at large, glosses Serres's analysis thus:

> Here truly is the 'Greek miracle' – one man dominates a mighty pyramid. In this 'theatre of measurement' invented through the simple act of placing a peg in the sand, it is as though everything changed place. The weak human overcomes ancient hewn stone, the mobile sun produces immobile geometric forms ... There is an interaction or communication between two

diverse partners (Thales, Pyramid) which involves a switching or exchanging of properties (weak/strong, mortal/durable). (Brown 2005: 220)

We are back, then, to the Archimedean image of leverage. The world's intelligibility holds itself together through an image of ontological balance. Whatever the world turns out to be – however and wherever we locate its sources of agency – this will always 'net out' as an exchange of equations: weak/strong, mortal/durable, cathedral/template, gigantic/infinitesimal, and so on. The use of a proportional imagination allows social theory to net out its descriptive projects in ontological fashion. It would appear, then, that a central tradition of our epistemo-ontological thought (the height, length and width of our social theory) works by reproducing itself as a sort of 'architectural optics of volumes', where epistemic knowledge is marginally netted out from exercises in surviving comparison.[2]

Notes

1. Philippe Boudon makes a distinction between architecture and architecturology (the study of architecture as a conceptual practice). According to Boudon, architecture confronts scale not as a given but as an epistemological 'shift': architects encounter scale and proportionality as something to work *with* rather than *upon* (Boudon 1999). Scale is something that one does to a project, rather than a geometric or physical constraint; it is a 'mode of shifting' one's conceptual take on an architectural challenge (Boudon 1999: 10). Thus, the criteria employed to relocate the giant red escalator in Yaneva's account would fare as one such 'mode of shifting'. They would provide an answer to the question 'How does the architect give measurement to space?', which is, for Boudon, the architecturological question par excellence (Boudon 1999: 15).
2. The netting out of ontology accomplishes *purity of form*: the birth of logos or reason as pure relationality. Thus, Serres observes how

   > Thales demonstrates the extraordinary weakness of the heaviest material ever worked, as well as the omnipotence, in relation to the passing of time, of a certain logical structure: of the logos itself as long as we redefine it, no longer as a word or statement, but, by lightening it, as an equal relation; even softer because *the terms balance each other,* obliterate each other so that all that remains is their *pure and simple relation.* (Serres 1995: 78, emphasis added)

   The ontological robustness of logic, then, appears in this context as the result of a proportional equation. *Proportionality is prior to relationality.* The world endures as an intelligible object as long as we can provide some kind of proportionate account of it.

   This proposition sets the place of 'measurement' in reason in a new perspective. Andrew Barry, for example, has brought attention to the central role of measurement in the history of mediations between science and political economy (Barry 1993). For Barry, the instrumentation of measurement has been key to generating political metrologies: 'measurement and other forms of scientific representation have been deployed in the regulation of social and economic relations over large "geographical" areas of space' (Barry 1993: 464). In his account this is a relatively recent historical phenomenon, in that '[i]f measurement has become a central resource for the regulation of space, it has only been so to a great degree since the mid-nineteenth century – the period in which science has become articulated with the moral, political and economic objectives of imperialism; and more recently with those of transnational industry and government' (Barry 1993: 467). My suggestion here, however, is that measurement has been integral to how all forms of epistemic knowledge have conceptualized themselves in the modern age. (Note that Serres's account is of course a modern account.) Measurement, or what I call proportionality, is the shape that modern knowledge takes every time it gets actualized.

2

The Strabismic Eye

Of course the importance of proportionality for architectural, and indeed socio-spatial reflection in the Euro-American tradition at large, has long been a matter of perspective – of optics.

For years the origins of perspective in the fifteenth century were traced back to the renaissance of classical proportionality. As Martin Jay has observed, 'Growing out of the late medieval fascination with the metaphysical implications of light – light as divine *lux* rather than perceived *lumen* – linear perspective came to symbolize a harmony between the mathematical regularities in optics and God's will.' Pictorial and aesthetic preoccupations shifted from a religious interest in objects to 'the spatial relations of the perspectival canvas themselves. This new concept of space was geometrically isotropic, rectilinear, abstract, and uniform' (Jay 1988: 5–6). Thus, famously, for Erwin Panofsky Renaissance perspective realized reflexivity as a spatial gaze (Panofsky 1993 [1927]). The difference between classical and renaissance perspective lies in the mode of occupying space and imagining spatial relations. In the Renaissance, perspective marks a mode of taking the world in by looking through it. This is different from the classical disposition of bodies in space, which remains anchored in the physical mimesis of experience and bodily movement. We may say that Renaissance perspectivalism introduces epistemological gradients to the way we look at the world: perspective does not drive us to a singular epistemological residence. There are differences between 'looking at' and 'looking through' something. The movement of the gaze through space – the achievement of depth and the skewing of vision through off-centred displacements – generates different sorts of friction. In this context, then, rather than, or beyond, comprehending perspectivalism as a geometrical or symbolic form as Panofsky did, it may be seen instead as a 'general capacity for producing effects' (Damisch 1997 [1987]: 41, my translation).

What kind of effects does the deployment of perspective produce? Very early on in the theorization of perspectivalism, Renaissance writers were already describing Brunelleschi's architectural use of perspective (for it is Brunelleschi who is widely acknowledged as having discovered the technique of perspectivalism) for its very special effects in making objects diminish in size. In this respect Hubert Damisch cites Antonio Filarete's famous *Trattato di archittettura,* where Brunelleschi's use of a mirror to help frame the lineaments of whatever the architect needs to represent is praised for 'making easily observable the contours of those things closer to the eye, whilst those that are farthest away will diminish proportionately in size' (cited in Damisch 1997 [1987]: 68). The observation is common: Antonio di Tucci Manetti, an early biographer of Brunelleschi, likewise describes perspective as a 'science which requires to determine well and with reason the diminutions and augmentations … of things close and afar' (cited in Damisch 1997 [1987]: 70–71). An acknowledged novelty of perspectivalism, then, seems to lie in the cultural salience lent to the technical capacity for making variations in size visible. Moreover, size becomes an effect of scoping: a consequence of zooming in and out of representation. Spectators can enter a picture's plane so long as they can keep certain proportions in place. The world inside the painting is therefore made to appear geometrically coextensive with the world outside, a world that invites us to engage and enter into its geometrical space. An ontological continuity between pictorial and world space is obtained through the friction and play entailed in making things big and small.

In its original formulation, the question of perspectivalism raised yet another cultural complex with epistemological significance, namely, the problem of *relational variance.* The experiment or demonstrations for which Brunelleschi is recognized as the discoverer of perspective involved two paintings of the Baptistery of St. John and the Palazzo de' Signori, both long lost. The only eyewitness account describes the Baptistery painting as being executed on a small wooden panel. Once the painting was accomplished, Brunelleschi drilled a small hole in the panel at the point that would represent his equivalent viewpoint on the Baptistery's plane (the vanishing point). He then invited spectators to peer through the hole from the back of the panel at a mirror held in front to reflect the painting (see Figure 2). The mirror, as Samuel Edg-

Figures 2 and 3. Experimental arrangement in Brunelleschi's first perspective picture. Sketches by Jorrín Montañés

erton has noted, played a crucial role in the experimental set-up, for it helped delineate 'the visual field by transferring the function of the eye to its surrogate, the vanishing point' (Edgerton 1973: 178). The vanishing point, suddenly denaturalized as the endpoint of visual cognition, was re-functionalized as its prosthetic supplementation. Viewers were thus reminded, Antonio Filarete tells us, that they would need to make a sharp use of that 'one eye' (the eye now re-functionalized as 'doer' of vanishing points) to best bring to life the full power of the perspectival illusion (Damisch 1997 [1987]: 69).

As Hanneke Grootenboer has observed, an important element in Brunelleschi's laborious experiment is therefore the way in which the use of this one-eye vision creates an illusion of depth at the expense of real depth. 'The first vision into pictorial space', writes Grootenboer, 'was, so to speak, *outside* of perceptual depth and resulted from the collapse of the view point into that of the vanishing point' (Grootenboer 2005: 53–54, emphasis in the original).

Brunelleschi's 'perspective' therefore took shape as a vexed supplementation: to the mirror reflection obtained by looking with one eye through the pierced hole, the viewer had to add the 'natural' gaze of her other eye. The view obtained was 'strabismic': it was the effect of each eye looking in different directions, and therefore of having to negotiate and fuse different perceptual fields. When years later Leon Alberti finally formalized the procedures for creating linear perspective, the illusion of perspectival depth was prescribed instead through the 'separation of the vanishing point and viewpoint and never again by means of their fusion' (Grootenboer 2005: 54). The perceptive field was designed instead as a geometrical continuum. To the classical binocular vision of the Albertian perspectivalists we must therefore add the strabismus of the original Brunelleschian experiment.

As James Elkins has put it generally for all kinds of mirror reflections (of which the Brunelleschian demonstration might fare as the inaugural exemplar), '[t]he mirror has a special kind of empty eye. It waits to see, but it cannot see without me to see it' (Elkins 1996: 49).[1] This one-eyed optics is intriguingly reminiscent of Hooke's microscopic vision, where one eye holds the scale of the miniature in view whilst the other is focused on the scale of representation. It further echoes the 'seeing double' at play in the Leviathan's optics. An eye is constructed that is therefore simultaneously internal and external to vision. Such a strabismic eye foregrounds the body (the body of the Brunelleschian viewer, the micrographer or even Hobbes's sovereign) as a figure of scale between the natural and the social worlds: an eye that looks straight and a second eye that looks astray. These are viewing subjects, moreover, that hold the world to account by virtue of a 'double vision', that is, two eyes, two views, and a compound (strabismic) double vision.

It remains uncertain whether Brunelleschi realized he needed to control the viewing distance for spectators to replicate his original point of view on the Baptistery (Damisch 1997 [1987]: 98; Kemp 1990: 13, 344–345). What Brunelleschi's experiment did accomplish, however, was to throw into relief the significance of *variation* as an epistemological figure. Variation was a produce of the prosthetic intervention: one had to tinker and adjust the mirror to obtain a proper sense of depth and geometrical coherence. There is a proper distance and location between our holding the mirror-world in view and the world's presentation or disclosure of its forms. Viewing the panel at a slight angle, for instance, would off-centre the drawing's geometric convergence and, therefore, its epistemological coherence: at an angle the vanishing point and the point of view would no longer be aligned. A subtle shift is thus introduced between the point of view on the world and the relational variance through which the view obtains.

The Mobile Eye

Of the famous realism of seventeenth-century Dutch art, Svetlana Alpers has observed that unlike the 'artificial perspective system of the Italians' (the Albertian solution), the 'wide vista' often afforded by Dutch composition 'presumes an aggregate of views *made possible by a mobile eye,* the retinal or optical has been added on to the perspectival' (Alpers 1983: 27, emphasis added). One could interpret the practice of Dutch artists, then, as rehearsing or re-enacting the Brunelleschian aesthetics of supplementation. For Alpers, the skill of double vision practised by Dutch artists (that is, adding the optical to the perspectival) enacted a visual culture where knowledge of the world was made available as a stand-alone, descriptive register in which 'meaning by its very nature is lodged in what the eye can take in' (Alpers 1983: xxiv) – that is, not in what the eye can see but in the amount of world that gets impressed on it: the worldliness of the eye.

The seventeenth-century Dutch eye, according to Alpers, encouraged therefore the viewer's total absorption by painting. Whilst the Italians were fascinated by the just proportionality of pictorial forms and therefore considered a painting 'an object in the world, a framed window to which we bring our eyes', the Dutch stressed instead the importance of 'the picture taking the place of the eye with the frame and our location thus left undefined' (Alpers 1983: 45). Thus, the 'eye of the northern viewer inserts itself right into the world, while the southern viewer stands at a measured distance to take it all in' (Alpers 1983: 85).

As an eye immersed in the world, the Dutch eye lacks scale: it does not seek to frame the world according to a human measure but simply takes the world in. Such disregard for scale is a characteristic of the visual culture of attentiveness that Alpers suggests was shared alike by seventeenth-century Dutch artists, for example Jan Vermeer, Pieter Saenredam or Jacques de Gheyn, and microscopists and optical experimentalists such as Leeuwenhoek or, most famously, Kepler:

> I want to consider at least three useful terms of comparison between the activity of the microscopist and the artists, terms that are based on notions of seeing held in common and posited on an attentive eye. First and second, *the double cutting edge of the world* seen microscopically is that it *both multiplies and divides*. It multiplies when it dwells on the innumerable small elements within a larger body ... or the differences between individuals of a single species. It divides when it enables us to seen an enlargement of a small part of a larger body or surface ... Third, it treats everything as a visible surface either by slicing across or through to make a sections ... or by opening something up to expose the innards to reveal how it is made. (Alpers 1983: 84, emphasis added)

Alpers's analogy between the early investigations of optical experimentalists and the gaze of artists rests on the potency of what she calls a 'mobile eye': an eye that moves elegantly and curiously across epistemic zones and regions, in and out of different scales of representation. The mobile eye cuts the world two ways: it multiplies with one eye what it divides with the other, and in doing so opens up a space for a third form of vision: a 'seeing double' that is more than one and less than many.

The mobility of the Dutch eye sets it apart from the strategies of representation in the classical Renaissance (Italian) perspectival tradition. The Dutch and the Italian may in this context be described as alternative itineraries or trajectories of the modern episteme. The optical descriptiveness of the Dutch world is set against the narratological perspectivalism of the Italians. It is indeed in these terms that Martin Jay has spoken of three 'scopic regimes of modernity' (Jay 1988), adding to the Cartesian perspectivalism of the Italians and the Dutch art of description a third form of baroque or anamorphic modernity.

The structural perspectivalism of anamorphosis offers a useful point of entry into what I have been referring to throughout as the complex strabismus of modernity. Anamorphic projections of objects are distorted such that a special device or manoeuvre is needed to restore the object to its original form by realigning the vanishing point and the point of view. They demand the spectator's participation to work over and actively re-engage the artwork's original aesthetic surface. Remember the Leviathan and Nicéron's dioptric device. Sometimes it is the use of a special kind of lens that does the trick of reconfiguration; sometimes observers are required to skew their vision, for example, by approaching the picture at a particular angle.

As Lacan famously argued, in anamorphic projections vision is confronted with a blind spot of conscious perception (Lacan 1979). An image is laid out in front of a viewer who nevertheless remains incapable of taking full cognizance of its underlying visual coherence. The object stares back from a point of view that remains oblique to us (Elkins 1996). Not surprisingly, the perceptual blindness or self-concealment of anamorphic images led to them being described as 'the secret of perspective': a technique through which one could 'camouflage an image rather than reveal it, making the image into a secret and the method itself into a magical art' (Grootenboer 2005: 102–103).

Like the Brunelleschian demonstration, the history of anamorphosis is closely associated with the vexations of one-eyed optics. The first known sketches of anamorphic projections are two drawings by Leonardo of an elongated baby's face and a single eye (Grootenboer 2005: 103). Leonardo's anamorphic projection of a single eye is of course a doubled eye, a distorted projection that requires our bending the page to have it recomposed into its proper shape: it is one eye, then, with two forms of vision (the distorted and the recomposed).

Another famous single/doubled eye is Mario Bettini's print *The Eye of Cardinal Colonna*. Bettini has the cardinal's distorted eye projected onto a surface and gets a cylindrical mirror to recompose the reflection into the archbishop's staring eye (Grootenboer 2005: 110). For Christine Buci-Glucksmann, Bettini's print of Cardinal Colonna's eye epitomizes the fundamental double structure of baroque vision (Buci-Glucksmann 1986: 41). The cardinal's eye is split between its distorted image and its mirror reflection. Such split between the *ana* and the *morph* opens up an interpretative space of excess, where vision is suddenly faced with the immense power of the gaze. In Margaret Iversen's formulation, 'The real in the scopic field is formed when the eye splits itself off from its original immersion in visibility and the gaze as *objet petit a* [as unattainable object of desire] is expelled' (Iversen 2005: 201). The cardinal's eye is the imago of the impossibility and excess of knowledge. A split eye signals the birth of the baroque as an aesthetic of the uncanny, an aesthetic 'which consisted in making something visible, in being a pure apparition that made appearance appear, from a position just on its edges' and which Christine Buci-Glucksmann, citing Paul Klee, describes as 'to see with one eye and consciously perceive with the other' (Buci-Glucksmann 1994 [1984]: 60). These analyses should not be read as mere psychoanalytic fancies, for as Keith Hoskin reminds us, such strabismic imperative was something well understood by the artists of the time: 'Both Leonardo and Dürer, when drawing their perspectival constructions, put literal eyes at each of the two viewing points' (Hoskin 1995: 153).

The baroque eye is therefore an anamorphic eye: a form of strabismus defined by the co-implication – and thus complexity – of a highly structured yet unstable perspective. 'The destiny of the baroque form', writes Hanneke Grootenboer, rehearsing Buci-Glucksmann's thesis, 'constantly solicits a double and doubling gaze … One eye is correctly and scientifically drawn, the other is deformed, swollen, almost fluid' (Grootenboer 2005: 111).[2]

There are good reasons to think that whereas the strabismus of vision is hardly an exceptional, baroque curiosity, its distorted capacities have underpinned the representational strategies of modernity for longer that we have cared to admit. Thus, employing what he calls an 'iconology of tracing', James Elkins has diagrammatized a number of celebrated Renaissance perspectives, only to discover that such paintings rarely if ever sustain a perfectly geometrical structure but are instead full of deliberate errors and mistakes (Elkins 1994: 234–235). Such mistakes demonstrate not a certain misunderstanding, on the part of artists, of how linear perspective works but, on the contrary, an illustrious understanding of how the artists wished to make it work. Artists displayed perspectival errors to their advantage for full aesthetic effect. The alterations were intrinsic to perspective as a rhetorical or allegorical form. They expressed the full potency of perspectivalism in practice. Following Pamela Smith, we may refer to these crafted, practical reorientations of perspectivalism's capacity to produce effects as instances of an 'artisanal epistemology' (Smith 2004: 8 and passim).

If northern art saw in the mobility of the eye – in the engine of strabismus – a vehicle for rendering visible the world's epistemic descriptiveness, it is not unreasonable to suggest a similar epistemic status for anamorphism, or indeed for Cartesian perspectivalism itself, in practice if not in theory. In all cases it is the *strabismus of knowing* that defines the kinship of the Brunelleschian experiment, the art of description and baroque optics as practical alternatives to the perspectival epistemology of Cartesian modernity at large, if not as its very subterranean constituent. The craftsmanship of perspectivalism appears in this light as a historical strabismic (deformed, unstable, vexed) project.

Double-Entry Vision

That the deployment of perspective may indeed be a question of pragmatism, that is, of the skilful use and display of a variegated set of *pragmata* or 'things', is something that Keith Hoskin (1995) has hinted at.[3] Importantly, in Hoskin's argument this pragmatic or instrumental configuration of the perspectival craft appears to mobilize, too, a notion of strabismic estrangement that in some sense would seem to precede the constitution of the modern *cogito*. Strabismus appears therefore as a form of practice that predates the visual-cum-cognitive culture of modernity.

Hoskin suggests that the development of the self as placeholder for a point of view in fact took place in the twelfth and thirteenth centuries, well before and independently from the development of perspective. Its coming-into-being involved and enrolled a complex apparatus of knowledge practices that fundamentally concerned pedagogy and writing, among them the 'rational reordering of textual space', which mobilized techniques such as 'paragraphing, the alphabetical ordering of lists, punctuation, the systematic layout of texts in columns along with subtextual devices like the gloss' (Hoskin 1995: 147). Other techniques included 'the development of the arabic numeral system' or 'the visualist separation of sight from sound … with a move among the scholarly elite towards silent reading, and away from the reading aloud which had been culturally dominant in antiquity. Silent readers tended also to become silent authors, abandoning the practice of dictating to a scribe' (Hoskin 1995: 147, 148). The whole gamut of techniques enabled the inscription of the 'viewing self' at a 'zero-point, whence it is never moved' (Hoskin 1995: 149). The epistemology of perspectivalism would therefore seem to display some pre-perspectival elements.

Of the various techniques identified by Hoskin, the epistemic structure of double-entry bookkeeping is worth a pause. According to Hoskin,

> double-entry as a system imposes on the reader of accounts a fixed point of view, hovering always in that space between the debits and the credits, surveying their regulated and regular layout, and projecting that regularity beyond the immediate page into journals and ledgers where, by meticulous cross-referencing, the mirroring process of recording can be extended in a process that theoretically need never end. (Hoskin 1995: 149)

Bookkeepers appear to have developed thus the skill of 'seeing double', hovering in the in-between of the inside and outside of the debit and the credit ledgers. Indeed, Hoskin goes on to argue that the emergence of such a 'book-keeping mentality', where the 'self is confronted with a very different epistemological world', seems likely to have contributed to the 'splitting of the self' characteristic of modern consciousness, where the self is split into interior and exterior accounts of itself (Hoskin 1995: 150, 151).

The doppelganger structure of bookkeeping assumed a curious inflection when transported to the realm of geometrical perspectivalism. As noted above, the development of perspective demanded two separate operations: an understanding of geometrical depth, and an understanding of relational variance. The former entailed the recognition that things diminish in size as they move away from viewers; the latter that the position of the viewers themselves is relative to other positions. Thus, whilst the Brunelleschian take on perspective required supplementing one's vision by moving in and out of the one-eyed optics afforded by the mirror reflection, the Albertian solution consisted in making the adoption of different viewpoints geometrically coextensive. According to Hoskin, it was this second operation that evinced the irrevocable splitting of the self. Here 'a second self now floats free of the immobilized first self, moves round to view from the side, measures and checks the viewing coordinates, and then returns whence it came, merging back into one' (Hoskin 1995: 153). The self stands unified as a geometrical *relator* in space. And yet the motility and curiosity of the self – taking supplementary and adjacent side-views to help make the construction of objects and the world around one geometrically robust – are in fact sustained in the strabismic eye as a distorted yet productive figure that redoubles itself as seen/seer from the sides.

Perspectives Inside Out

Around 1670, the Dutch artist Cornelius Gijsbrecht produced a number of paintings that played on the rhetorical power of perspectivalism to startling effect. *Trompe l'Oeil Letter Rack,* for example, masterfully displays a three-dimensional letter rack that bodies itself forward in space. Like all trompe l'oeil paintings, it tricks us into seeing a number of objects that apparently hang out of the picture plane and invade our own physical space. The trick is here twice enfolded, because some of the letters and papers hanging from the rack are partially hidden or veiled by a curtain. The curtain supplements the perspectival trick: it generates a false sense of depth to a painting whose entire mission is to empty itself out of depth. The illusion of the trompe l'oeil is sustained in making us believe that the objects are outside rather than inside the pictorial plane.

Hanneke Grootenboer has commented on this painting by Gijsbrecht and other seventeenth-century Dutch trompe l'oeils apropos their capacity to turn perspective inside out (Grootenboer 2005: 54). In trompe l'oeil paintings, Grootenboer argues, the vanishing point and the point of view are made to coincide. In this convergence, similar to the one prompted by the mirror in the Brunelleschian demonstration, the one eye that looks through the peephole encounters its own gaze at the other end (the vanishing point) of the perspectival path. Thus, rather than being invited into the picture, our perspectival gaze is in both cases forced instead to bounce off the picture plane. The 'vanishing point to which the viewer's eye is directed', writes Grootenboer, 'can never be reached – or, for that matter, seen – and collapses with the point of view from which seeing is made possible' (Grootenboer 2005: 54). We think we are looking at a perspectival painting, yet we are not allowed to rest our perspectival gaze at its natural resting place: the vanishing point. Our perspective is instead violently thrust back at us, or as Grootenboer puts it, is 'turned inside out'.

Trompe l'oeil paintings are a meeting place for what, following Lacan's famous description in *Seminar XI*, Grootenboer calls the *reversibility* of the gaze. The surface of a trompe l'oeil painting captures the encounter of the vanishing point and the point of view, so that the perspectival organization of painting displays simultaneously an inside/outside structure. She offers an eloquent description of how this structure operates with the example of a glove:

> If we turn the finger of a glove inside out, its structure will remain exactly the same but will now be articulated by its reverse side. Previously enveloped by the leather, the lining of the glove will emerge. Exteriority and interiority are reversed without actually changing the structure of the glove. Elaborating on this metaphor, we may imagine the tip of the glove's finger as a vanishing point that once pulled out reveals the other side of the point, which normally falls beyond the horizon. Moving the finger of the glove back and forth, we see how the vanishing point can merge with the point of view when the structure within which these points are normally separated is mapped out. (Grootenboer 2005: 55)

The surface of a trompe l'oeil painting therefore becomes a meeting place for two perspectives: the perspective that is hollowed out in a forward direction from the painting's interior, and the perspective the viewer holds from outside the painting. We can no longer speak of a *vanishing point* and a *point of view,* for these descriptors properly belong to the tradition of linear perspectivalism: *inside* a painting and *outside* a painting are epistemological locations defined within the parameters of an Albertian geometrical grid.

One could rehearse instead the argument that two distinct pictorial objects are in effect making an apparition in the trompe l'oeil painting: one canvas, two pictorial forms. If we follow Grootenboer's metaphor, the inside of the glove's finger is a different object from its outside. They are objects that share a perspectival structure – they share a point of view on what is inside/outside in each case – but they are ontologically distinct objects. These objects are not differently located within the same geometrical plane, but they summon different topological fields.

Another painting by Cornelius Gijsbrecht helps illuminate this point. In *The Reverse Side of a Painting* (c. 1670) Gijsbrecht presents a painting whose canvas has been turned around. We see a wooden stretcher, six nails holding the frame in place, and the back of a canvas proper. But there is, of course, no image. Grootenboer has aptly described the viewer's shock when confronted with this picture:

> If we follow our inclination to turn this canvas around in order to see what is represented on its front side, its shock effect would reside less in the deception, and more in the discovery that there is nothing there to see. Nothing, except for the same image, back as front. (Grootenboer 2005: 59)

Figure 4. Cornelius Gijsbrecht, *The Reverse Side of a Painting* (c. 1670), Statens Museum for Kunst, Copenhagen, Creative Commons BY 3.0

To be sure, the picture whose negation Gijsbrecht painted is a different object from the actual frame and stretcher we would encounter if we were to flip the painting around. They hold the same perspective (they index the same presentation of the world: the reverse side of a painting) but they do so from distinct epistemological and ontological positions: a human and an object-centred point of view. Thus, whereas *The Reverse Side of a Painting* is the view we hold of the picture as viewers, that is, a view that obtains through an epistemological action (the act of eliciting the painting as object), the back side of a painting, on the other hand, elicits not an epistemological point of view, but an ontological position: an object (the wooden stretcher) that no longer requires the epistemological elicitation of a viewer to come into existence. *The Reverse Side of a Painting* and the reverse side of a painting are therefore different epistemological and ontological points of view, respectively, on the same epistemic object.

The Reverse Side of a Painting's masterliness lies in Gijsbrecht's sophisticated problematization of the representational strategies of the linear perspectivalist tradition. Like Velazquez's *Las Meninas* or Vermeer's *The Art of Painting*, it is a cunning work of baroque intelligence that subsumes its representational motif in a dazzling display of double relations (inside:outside / object:human / epistemology:ontology), and in so doing endows the notion of the duplex itself with epistemic status. (We shall return to the epistemic status of the duplex again in Chapter 4.) Gijsbrecht's boldness forces us to take residence in the epistemic space of the painting's liminal screen as a guarantor and purveyor of reasonableness. Oscillating between an interior and an exterior perspective, an ontological and an epistemological point of view, the trompe l'oeil's very *reversible* structure emerges therefore as the only possible comfort-zone for stabilizing, if transiently and fragilely, the turbulence and confusion of all such double movements. It is the painting's reversibility that holds all such reversions meaningful. Reversibility operationalizes the task of conceptualization for baroque reason. It is a concept that allows us to flip between an epistemological and ontological point of view.

The trompe l'oeil's status as a limit-holder – a figure of the very in-betweenness of baroque reason – distracts spectators from another important epistemic operation indicated by Gijsbrecht's painting and the genre at large. Trompe l'oeil paintings, we have seen, hollow out their own perspectival structure in a forward movement, emptying themselves outwards by turning their perspective inside out, as Grootenboer puts it. Whereas in the classical perspectival tradition, the function of perspective has been naturalized as a cognitive quality of space (a quality marking the geometrization of thought), trompe l'oeils show instead how perspective may in fact be disembedded from space and in such a condition make itself available for use as one optical device among others.

Trompe l'oeil paintings thus point to a quality of perspective as an operator, an instrument of intervention in our cultural and visual field. In these paintings, as Hanneke Grootenboer has put it, 'perspective reveals itself as unfolding the objects' visibility, and not their mere representation ... Itself remaining invisible, perspective makes us forget its structure, and even its presence, only to reveal what it makes visible' (Grootenboer 2005: 163). Perspective functions thus as a topological structure wherein objects call out their mutual co-implications as they index and point towards each other. Rather than us holding a perspective on the world, it would seem that the holding of a perspective is itself defining of our subjectivity vis-à-vis the world. The effect is analogous to that elicited by anamorphic paintings, with which trompe l'oeils share the kinship of strabismus. In an anamorphic painting, our subject position is determined by the point of view itself: We may opt to take a position perpendicular to the painting's surface, in which case the anamorphic projection will appear smeared and distorted. We will be seeing nothing. In effect we would have therefore opted for assuming a subject-less position: the position from wherein nothing becomes visible. Alternatively, we may engage with the painting and attempt to assume its own point of view, which might require us to bend the lamina or come up close to the canvas and skew our vision diagonally across its surface. Slowly, gradually, the anamorphic distortion will recompose. The painting will disclose and elicit its own point of view. We will now be seeing the distorted image, but it will have become visible 'from the painting's point of view' (Grootenboer 2005: 131). We may therefore say that the strabismus of anamorphosis and trompe l'oeil paintings works as the analytics that elicits 'perspectivalism' itself as an analytic – a point of view on/of the point of view, or in other words, the perspective's perspective. It is, moreover, a prosthetic perspective, whose completion (always partial and elusive) calls for a supplementation: an optical lens, a cylindrical mirror, an object staring back at ourselves.

Trompe l'Oeil Anthropology

Trompe l'oeil and anamorphic paintings invoke a permanent sense of incompletion. They demand acts of supplementation on the part of viewers, who must bend the lamina or skew their gaze. Theirs is therefore an aesthetic of elicitation, of calling out for completion, and of pending closure.

It is perhaps not coincidental that James Weiner (1995) has picked up on this aspect of anamorphosis to expound on a model of social life as a theory of caducity. What Weiner calls 'caducity' describes the processes and analytical figures of social life in light of their maturation, decomposition and detachment. It aims to capture how social forms fail or fall away 'after [their] descriptive and theoretical fertilizations have been made' (Weiner 1995: 4). Caducity therefore works here as a cipher of incompleteness. It is what an anthropological anamorphosis of, as opposed to an anthropological perspective on, social life might look like.

Weiner builds on a vast body of Melanesian ethnography to rethink the theoretical status of social relationships. What does a social relationship look like if it is emptied out of its expectations of (perspectival) completion? In its place Weiner offers a model for thinking of social life as a long chain of substitutions and displacements, where what people exchange and substitute are versions or metonymic bodily tokens of themselves. Weiner aptly glosses it as a 'hermeneutic of embodiment' (1995: xvii): token bodies that mature and decompose, cast off and re-incorporate, mutate and extend, pop up and disappear. Indeed, making things disappear – coming to terms with the indissoluble role of detachment as both a theory and form of action – is what Weiner, marrying Lacan and Strathern, hopes to establish:

> What Lacan introduced was the idea that to make this whole [the whole of the self, personality, the ego], something must be detached from it. For him, the critical act of perception was the making of a cut, of which the model was the specular image, the cutting off of the scopic field by the operation of that most relational of organs, the eye. And what Melanesians present us with, according to Strathern, is merely the practical, productive consequence of such an understanding: they strive to detach parts of themselves, they aspire to a partiality and excentricity of perspective, to maintain the externality of the various sources of the self, to *not* introject them, to maintain the multiplicity of compositional influences on the self. (Weiner 1995: 15)

'Everything has a detachable part and a left-behind part', Weiner notes at one point (1995: 15). In a Lacanian turn, he picks up the image of the left-behinds to make a general argument about the caducity of social life. 'To be human', notes Weiner, 'is to be temporal, which is to say that we look forward to the completion of our acts … Because this anticipation of form precedes its visual confirmation, there are always parts or regions of the body that escape the mirror, that are not retained by the subject in the formation of its ego ideal' (1995: 19). These discarded parts therefore work, also, as distortions of the subject: 'although they maintain the shape of the body's geography, they do so in a perspectival, nonproportional way, as an anamorphic projection distorts the proportions of the depicted object' (1995: 20).

The resort to anamorphosis and (non) proportionality in Weiner's argument makes for a suggestive reformulation of how detachment works. In the Melanesian model of sociality, 'detachment makes the person incomplete … and therefore [inclined to] seek completion with another' (Strathern 1988: 222). It is therefore both a sign of anticipation and de-formation – an index of the form-to-be. The anamorphic, as Weiner points out following Lacan, signals this becomingness of form. The form is tensed against its own elicitation or projection outwards. It everses or hollows itself outwards in response to a residual or displaced (anamorphic) perspective held on it. Importantly, however, in propelling itself outwards towards completion, the form-inducing process shows its moments of disjuncture in *dis/proportional* fashion. Short of completion (i.e., of proportional integrity and wholeness), the form thus expresses its disfiguration or disproportionality. On this basis, Weiner reformulates the project of anthropology as being concerned 'with a consideration of the *differential proportions that meanings take in human life*' (Weiner 1995: 25, emphasis in the original).

Weiner's anthropological anamorphosis of social life offers a general model for critical thought. What would happen, his approach invites us to consider, if we were to think of sociological analysis as an unfinished form of aesthetic elicitation? If we imagine the classical objects of political economy (the public, knowledge, the market) not as Renaissance paintings but as trompe l'oeils or anamorphic projections – if we were to everse our perspective on them?

What, in sum, would the public, knowledge and the economy look like if seen with strabismic eyes?

Notes

1. The place of the uncanny is thus intuited in the work of optics. In this respect Andrea Battistini recalls an early observation of Emanuele Tesauro, who 'marked the maximum wit of the optical emblems, "which, for *certain proportions of perspective,* through strange and ingenious appearances, make you see things that you do not see"' (Battistini 2006: 19, emphasis added).

2. David Topper has argued against what he calls the 'postmodern' use of anamorphosis for sustaining subjectivist or relativist epistemological positions (Topper 2000). A postmodern account of anamorphosis, in his rendering, would emphasize the either/or version of an image: either you see the twelve sultans, or you see Louis XIII. Instead, he makes a cognitive argument about the dual nature of visual perception. Like James J. Gibson, he suggests that human perception can hold the 'concurrent specification of two reciprocal things' or 'in-between perceiving' (Topper 2000: 118,

116). A classic example is the way we hold together, in one integrated vision, the flat-depth distinction between a painting's surface and the surfaces of the objects represented inside the painting (Topper 2000: 117). Notwithstanding the fact that some anamorphs are so distorted that their initial viewing requires a wholesale surrender of 'concurrent' perception, I think his argument about 'in-betweenness' is nonetheless inherent in the historical analytic of reversibility: the mode of knowledge that can hold simultaneously internal and external expressions of itself.

3. My thanks to Marilyn Strathern for bringing Hoskin's article to my attention.

3

Reversibility/ Proportionality

> At the beginning of the seventeenth century,
> during the period that has been termed,
> rightly or wrongly, the Baroque, thought
> ceases to move in the element of resemblance.
> —Foucault, *The Order of Things*

Sometime in 1600 Michalengelo Merisi (Caravaggio) painted his *Narcissus*. The story of Narcissus, it is well known, was of great interest to painters, for it provided a myth of origins for the invention of painting: 'I used to tell my friends', noted Leon Alberti in his foundational treatise *On Painting*, 'that the inventor of painting, according to the poets, was Narcissus, who was turned into a flower; for, as painting is the flower of all the arts, so the tale of Narcissus fits our purpose perfectly' (Alberti 1991 [1435]: 61).

Some recent radiographic research on the composition of Caravaggio's *Narcissus* shows that the master must at some point have changed his mind about Narcissus's body posture and composure as he looked at his reflection on the water:

> It appears that in the original version, the image of Narcissus in the water was a faithful reflection of Narcissus the man, undergone a 180 degree inversion. On second thoughts, however, Caravaggio decided to adjust the reflection, raising the knee and the face's outline ... [It] has been suggested that Caravaggio, positioning himself as Narcissus would have, employed a set of mirrors to capture his reflection as laid out by the experimental setting. According to such an interpretation, the painting would take as read the presence of Caravaggio himself within the composition. In other words, Caravaggio's intent was to represent not a painter's take on the scene, but what the painter himself would see if he were to take Narcissus's position. (Ordine 2008 [2003]: 219, my translation)

Figure 5. Michelangelo Caravaggio, *Narcissus* (c. 1600),
Galleria Nazionale d'Arte Antica, Rome

Caravaggio thus painted what the reflection would look like *from a point of view interior to the painting*. For Nuccio Ordine, Caravaggio sought to problematize the nature of mimesis, which moreover is a most appropriate theme, given Narcissus's own fame as a deer hunter (Ordine 2008 [2003]: 220).

The story of Narcissus, the hunter who fell trap to his own hunting impulses, has a distinguished genealogy in the classical lyrical tradition. Perhaps the most famous of such lyrical stories is the myth of Actaeon, who himself became a deer and was devoured by his own hounds. Actaeon's story has been told many times, perhaps most famously by Ovid in *Metamorphoses* 3.13. Around the time Caravaggio painted his *Narcissus,* the story of Actaeon was being told again, this time by the heretic philosopher Giordano Bruno in a dialogue titled *The Heroic Frenzies.*

In some respects, Bruno's effort in *The Heroic Frenzies* is no different from the classical lyrical tradition, in that his story is brought to bear on the metamorphoses that body and soul must undergo in the search for true knowledge. It is a story that spells out the ambiguity between the *intus* and the *extra,* the hunter and the prey, the interior and exterior dimensions of all human-nature and human-divinity relations. But Bruno's *Heroic Frenzies* lends an unsuspected dimension to the relational complex. Bruno is the first Renaissance thinker to confront the problem of the infinite head-on. And he takes the problem of infinity within, into the depths of the human form:

> So we are led to discover the infinite effect of the infinite cause, the true and living sign of infinite vigor; and we have the knowledge not to search for divinity removed from us if we have it near; it is within us more than we ourselves are. In the same way, the inhabitants of other worlds must not search for divinity in our world, for they have it close to and within themselves, since the moon is no more heaven for us than we for the moon. (Bruno 1995 [1585]: 191)

Searching for knowledge in the interiorities and profundities of the infinite places Bruno at the verge of what Ordine has called 'the dimension of the umbra'. Bruno's is a philosophy of the shadow, where the ontological and the epistemological confound themselves in a complex of 'metamorphoses and reverberations' (Ordine 2008 [2003]: 222, 199): for example, where Actaeon's hunt for knowledge confronts its own ontological dissolution and infinitesimal transformation. It is also, then, as the stories of Narcissus and Actaeon remind us, an anthropology of hunting and predation, of mimesis and frenzy.

In the rest of this chapter I shall look in more detail at Bruno's philosophy of the shadow, and in particular at how his confrontation with the infinite prompted him, in ways that rehearse Caravaggio's adjustment of the perspectival angle, to generate a perspective from a point of view *interior* to the epistemological itself. Bruno 'unbundled' the epistemological into a variety of points of view, some of which would cease to qualify as epistemological thereafter. It is the work of such unbundling that I refer to when I speak of the modern complex of strabismus.

Un/Bundled

Strabismus developed the epistemological magic and productivity of two prior 'epistemic engines', proportionality and reversibility, in full potency. Reversibility belongs to the epistemological cluster of figures making up what in *The Order of Things* Foucault called the sixteenth-century Renaissance episteme of 'resemblance', in contradistinction to the episteme of classical 'representation' (Foucault 1970: 16–17). In sixteenth-century philosophy, Foucault tells us, the central figures of the resemblance episteme were 'convenience', 'emulation', 'analogy' and 'sympathy' (17–24). In their different ways, they all expressed modalities of resemblance: ways in which the qualities of things are transported and mirrored between human and nonhuman objects and agencies, and in which the world communicates itself to itself, projects its forms in perpetuity, and reproduces the order and stasis of the cosmos.

'Convenientia', for example, 'is a resemblance connected with space in the form of a graduated scale of proximity' (17). Thus, under the spell of convenience, the qualities of body and soul gravitate towards each other due to their propinquity, their sharing of movements and tendencies. The adjacency that bodies and souls share lends them a quality of intimate cohabitation, as if they were concatenated together in an 'immense, taut, and vibrating chain' (18). Emulation, on the other hand, enables resemblance without connection or proximity. It is set in motion through the mechanics of imitation: 'emulation is a sort of natural twinship existing in things; it arises from a fold in being' (18–19). The third figure, analogy, takes the powers of convenience and emulation to new heights. Here resemblances need not build on adjacency or imitation but are free to develop and extend along the 'more subtle' space of 'relations' (20). Through analogy 'all the figures in the whole universe can be drawn together' (21). But there is a caveat, a clause, to how analogy deploys its magic. All analogical experiments must at some point pass through a privileged gateway. 'This point is man: he stands in proportion to the heavens, just as he does to animals and plants, and as he does also to the earth, to metals, to stalactites or storms' (21). Or as he puts it a little later: 'The space occupied by analogies is really a space of radiation. Man is surrounded by it on every side ... He is the great fulcrum of proportions, the centre upon which relations are concentrated and from which they are once again reflected' (22).[1] The fourth and last form of resemblance is sympathy. Sympathy is a 'principle of mobility' that draws all things alike together. It 'excites the things of the world' in unison, creating a community of sameness in difference (22). The danger of sympathy, however, is that if left unchecked 'it would reduce the world to a point, to a homogeneous mass, to a featureless form of the Same' (23). Which explains why sympathy needs to be, and is in practice, counterbalanced by antipathy (23).

Let me comment on two additional characteristics of this sixteenth-century Renaissance episteme, as described by Foucault. The first concerns the sovereignty of the system of resemblances. This falls under the jurisdiction of the sympathy-antipathy binomial. Because of the capacity of sympathy to bring the world as a whole unto itself, to fold the world into a converging and unique singularity, and because of the contrary power of antipathy to disperse the world into a disaggregated molecular infinity, all forms of resemblance are ultimately secondary to and derivative from the tensional dis/aggregation accruing between the sympathetic and the antipathetic: 'The whole volume of the world, all the adjacencies of "convenience", all the echoes of emulation, all the linkages of analogy, are supported, and doubled by this space governed by sympathy and antipathy' (24). The world reflects and reverberates itself in and out of shape in accordance to the laws of an opposition between sympathy and antipathy.

The second figure I would like to comment upon, again following Foucault, is what I have been calling 'proportionality'. The endless reverberation of similar forms to which resemblance subjected the flow of the world generated a sense of epistemological claustrophobia: everything resembled everything else in a true ontological hall of mirrors, where knowledge moved back and forth between similar / imitative / emulated / analogical / adjacent forms. Knowledge proceeded thus 'by the infinite accumulation of confirmations all dependent on one another', thus condemning itself 'to never knowing anything but the same thing, and to knowing that thing only at the unattainable end of an endless journey' (29).

Infinity

Renaissance thought, however, found a way out of such infinite regression. It required a change of scale. The endless associative chain of resemblances was put to an end by confronting it with a macrocosmic superiority: 'everything will find its mirror and its macrocosmic justification on another and larger scale' (Foucault 1970: 30). The existence of such a domain, an immensely superior yet clearly delimited higher-order world, in turn delimits ours: the chain of resemblances must end somewhere, because at some place (at the *limit*) the world reaches its abyss and becomes something larger than itself. Here thought encounters the possibility of its continuity via a relation of magnitude, in an order of reality that is continuous yet dimensionally different from ours. Beyond the limit, our relational logic becomes relational imagination.

Proportionality traverses fourteenth- to sixteenth-century mystical and magical rationalism. It provides the necessary dimensioning, the worldling environment, for the 'fundamental configuration of knowledge' as the 'reciprocal cross-reference of signs and similitudes' (Foucault 1970: 32). The world can hold itself together as some kind of reversible eternity, locked up in its own chain of perpetual resemblances, because it has a size of sorts, a dimension and volume and magnitude that is proper to its ontology: knowledge of the world comes with its own height, width and length. In Renaissance times, proportionality provided a means for gaining ontological purchase over the world's knowledge. Ontology is proportionate because to know the world one's knowledge must begin and end somewhere. But what would happen to knowledge if the very possibility of an infinite world – worse still, of a multiplicity of infinite worlds – were to enter the picture? What if infinity became a source of ontology? What would the proportions of the world then be?

Notwithstanding its Renaissance ascendancy and connotation, the question of infinity is one that holds some important lessons for contemporary social theory. For example, in certain intriguing analogies between the management of infinity as an ontological category in Renaissance times and the rise of a cultural economy of innovation in our times, knowledge is imagined as an inherently infinite source of ontological creativity, spontaneity and optimism (cf. Nowotny 2007). I do not mean to be flippant: as we will see, the management of the infinite threw into relief problems about the capacity of the intellect to produce explanations that would render the world into a dimensionally intelligible object. It confronted thought with problems about the distribution, apportioning and scales of the human and nonhuman forms that populated the universe. These are questions about the proportions of the infinite, of where and when things start and end, whose epistemic relevance still looms large over the sociology and politics of modern knowledge.

The question of the proportions of the infinite was most famously articulated during the Renaissance by Giordano Bruno. For a number of reasons, Bruno's oeuvre happens to be a fascinating place to start exploring and reflecting on the convergence of the infinite, the proportionate, and the ontological coming-into-being of knowledge in an age of neo-baroque confusion like our own. Although for many years Bruno was characterized as a hermetic and mystical philosopher, a characterization that Francis Yates (2002 [1964]) famously used to argue for the occultist legacy in later classical and modernist philosophy, today Bruno's work may in fact be read as imaginatively anticipatory of many of the philosophical and ontological questions that have taken hold of contemporary social theory. Bruno's oeuvre is of particular interest because of his concern with multiple and infinite worlds, animism, and the monadic or atomic structure of the universe, themes that have all received renewed attention in recent social theory, where a new imagination of the imitative, of the contagious and the sympathetic, of proliferation, association and mimesis, is taking hold in sociological explanation.[2] To offer just one example, in the mid 1580s Bruno developed an interest in the calculus of infinitesimal quantities. In Paris he gained the acquaintance of Fabrizio Mordente, the 'god of geometers', who had invented a compass with adjustable arms. Fascinated with the possibilities the compass offered for calculating infinitesimal transformations, he offered to translate Mordente's work into Latin. In an extraordinary creative move, his 'translation' acquired unexpected philosophical purchase. Ingrid Rowland, who has recounted the episode, tells the story thus:

> Bruno used the word 'translation' (*translation*) in another sense: to describe the changeover from circular to linear motion and vice versa (for translation from one language to another, he actually used the Latin word *traductio*). This kind of translation was the goal toward which he directed all his own involvement with the reduction compass, which for him was really an involvement with geometry. He used Mordente's instrument to divide arcs and chords of a circle into fractions, and then divided the fractions into fractions until he reached the level of infinitesimal units; this was the place where 'translation' occurred. (Rowland 2008: 195)

Bruno's *translation* has an uncanny resemblance to the concept of 'translation' as used in actor-network theory by Bruno Latour or Michel Callon—that is, a nexus or temporary assembly-point for transformative dynamics (Callon 1986; Latour 1983). In Chapter 1 we saw how Latour's use of translation, for instance, brought his theory alive as an 'architectural optics of volumes', in Serres's wonderful phrase. And it is indeed the world's new voluminousness, its expanded sense of infinity, that Bruno is theoretically struggling to come to terms with – thence the vitality and relevance of his thought for contemporary social theory. All in all, as Hilary Gatti has put it, Bruno's 'daring and uncompromising development of universal infinity launched into the post-Copernican cosmological debate a discussion which ... is still ongoing', not least because of his being an early propounder of the 'dynamic, vitalistic concept of matter' (Gatti 1999: 76, 8). Thus, while Latour and Deleuze have seen in Gabriel Tarde a forefather of contemporary post-Durkheimian social theory, and Tarde himself saw in Leibniz a forefather of post-Kantian sociology, Giordano Bruno is without doubt the sociological forefather of them all.

Bruno's encounter with the infinite is of particular interest to social theory, I would like to argue here, because it stands as a reference point for the geometrization of the sociological imagination thereafter (Saiber 2005). Whilst in most Renaissance thought proportionality provided the means for making sense of the world's ontology, Bruno's encounter with the infinite led him to take proportionality *inside* the world itself, so that the proportion was no longer what the world must measure up to, but the mode of measurement itself.

Here one particular text of Bruno's deserves commentary, most notably for its implications for anthropological theory. I am referring to *De vinculi in genere*, 'A General Account of Bonding', where Bruno maps out his theory of relationality (Bruno 2004 [1588]). Relationality, or bonding, as Bruno calls it, is the central figure of his cosmological order, but even more importantly it is the organizing principle of his vision for civil life, for there can be no understanding of what civil life is without some understanding of how bonding works, or indeed of what it might be (Bruno 2004 [1588]: 145). For Bruno, relationality is the source of all agency, of all ambitions and movements, of all propensities, 'which vivifies, soothes, caresses and activates all things; which orders, generates, rules, attracts and inflames all things; and which moves, reveals, illuminates, purifies, pleases and completes all things' (146). Bonding is Bruno's analytic of resemblance, and in this guise it takes shape as a modal disposition: there are different modalities of bonding, of different intensions and inclinations each. Thus Bruno speaks of beauty, for example, in terms of 'a special symmetry or of some other incorporeal aspect of physical nature, [which] occurs in a myriad of forms and arises from innumerable ordered patterns' (149). Indeed, such multiplicity defines the very working of nature, 'which has spread about many bonds of beauty, happiness, goodness, and the various contraries of these dispositions, and which widely distributes them separately according to the numerous types of matter' (147).

There are different forms of bonding, but bonding itself is also of a complex nature: 'a bonding power is not simple or reducible to only one thing, but is composite, variable in nature and composed of contraries' (147). Complex and intricate as it is, bonding is also fugitive and elusive. 'Bonds are so subtle, and that which is bound is so barely sensible in its depths, that it is possible to examine them only fleetingly and superficially' (154). Their elusiveness is also indicative of their modifiability, their continuous changing forms—that is, of their function as a 'translating' device, as defined above.[3] Bonds belong thus to the subsequent. Importantly, it is this subsequence that gives bonding a shape and form of sorts. It provides the structure for its accommodation or internal fit to the world as we experience it:

There is one type of bonding in which we wish to become worthy, beautiful and good; there is another type in which we desire to take command of what is good, beautiful and worthy. The first type of bonding derives from an object which we lack, the second, from an object which we already have. These two types bind both what is good and what is thought to be good, although *this bond always occurs in some proportional or suitable way.* (152, emphasis added)

Bruno's insight at this point is worth a pause. Relational life, he says, is always proportional to its object. It seeks an expression of suitability; it longs for a form *adequate* to its desires or will. It demands of the world some sort of dimension. Later in the text, he writes that 'social types of bonding require *a degree of size* on which the form and the power of the bond depends' (166, emphasis added). The world, Bruno tells us, is proportional to our social life. There is a proportionality to the world and to our modes of encountering, describing and accommodating to it.

I noted earlier how Bruno's use of proportionality as a *tool* for placing knowledge in hold of measurement captured and in some respects epitomized the moments of epistemic instability that would later bring about the collapse of Renaissance thought. The way in which *measurement* became at once a form of representing the ontological *order* of resemblances and yet, at the same time, of holding ontology itself to rational calculation (to the ratio of measurement) generated the conditions of possibility for such epistemic transition. Foucault has described the role that measurement and order played in the bodying forth of rationalism over resemblance-thought in the seventeenth century (Foucault 1970: 53–58), especially in the function ascribed to both as *modes of comparison:*

Resemblance, which had long been the fundamental category of knowledge … became dissociated in an analysis based in terms of identity and difference; moreover, whether indirectly by the intermediary of measurement, or directly and, as it were, on the same footing, comparison became a function of order; and, lastly, comparison ceased to fulfil the function of revealing how the world is ordered, since it was now accomplished according to the order laid down by thought, progressing naturally from the simple to the complex. (Foucault 1970: 54)

This is a fundamental point. For Foucault, the operations upon knowledge hitherto performed by resemblance in Renaissance thought were gradually transformed into those performed by a functional relationship (between order, on the one hand, and measurement, on the other) in classical epistemology. Foucault calls this functional relationship *mathesis,* 'the science of calculable order', 'of which the universal method is algebra', the study of structure, relation and quantity (Foucault 1970: 72, 71). In Bruno, we have seen, such functional relationship is well delineated in his idiom of 'proportionality', which Bruno makes work as an expression of 'bonding' or relationality. Apropos of such an algebraic imagination (the organization of relations, structure and quantity in a mode of description), he writes for example that '[t]he bonding agent is said to be predisposed to bonding in three ways: by its order; by its measure; and by its type. The order is the interrelation of its parts; the measure is its quantity; and its type is designated by its shapes, its outlines and its colours' (Bruno 2004 [1588]: 151). But importantly, for Bruno proportionality is a means too for describing how similitude and resemblance work: it is the *how* behind the world's proliferation, multiplication and ramification into new shapes, modalities and dispositions. In the 'proportion' Bruno finds a tool for reconciling the analytics of science and the conditions of possibility of resemblance – a tool for not despairing when confronting the infinite.[4]

What makes Bruno so pertinent to contemporary social theory is this ability to describe the world in a conceptual language that is at once radically open to change and multiplicity and yet *interior* to its own mode of description, that is, capable of re-proportioning and internally accommodating its forms and shapes to the objects at hand. He spoke thus of bonding occurring in a 'suitable way' (Bruno 2004 [1588]: 152). To make forms suitable for each other was analogous to equating them to each other. They suited because they were *ad-equate* to each other. Indeed, the legacy of adequation would haunt modern thought thereafter. The consolidation of perspectivalism that took place during the Baroque reinforced, for example, the 'distinction between *appearance* and *essence,* which is normal in Western thought, [but] became accentuated in baroque mentality and constituted the basis for organizing [a] "tactic of *accommodation*" reflected in morality and politics' (Maravall 1986: 194, emphasis added). Because, as the Spanish poet Quevedo put it, the illusions of perspectivalism meant that 'farness and proximity deceive sight', baroque culture developed a sort of *pragmatics of adequation:* an epistemic shorthand, designed to zoom in and out of reality, that worked as a 'system of accommodation precepts' for the world (Maravall 1986: 196). In the terms used in Chapter 1, the world obtained as an architectural optics of volumes, where epistemic objects were ad-equated to—that is, set as a ratio of—each other.

The World Inside Out

The world that Bruno was born into had a size and proportion—an ontological height, length and width—that were taken for granted, even though their elucidation was a matter of disputation. The proportions of the world were a problem to wrestle with, rather than to dispose of. Perhaps for this reason, when Bruno had to confront the infinite he opted not to throw the baby out with the bathwater. He moved the proportional imagination *inside* the world (to a radical, infinite degree, we should hasten to add), so that it became its mode of description rather than its framework of explanation.[5] Bruno turned the world into a giant laboratory by devising the epistemological conditions for thinking of the world as a place unto itself: proportionality, shadows, infinity, memory, intensiveness.

The use of the proportion to turn the world inside out found a variety of applications. Employed in optics, we saw in Chapters 1 and 2, it enabled the illusion of variations in size to produce perspectival effects. The world's harmony and balance was thought to be manifest in proportional forms whose beauty would become visible *from the proper point of view*. The point echoes what Deleuze, in his lectures on Leibniz, had to say about the rise of perspectivalism in the development of projective geometry: 'What produces a point of view?' Deleuze asks as he recalls Leibniz's thought, '[Answer:] That regional *proportion* of the world that is clearly and distinctively expressed by an individual in relation to the totality of the world that is expressed confusingly and obscurely' (Deleuze 2006 [1980/1986/1987]: 37, emphasis added, my translation). In other words, we get a proper view of the world when we can apportion its forms into a fitting and just alignment. Interestingly, however, in his book on the expressiveness of Baroque thought as a philosophy of curvature and sensuous shadows, which represents Deleuze's mature reflections on Leibniz (Deleuze 1993), this very same thought is rendered somewhat differently: 'every point of view', Deleuze writes there, 'is a point of view on variation. The point of view is not what varies with the subject ... it is, to the contrary, the condition in which an eventual subject apprehends a variation (metamorphosis), or: something = x (anamorphosis)' (Deleuze 1993: 20).

What is at stake in the holding of the world as an ontological infinitude of variance, Deleuze realizes in editing his lecture notes on Leibniz for publication, is not the movement of proportional changes through which the world transforms itself, but the *condition of variance itself*: 'The infinite presence in the finite self is exactly the position of Baroque equilibrium or disequilibrium' (Deleuze 1993: 89). Baroque thought, therefore, is no longer interested in the proportions through which the world holds itself together, but in the distortions and disproportions— the infinite predicament of the shadow, as Bruno saw it—that call for its deformation (anamorphosis). It is the anamorphic, the politics of the gigantic and the exaggerated—of variance as a sense of amplitude, expansion and/or subsequent contraction—that characterizes and is worthy of commentary in modernist thought. The anamorphic becomes the distinguishing characteristic of modern society.

Aggrandizements and Miniaturizations

'The task of perception', Deleuze writes of Leibniz's theory of perception (whilst paraphrasing Gabriel Tarde), 'entails pulverizing the world, but also one of spiritualizing its dust.' The *differential orders* of pulverization, from dust to world and back again, are what constitutes the world as a process of becoming, '[f]rom the cosmological to the microscopic, but also from the microscopic to the macroscopic' (Deleuze 1993: 87, emphasis removed). From Bruno to Leibniz to Tarde and Deleuze, the epistemological imagination of modernity has been concerned with making 'knowledge' appear as a significant and visible epistemological object through 'differential relations among ... differentials of other orders' (Deleuze 1993: 90). In other words, knowledge was recognized as an epistemic object when 'relations' were seen to *escalate out* of prior relational orders. And yet we must caution against taken-for-granted expectations that such 'other orders' should indeed be the result of scopic aggrandizements or miniaturizations—'from the microscopic to the macroscopic', as Deleuze put it. For—echoing the epigram with which this book opens—not doing so 'runs the risk of failing to see the work that aggrandisement does in human affairs'. Indeed, writing about the strategic movements through which anthropologists create and demarcate their objects of analysis, Marilyn Strathern observes that 'in the facility to switch frames not across epochs but across scales ... [it] is equally possible to change what is seen / known by focusing on detail as by enlarging one's scope. *Miniaturisation and magnification both appear as transformative;* such transformation keeps the knowledge that each moment has so to speak emerged from the other' (Strathern 1995b: 6, emphasis added).

The epistemological work invested into demarcating and delineating the production of knowledge has in this light consisted in opening up spaces for its intelligibility through mechanisms of amplification and/or contraction, that is, through tactics of optical re-accommodation. Whenever an image of knowledge has been held stable and made to appear effective, our anthropological categories have undergone a coterminous re-proportional transformation.

In the modern age, knowledge of the world has therefore consisted in the production of its own sense of self-aggrandizement or self-deformation. Thus, that the modern condition is characterized and reproduced through its own sense of self-aggrandizement is inadvertently replicated in what is perhaps the most trenchant and sophisticated critique of modernity to date, Bruno Latour's argument about our historical nonmodernity (Latour 1993). For Latour, famously, the modern constitution, the sociological imagination of a complex matrix of relations between nature, society and divinity, is premised on the alleged ontological discontinuity between objects and forms of knowledge (between human and nonhuman beings) whose coexistence is in fact mangled up and ontologically impure throughout: 'The essential point of this modern Constitution is that it renders the work of mediation that assembles hybrids invisible, unthinkable, unrepresentable' (Latour 1993: 34). For moderns, hybridity is a fact never to be awarded ontological recognition.

What is interesting about Latour's own description of this constitution of proliferating yet self-annihilating hybrid forms is the terms through which the 'ontological' itself appears as a recognizable knowledge-form. Nature and society are awarded ontological recognition because they are *separated* from one another, and because their success at recruiting candidates to their ontological cause relies precisely upon generating a sense of *removal* from each other: 'the Constitution provided the moderns with the daring to mobilize things and people on a scale that they would otherwise have disallowed. This modification of scale was achieved not—as they thought—by the *daring separation of humans and nonhumans* but, on the contrary, by the *amplification* of their contacts' (Latour 1993: 41, emphasis added).

Thus, whether one is a modern or a nonmodern, one's sociological imagination is always premised on the capacity to think ontological distinctiveness (as a pure or even as a hybrid form) through a process of aggrandizement or miniaturization. Ontology *grows* (as a self-recognizable knowledge-form) at the expense of its remainders, and this growth takes a proportional form: 'The scope of the mobilization [the capacity to recruit ontological friends to one's cause] is *directly proportional* to the impossibility of directly conceptualizing its relations with the social order' (Latour 1993: 43). When it comes to think of ontology, then, one always has to think of it as a proportion of something else.

In a beautiful image, Michel Serres has described Thales's inauguration, his emplacement of the peg in the sand, as 'a strange thing full of water': the creation of a 'logos-proportion' capable of providing accounts of 'objects whose appearance and birth are independent of us and which develop by themselves in relation to other objects of the world', things that are born from air, fire or water and do not attend to the laws or rules of kings or gods. The Nile floods that Thales witnessed washed away the fields' crops, and his 'proportion' came to the rescue of, indeed, a strange world full of water: a world that demanded a new logos to measure the land, re-establish the cadastral register, and net out the outstanding balances between creditors and debtors (Serres 1995: 122).

Today the proportion has dried up the world again. In their examination of the status and place of atlases in the history of objectivity (and the wider history of epistemology), Lorraine Daston and Peter Galison have aimed for a type of explanation that is 'on the same scale and of the same nature as the explanandum itself'. In their own words,

> If training a telescope onto large, remote causes fails to satisfy, what about the opposite approach, scrutinizing small, local causes under an explanatory microscope? The problem here is the mismatch between the heft of explanandum and explanans, rather than the distance between them: in their rich specificity, local causes can obscure rather than clarify the kind of wide-ranging effect that is our subject here … Looking at microcontexts tells us a great deal—but it can also occlude, like viewing an image pixel by pixel. The very language of cause and effect dictates separate and heterogeneous terms: cause and effect must be clearly distinguished from each other, both as entities and in time. Perhaps this is why the metaphors of the telescope and the microscope lie close to hand. Both are instruments for bringing the remote and inaccessible closer. But relationships of cause and effect do not exhaust explanation. Understanding can be broadened and deepened by exposing other kinds of previously unsuspected links among the phenomena in question. (Daston and Galison 2007: 36)

The call to attend to the problems of 'The mismatch between the heft of explanandum and explanans', as they put it, is of course a call to re-describe the weights that inhere in the forms of the explainer and the explained; in other words, a call to creatively reimagine the dis/proportions that exist in the languages of social-scientific description. We need, they are suggesting, forms of description that escape our proportional imagination.

■ ■ ■

My aim in Part I has been to set in historical continuity the anthropological imagination of the production of knowledge as a re-proportional exercise, and to delineate the role that 'proportionality' and 'reversibility' have played and continue to play in the modern imagination of theory.

Reversibility owes its distinctive epistemological efficacy to the Renaissance imagination. Inflected with genealogical qualities at once magical, mystical and logical, the episteme of reversibility-resemblance is finding a new lease of life in contemporary theories of mimesis, of contagion and sympathy, of the *agencement* of material proliferations and associations. Reversibility is a useful port of call for explorations of ambiguity and double vision in everyday sociality. Like Giordano Bruno, however, we might do well to remember that the work of reversibility is always haunted by a proportional legacy. As he put it, to bond with the world in any of its manifestations is to decant the terms of our mutual 'suitability', to get an appreciation of how the world and our selves proportion each other's projects out. We cannot, in sum, escape the proportion. Some of our finest efforts, like Bruno's or Deleuze's or Serres's, are perhaps best described as visionary explorations of its limits, as well as lucid realizations of its burdens and toll.

Part II of the essay explores the reach of strabismus (reversibility and proportionality) in giving anthropological form and shape to the configuration of modern political economy. Chapter 4 looks at the ontological tension between politics and society that has historically nurtured the ghostly character of modernity's political ontology. Chapter 5 redescribes the stressful relation between production and reproduction in the new 'social' capitalism of immaterial labour and networked production. Finally, Chapter 6 explores the blurring distinction between the insides and outsides of society and economy under neoliberal governance and science policy in particular.

Notes

1. On the anthropological imagination of the relational relativity of man as the great 'fulcrum of proportions', see Corsín Jiménez (2003a). Ortega y Gasset beautifully captures the impact of the Galilean re-description of man as a figure of proportionality when he says that it '*magnified* the size of man in the universe' (Ortega y Gasset 1996 [1956]: 240, emphasis added).

2. Sociology, for instance, especially through the work of Bruno Latour, is witnessing a resuscitation of interest in Gabriel Tarde's neomonadology (Tarde 2006), in particular his concern for the molecular and infinitesimal traces that make up the social (Barry and Thrift 2007; Candea 2010; Latour 2002; Toews 2003), which echoes Bruno's interest in the corpuscular and its legacy. Following the lead of actor-network theory and post-phenomenological scholarship (Law 1999; Strathern 1996), there is also increasing interest in nonhuman and posthuman forms of agency, including a renewed interest in animism (Willerslev 2007) and the ontological agency of material forms (Holbraad 2005), whilst in anthropology this scholarship has developed into a wider concern for so-called multiple ontologies (Henare, Holbraad and Wastell 2007; Scott 2007; Viveiros de Castro 2003).

3. An aspect of the work of relationships that echoes, again, Gabriel Tarde's insistence on the molecular modifiability of the social; see for example, Barry (2010).

4. There are, of course, multiple stories about the sources of agency that enabled such transformation of proportionality from a natural form to a mechanical or instrumental tool. Horst Bredekamp, for example, has brought to attention the role played

by the bizarre inventories of *Kunstkammers* (cabinets of curiosities and wonders) in organizing a spatio-temporal transition between antique philosophies of nature and the rise of mechanistic philosophy in the seventeenth century. Bredekamp cites thus René Descartes, who 'could see "no difference between machines built by artisans and objects created by nature alone"'. His words, adds Bredekamp, 'indicate that, like other philosophers of nature, he too had been impressed by the *Kunstkammer*, which for three generations had been using its mute images to depict the transition from natural formations to art forms' (Bredekamp 1995 [1993]: 39). Inside the cabinet of curiosities, then, the proportionality of natural forms was spatially juxtaposed to the emerging proportionalities of human affairs. The cabinets thus formatted proportionality's transition from an ontological to an epistemological form.

5. The larger history of mathematical transformation of the proportion from 'problem' to 'equation' has been told by Reviel Netz (2004). Netz describes how early Greek mathematics, such as Archimedes', foregrounds the proportion, whilst later, medieval mathematicians such as Omar Khayyam used proportions as tools to produce equalities (Netz 2004: 169). The 'proportion' thus underwent a long historical transformation from being the background or context against which the work of mathematics proceeded, to becoming a tool for performing other operations.

Zoom Out

The Science of the Just Proportion and the Just Proportions of Science

In *Hatred of Democracy*, Jacques Ranciére noted that

> The distribution of knowledges is only socially efficacious to the extent that it is also a (re)distribution of positions. To gauge the relation between the two distributions, one must therefore have an additional science... political science. [...] But this science will always be missing the very thing that is necessary for settling the excess constitutive of politics: the determination of the just proportion between inequality and equality. [...] But there is no science of the just measure between equality and inequality... The republic aims at being the government of democratic equality by dint of a science of the just proportion. (Rancière 2009: 68–69)

Ranciére's invocation of the image of the Republic should not come as a surprise, for classical thought indeed placed proportionality at the very centre of political thought. There was nowhere to be community if there was not first equality of positions, so that nobody could claim an innate advantage over anybody else and exchanges balanced out. Thus Socrates tells Callicles

> that heaven and earth and gods and men are held together by communion and friendship, orderliness, temperance, and justice; and that is the reason, my friend, why they call the whole of this world by the name of order, not

of disorder or dissoluteness ... for all of your cleverness, [you] have failed to observe the great power of geometrical equality amongst both gods and men: you hold that self-advantage is what one ought to practise, because you neglect geometry. (Plato 1977: 508a)

The requirement to observe geometry as a principle of political behaviour in the classical context in fact led Michel Serres to propose an alternative translation for Euclid's *Axioms*: 'So the term *Axioms* is the worst possible translation of Euclid's original title: Κοιυαι έυυιαι (*Common Notions*), which deals with equality.' A *koine* or community 'no longer means the usual or common denominator, but *that which characterizes the public*. The whole body of descriptions or implications of equality, its attributes, operations or properties, constitute indispensable notions for the setting up of the said community' (Serres 1995: 116, emphasis added). A community is where we find a proportional and equivalent configuration of its membership – where commensality and commonality obtain in an equation of political justice. The proportion is therefore the ethic and aesthetic of political hope and harmony. It is the operational function (the epistemic engine) animating the ascension of social relations into *public* relations. It is what may ultimately legitimate speaking of the commons as a geometrical axiom of political ethics. There is a science of the just proportion because there is no knowledge that is not always, already, internally accommodated and proportioned to a justly aesthetic.

Part II

Common World

4

The Political/
Phantasmagoria

> Deities, angels, specters, and ghosts … what to make of
> these creatures rising from the pens of radical thinkers
> in the twentieth century (Walter Benjamin, Jacques
> Derrida, Sheldon Wolin, and Marx, in the nineteenth
> century) as they attempt to grasp our relation to past and
> future, and in particular as they attempt to articulate the
> prospects for a postfoundational formulation of justice?
> —Wendy Brown, 'Specters and Angels at the End of History'

In a number of places today, the productivity of knowledge is manifest-
ing itself as a source of commensality, especially in the way in which the
capacity to produce more knowledge and make it available is taken as
an index of social wealth and abundance (Benkler 2006), as if indeed
knowledge were a sociological object per se. The relational economy of
knowledge at work in, say, 'commons-based systems of peer production'
(Benkler and Nissenbaum 2006) produces geometrical superpositions
not unlike those Serres described for the classical period, where knowledge, sociality and politics converge in a sociological commons. Take,
for instance, Google's project of becoming the world's online library. As
reported in *The New Yorker* magazine (Toobin 2007), Google's ambi-
tion is to digitize every book ever published, currently estimated to be
at least 129,864,880 volumes (Taycher 2010). The project has raised
concern over, and opposition because of, issues of intellectual property
rights, in particular regarding the terms in which knowledge is said to
inhabit the public domain (Picker 2009): Who owns knowledge in a
book with uncertain copyright status? How does an electronic version
of a book relate to its physical content?

The challenges that Google's incursions pose to the Internet's new
'community of knowledge' do not, however, stop at questions of intel-

lectual property rights. Google's project signals too to the novel ways in which the revolution in information and communications technologies is causing the obsolescence of many of the classical categories of political economy: the state, the market and private property have all suffered important conceptual distortions. In fact, it is no longer clear that these categories serve their purpose any more, as a new cohort of discursive interventions – 'ambient intelligence', 'sensor networks', 'responsive environments' – is taking over as definitory of how we imagine our political communities today, with microprocessors, sensors and software-sorting devices traversing and organizing our ecological and cultural habitats. These interventions all index an expansion of the idea of stakeholder-ship capable to accommodate a view of intelligence as, in the words of Nigel Thrift, an atmosphere or a 'proto-environment' that has 'taken some of the characteristics of weather.' (Thrift 2012: 154, 155) Thus, as Siva Vaidhyanathan and others have argued (Vaidhyanathan 2011), in this context Google's project entails yet another structural transformation of the public sphere (of which more below), where the boundaries of the forms of knowledge that are public and common to all modify not only their shape and contours, but their very capacity to generate their own changes thereon.

These are new 'recursive publics', as Chris Kelty calls them (2008), where the sociological notion of a 'public' is now at once social and infrastructural, political and material: by sharing information, code or open-access content, bloggers, free software programmers or scientists build, shape and modify their own public sphere. The technological infra-structure of the new public sphere therefore gives it the capacity to catch its own breath; there is only a public insofar as it has the capacity to 're-mix' its own conditions of possibility as a socio-technical project (Lessig 2008). Thus, if the new public sphere does indeed deliver sociological utopias, it is because the knowledge/commensality equation has relo-cated from an exclusively political topos to an infrastructural one.[1] Code is the new language of hope, and the political takes shape as a network of techno-environmental connections. The productivity of the social is now truly and inherently metrological (Barry 2001), and the public ap-pears as an internal moment of a technological economy. The implica-tion is that the economy carries its own democratic potential within, which can be best realized if visualized and made explicit through the application of networked sensoriums. The proto-environmental net-work awakens thus the democratic impulse that lies dormant within the economy. Welcome to the land of sentient capital!

An interesting side effect to this techno-animated conception of dem-ocratic sociability concerns the way in which the network-informed spontaneity of knowledge becomes a surrogate for political hope and social ethics. Mike Featherstone and Couze Venn, for example, have recently written about the epistemic change that digital networking may be effecting in our concept of knowledge (Featherstone and Venn 2006). The technological capacities of online communications, they argue, are bringing about a de-cadence of knowledge, a shift towards non-linear and a-synchronic, autopoietic and vitalistic modes of knowing. Indeed, knowledge itself as an epistemological enterprise may be gradually assuming the form of an existential politics, a 'worldling, inventive and generative' politics that builds on an ebullient and spontaneous economy of networked information. If the promise of a 'global public sphere' was ever a precondition for the aspirations of social emancipation, then with the modular structure of the Internet we have instead leapfrogged directly into the age of 'global public life' (Featherstone and Venn 2006: 11).

What remains essentially unexamined in the novel conceptualization of knowledge as a stream of vitalistic and spontaneous network associations, however, is the very conception of 'democratic accountability' at play here, that is, the very notion that 'knowledge' and 'the social' are indeed objects liable to hold each other to theoretical commensurability via the injunction of 'the political'. Said differently, we may want to ask what makes 'knowledge', 'the social' and 'the political' today into sociological objects to be summoned in contexts of democratic accountability, distributive justice or political ethics. What makes them adequate descriptors or proportionate objects for each other?

Public Choice Therapy (and Theory)

Knowledge, to begin with, occupies a curious place in economic theory. It fares as both theoretical commodity and methodological infrastructure; it has 'dual functionality as a human need and an economic good' (Hess and Ostrom 2006: 13). Take its role in social or public choice theory. Kenneth Arrow laid out social choice theory in its programmatic form in 1951 (Arrow 1951), motivated by a fundamental question of political sociology: how to produce cogent aggregative judgments about, say, social welfare, collective interest or aggregate poverty (Sen 1999b: 349)? In other words, how do we know what society needs? The difficulties involved led Arrow to ultimately state the impossibility of social choice: there is no transparent mechanism for mapping society onto available information. More recently, however, Amartya Sen has advanced a programme for broadening the informational basis of social choices, such as the use of interpersonal comparisons of well-being and individual advantage (Sen, 1999b). The more we enrich our information with human-centred, culturally sensitive data, Sen has suggested, the more our choices will resemble social knowledge: public choice will equal public knowledge.

The development of public choice theory over the past fifty years, then, has shown the inevitable theorization of knowledge as a necessary infrastructural requirement of our economic and political models. In public choice theory, the 'going public' of knowledge marks both an epistemological necessity and a requirement of political accountability. As an episode in the history of economic ideas, the transformations the word 'public' has undergone in public choice theory signal therefore the coming to terms of economic theory as political epistemology.[2]

A useful port of call in such transformations is the so-called pure theory of public expenditure, first outlined by Paul Samuelson in 1954. In elaborating it, Samuelson distinguished between 'private consumption goods' and 'collective consumption goods, which all enjoy in common in the sense that each individual's consumption of such a good leads to no subtraction from any other individual's consumption of that good' (Samuelson 1954: 387). The line distinguishing private from public consumption was therefore originally placed on rivalry: my consumption of a good should not rival the consumption of others. Another twenty years passed before the principle of rivalry was further discriminated. In 1977 Vincent and Elinor Ostrom developed a twofold classification where goods were defined by both the varying degrees of 'jointness of use' (i.e., rivalry) and exclusion (the use of a good excludes others from accessing it) (Ostrom and Ostrom 1977). An important point to make about this distinction between rivalry and excludability is that it leaves questions of property aside (Hess and Ostrom 2003: 120–121): public and private in this formulation do not constitute and are not envisaged as property regimes. They are categories of sociological consumption.

Indeed, perhaps the most remarkable feature of the economic theory of public goods is that it defines publicness in terms of use or consumption. Non-rivalry and non-excludability are both consumption functions: it is an agent's private access and enjoyment of a good that creates the notion of publicness as a 'residual category' (Kaul and Mendoza 2003: 80). If the public were a cake, it would be much larger than any slice one individual could ever eat. Public goods are therefore goods that come into existence by virtue of being 'extracted' from the market through the forces of demand: someone eats a slice of a cake that remains otherwise available for others to try. The larger cake is a *residue* or leftover of consumption. This is significant for one principal reason:

it leaves unaccounted how the goods are assembled or manufactured to start with; in other words, who and how the cake was baked. This omission is hugely ironic because, as it turns out, the history of the idea of public goods is inextricably bound to the history of the state as a fiscal agency (Desai 2003). It is the state that has historically been most involved in the production – and sustenance – of public goods.[3]

The origin of institutional interventions in the economy (by the state, church, private capitalists) runs in parallel to what E.P. Thompson famously called the rise of the 'moral economy of the crowd' (Thompson 1971). At the turn of the eighteenth and nineteenth centuries, when the exponential growth of industry crowded populations in and around the fringes of expanding urban centres, a moral sentiment of economic injustice set the precedent for the imagination of what we would call today the public domain. Thompson boldly observed that these sentiments were in fact 'market' inspired, in the sense that what most participants in eighteenth-century food riots in England wanted was for market traders to respect the (paternalistic, Statute) laws of the market. These laws established proper marketing procedures to prevent farmers and middlemen from striking underhand deals outside the marketplace, such as withholding corn from the market to push its price up, or selling large quantities of it on a small sample basis to foreign buyers. Most rioting aimed therefore at 'setting the price', that is, at trying to get the market to work properly (Thompson 1971: 108). Thus, insofar as the state had to move in to compensate for the upheaval created by the establishment of free trade and the subversion of the paternalistic model, the provision of goods with a remit of 'universal beneficence' (the closest thing to what a public good is today) faithfully mirrored the moral sentiment of the original 'market' economy. In other words, the move from a 'moral economy of provision' to a 'political economy of free market' (Thompson 1971: 128) in fact accomplished a reinvention of 'the statutory market' as 'public domain', a move given historical and sociological credence by the transition from the Poor Law era to the welfare state (Harris 2002; Trattner 1998).

The rise of the welfare state as a sociological object came hand in hand with the rise of moral individualism. Although no doubt part of a much larger and complex historical economy, the constitution of the public domain as a concern of welfare economics in the nineteenth century ran parallel to, if not actually capturing, the moment when the idea of society 're-distributed' itself into a political economy of rights-bearing individual claimants; that is, when the concept of 'social justice' (versus, say, charity or reciprocity) finally consolidated (Fleischacker 2004; Jackson 2005). According to Jose Harris, for example, Edwardian social reformism 'subordinate[d] the analysis of specific social problems to a vision of reconstructing *the whole of British society,* together with reform of the rational understanding and *moral character of individual British citizens* ... both policies and people were means to the end of attaining *perfect justice and creating the ideal state*' (Harris 1992: 126, emphasis added). In a similar vein, writing on the historical anthropology of the rise of English individualism in the nineteenth century, and in particular on the place of Matthew Arnold's writings on the role of the state in the 'democratisation of culture', Marilyn Strathern has observed how '[r]egulation and order ... here externalised in the idea of a system of laws encompassing the individual person. The social order which thus exists beyond the individual is a collectivity presented to the person as the field of rights and duties by which he/she is defined' (Strathern 1992: 109). Walter Lippmann put the point eloquently when noting that from the point of view of individual agency, 'each of us, as a member of the public, remains always *external.* Our public opinions are always and forever, by their very nature, an attempt to control the actions of others from the *outside*' (Lippmann 1993 [1925]: 42, emphasis added). We are defined relationally and internally as individual members of a collectivity by our (right-bearing) abilities to conceptualize society as an organic whole from the outside.

In the United States, the federal government's emergence as a major dispenser of welfare aid in the nineteenth century took the shape of public land distributions (Trattner 1988). In this context, the political economy of the public domain became modelled on what Arthur Schlesinger Jr. has called a 'hand-out system' (cited in Trattner 1988: 350), where the idea of public wealth stood somehow as an imaginary *spatial outside* from which one could extract or exploit national or commercial riches.[4] The utopianism of the frontier ideology was thus translated into a concrete, self-expanding landholding patrimony (Iglesias 2006), against which a nation of settlers constituted themselves as citizens by staking out their claims. The public domain and the republican ideal thus gained conceptual independence insofar as they mirrored the individual labouring aspirations of an agrarian society (Huston 1998).

If we establish that Western society created itself as a total economic object by externalizing its own internal public, that is, by turning its moral sentiments about market justice inside out into a political economy of market distributive rights, it follows that about the same time, economic intelligence must have had to confront the problem of collective preferences: how to measure collective welfare when only the agency of individual consumers is visible sociologically. Indeed, the very nature of this problem in fact signalled the birth of the marginalist revolution in economics in the 1870s, 'when the analysis of subjective utility had grounded value theory on the demand side ... [and the] focus was no longer on the duty of the sovereign, but on the demands of the individual consumer. The public sector appeared no longer as an awkward, albeit necessary, exception to the laws of economics' (Musgrave 1985: 8). Instead, public provision became a problem of efficiency in use and allocation, which made society disappear as a total sociological object. Thenceforth 'society' appeared only on the margins of every economic transaction as a remainder to the operation.[5]

The problem of collective preferences points to economists' efforts to look for the social good, even as the social good seems to aggregate and disaggregate mysteriously into all types of social agencies: now a public, now a market; now an individual, now a moral sentiment; now a political artifice, now a subjective choice. Marginalism solved this problem for public economics by positing the state as the invisible agency behind the production and sustenance of the public domain. Desai has called this phantasmagoria 'the Samuelson fiction': the idea that there exists 'a collective mind, an ethical observer to whom preferences are somehow known' (Desai 2003: 72) Although the consequences of not acknowledging the political bargaining processes shaping fiscal decision-making had in fact been noted by Knut Wicksell in 1896 (Musgrave 1985: 9–15), for most of the twentieth century the problematic nature of the collective mind that undertakes to adumbrate collective preferences was barely taken notice of – although it would, in time, lead to the development of the 'sociology of knowledge' as a field of inquiry concerned with the types of intelligence through which society comes to 'know' itself, a point to which I shall return below.

In terms analogous to the Leviathan's hiding of its own aesthetics of representation, the 'Samuelson fiction' effectively disguised that the public domain was but the ethical dioptric artefact through which the 'moral economy of the crowd' had been travestied into the 'political economy of free trade'. The point is echoed in Carl Schmitt's trenchant critique of the liberal state. Schmitt's obsession with Hobbes's Leviathan – and the notion of politics as a theological play – rests precisely on this notion of the state as an agency that 'acts in many disguises but always as the same invisible person' (Schmitt 2005 [1922]: 38). In fact, the question of aggregation, known to Durkheim and Mauss as a fictive sociological ethics, was also what led them to insist that the problem was equivocally conceived, for the question to ask was not how or which economic values represent societal choices but how social relationships devolve themselves into economic, religious or political values (e.g., Durkheim 1974; Mauss and Hubert 1964). In this light, it was clear that 'public choice' was the name of an (economic) ethics for a society that had never needed one. The ethics of the public domain was nothing more than the aesthetics of marginalist economics.

The Rise of Political Ethics

The challenges posed by Google's adventurous online interventions go to the heart of what Nico Stehr has called a new 'knowledge politics' (Stehr 2003). Stehr's project inscribes itself in a recent 'governance of science' debate (Fuller 2000; Irwin and Michael 2003; Nowotny et al. 2005; Nowotny, Scott and Gibbons 2001) interested in exploring how the reconfiguration of the relationships between government, industry, universities and emerging amateur- and do-it-yourself techno-scientific communities is transforming the public sensibilities and institutional cultures through which society comes to 'know' itself. The formulation may be facile, but the point is not. What the debate on the governance of science brings to attention is the extent to which society's political awakening to the relevance of knowledge bears on our democratic imagination – and how this imagination today revolves around different invocations and ideas of the forms that *publicness* takes:

> The by now constant and controversial public debates about the consequences of new scientific knowledge and technical artifacts and calls for their regulation and administration are expanding the public sphere in modern societies. The organization of the public sphere is changing, participatory demands and contribution to the regulation of knowledge are bound to become more routine and, more generally, we will see significant transformations of the political culture and the re-alignment of the major institutions of modern society as the result of the emergence of knowledge politics as a new field of political activity. (Stehr 2003: 652)

For Stehr, the assemblages emerging around new knowledge/society relations take the *public* as their central, organizing, political trope. The Public takes shape here as the place where knowledge and society contrast each other's politics. Helga Nowotny and her associates corroborate the diagnosis and call these contrastive spaces of knowledge/society encounters *agora*, re-invoking the classical Greek term to capture the new, emergent forms of associative politics that are starting to intervene in the world of science (Nowotny, Scott and Gibbons 2001).

The use of the vocabulary of classical political ethics (*agora*, public sphere, republican decision-making processes) to describe the sociological spaces where knowledge/society relations are assuming new forms is, no doubt, worthy of attention in itself, and may call for an interesting re-evaluation of the historical sociology of the public sphere. As noted in the Introduction, we may for instance gain insight into the current *rise of the public* as a sociological and political object by comparing it with Hannah Arendt's famous rendering of the *rise of the social* as the historical moment when social life abandoned the realm of the household (*oikonomía*) and moved into the *polis* or public sphere (Arendt 1998 [1958]). For Arendt, the concept of 'society' emerged around the eighteenth century as the organization of social life was formalized as a matter of *political economy* – that is, when the management of household affairs (*oikonomía*) went public (1998 [1958]: 45). Extending Arendt's analysis, we may argue that the current interest in the *political* value of knowledge marks the moment when 'political economy' itself is now taken wholesale *outside society* and sanctioned as a self-validating *ethical* object. In other words, ethics has become the mode of organization of the social *after society* – a mode of organization that Foucault famously termed 'governmentality' and that appositely takes 'political economy as its major form of knowledge' (Foucault 2007: 108).

If there is no knowledge that is not at the same time a political economy form, then our only avenue for producing new knowledge – that is, for producing new social forms – requires a super-socialization of our social thought. Hence the 'rise of the public' and other analogous ethical idioms: talk of trust, responsibility and ethics naturalizes the economy by socializing it from within, making the economy appear as a naturally ethical object, a super-social (i.e., ethical) domain.

Here I am suggesting that, in the long perspective of historical sociology, the new language of publicness and ethics provides the sociological vocabulary through which the 'knowledge society' re-socializes the economy. This process of re-socialization is necessary because, as Marilyn Strathern has suggested for the naturalization of 'choice' as a social category in post-plural Euro-American culture, '[w]hen nature becomes a question of cultural style and culture the exercise of natural choice, the one ceases to be "inside" or "part of" – contextualised by – the other' (Strathern 1992: 176). Substitute 'economy' for nature and 'ethics' for culture and the poignancy of the equation remains. The point is that parlance of a 'knowledge economy' or a 'knowledge society' cancels all possible terms of reference for sociological analysis. The knowledge society appears in this context as an emblematic ethical society because the very capacity to know society is glossed as an exemplar of public and communicative rationality (Delanty 2001; Habermas 1970): a society where transparency, trust, governance, responsibility or collaboration dictate the proper ways for thinking about and organizing the social.

In this context, the widespread use of consultation exercises such as 'upstream engagement', 'society in science', 'benefit-sharing' or 'participatory development' programmes contributes to the conceptualization of the ethics of democratic participation (namely, public opinion) as an open assembly of different perspectives.[6]

It is perhaps worth remembering, however, that both perspectivalism and public opinion are paradigmatic baroque tricks. Perspectivalism, we saw in Chapter 2, afforded its trick of comprehensible vision through a gesture of political illusionism – the illusions of a socially and geometrically distributed world. As Elizabeth Povinelli has put it, through 'public reason perspective becomes perspectival; moral obligation and its conditioning of freedom opens to a broader moral horizon, the I-you dyad to a we-horizon, most notably the we-horizons of the nation and the human, the national and the cosmopolitan' (Povinelli 2001: 326). The trick of perspective, in other words, splits the world into a grid of epistemo-geometrical locations and locative subjects.

Analogously, throughout the seventeenth century, consultation exercises in public opinion became the stock-in-trade of absolutist monarchies, such as that of Spain's Philip IV. Indeed, the idiom 'current opinion' was formed at this time, and thinkers such as Hobbes and Pascal are known to have observed that 'the world is governed by opinion' (Maravall 1986: 98). 'Opinion' emerged in this context as a compulsive obsession of governors and political theorists – a heightened index of changing sociological awareness. If Society was a geometric whole, 'perspective' was the visual vehicle for its comprehension, and 'opinion' the vehicle of language and communication. José Antonio Maravall thus noted, in his famous essay on the historical Baroque, 'Baroque culture thus sets itself the task of moving its addressee … One of the means that proved effective in reaching this objective … consisted in introducing or implying and, to a certain extent, *making the spectators themselves participants in the work*, which succeeded in making the spectators almost its accomplices' (Maravall 1986: 75, emphasis added). An example he cites is the technique of 'turning the spectator into a coauther [sic], making use of the artifice by which the work changes *along with the viewer's perspective*' (Maravall 1986: 75, emphasis added). Likewise, Lois Parkinson Zamora and Monika Kaup, in their recent anthology and review of the Baroque's actuality, observe that 'Baroque forms invite *participation*' (Zamora and Kaup 2010: 26, emphasis in the original). In this context, then, the tropes of perspective, consultation and participation fare as symptomatic effects of a baroque cultural epistemology.

What remains distinctive and characteristic of our age, however, is that today coevality of perspectives summons the public as *ethical* status

(Wilsdon, Wynne and Stilgoe 2005: 40). Thus, there is a new political economy of knowledge whose very economic value lies in its alleged *public* status as ethical knowledge. In this fashion, the 'rise of the public' is a characteristic signal of a political era when all decisions about what is (social) knowledge – that is, all decisions concerning the politics of recognition – are left to the politics of the economy. Defining knowledge as a public good – indeed, speaking of it as 'public knowledge' – is a 'political economy' move (in Arendt's ironic formulation): it is making 'knowledge' appear in the political sphere of the economy and constraining its definition to the terms of such a sphere. It is reducing knowledge to the realm of institutional resource allocation. What Alan Irwin has called the new 'politics of public talk' (Irwin 2006) is therefore a perversion of what academics once knew as the 'sociology of knowledge': a *realpolitik* version of a social theory about modernity. This is why we may speak of *political ethics* today as an anthropological assemblage in its own right (Corsín Jiménez 2008a).

The Public, then, is what is left of sociality when economics takes the appearance of politics. It is social life after society itself – and after the economy, too, in that our sociological categories have become fit for explaining little else but economic relations. There is, of course, a certain redundancy to this political emergence of the public as an ethical object. We could summarize it by saying that it is a politics deployed twice: as politics and as a Public. I refer to it as an anthropology of political ethics.

Phantasms

As noted above, the rise of the public may be characterized in terms of the disembowelling – the turning inside out – of a community's political consciousness. In Arendt's description, this is what the displacement and transformation of the household (*oikonomía*) into a political object effected: the turning inside-out – the bringing out from the life of domestic interiority to the spaces of political exteriority – of the life of labour. The threshold or umbra dividing the inside and outside of the *oikonomía* collapsed. The social form of Labour was therefore left without shelter and objectified into a category of Political Economy. The age of Labour is therefore an age of homelessness, of vagabondage. 'Today', writes Paolo Virno, 'all forms of life have the experience of "not feeling at home", which, according to Heidegger, would be the origin of anguish.' The economy sources thus our existential anguishes: 'there is nothing more shared and more common, and in a certain sense more *public*, than the feeling of "not feeling at home"' (Virno 2004: 34, emphasis in the original). Out from the shelter of the household, our destiny today is to blindly roam the wilderness of a public economy. The key here is the movement through which this is sociologically imagined: the exteriorization, or the opening up and exposure, of our social entrails.

Jürgen Habermas's account of the historical transformation of the public sphere similarly rehearses images of interior and exterior displacements (Habermas 1989). Habermas's account is well known for outlining the structural conditions under which the public sphere came into existence and, eventually, deteriorated. In the middle ages, a ruler's 'status attribute' indexed his 'representative publicity'; the ruler was on display as a public symbol (Habermas 1989: 7, 8). Against this background, the first structural transformation came about between the seventeenth and eighteenth centuries with the rise of the liberal bourgeois public sphere, which institutionalized a space for rational-critical communication among private people. Importantly, the coming-into-being of the bourgeois public sphere, in Habermas's account, further required an alienating division of the person into public and private: the former, a political rational *bourgeois* whose affairs were stately; the latter, a familial, intimate *homme* (Habermas 1989: 55). The 'coffee houses, *salons*, and *Tischgessellschaften*' that concentrated public debate were thus demarcated from the 'subjectivity originating in the interiority of the conjugal family' (Habermas 1989: 51). The second transformation came about through a 'refeudalization' of society and an associated 'neomercantilism' in the nineteenth century, whereby new private corporations assumed public powers while the state undertook to intervene paternalistically into the realm of the family. In effect, an 'externalization of what is declared to be the inner life' took place (Habermas 1989: 142, 159).

Arendt's and Habermas's dynamic equations between interior:exterior lifeworlds brings us back to the question of reversibility. That reversibility returns at this stage in the argument is not coincidental, for I want to argue that its very sociological imagination is central to the way Euro-American modernity has conceptualized the sphere of the political. Reversibility is the natural language of modern political sociology, and the only idiom left to the Euro-American sociological imagination for methodologically describing the elusiveness of social life.

The reasons for this have been frequently rehearsed, although seldom in these terms. Giorgio Agamben's recent exploration of the theological underpinning of governance and economy is a notable exception and source of inspiration (Agamben 2008).

In his extraordinary archaeology, one of Agamben's points of departure is the shifting location of *oikonomía* from Greek to early Christian and, later, scholastic and theological thought. For example, an incipient reminder of the economy's performative character is found in Corinthians, in Paul's announcement of his evangelical mission, where he employs the word 'economy' to describe his own role as 'administrator in charge' (Agamben 2008: 37). Paul's work as an apostle, Agamben observes, is not to make known a divine plan or will, but to administrate the disclosure and publicity of the good news. Therefore the reference to economy here is simply to the relatively menial organizational and executive task of administering or disclosing the mystery of salvation – an economy *of* mystery. As Agamben points out, the first and most startling consequence of this is that the early Christian messianic community self-consciously represents itself as an economic and not a political movement: a community of God-sent administrators (Agamben 2008: 41). Over time, however, as Agamben's laborious genealogical excavation shows, the meaning of the term economy gradually shifts to refer to the one activity that disposes and manages the internal and mysterious organization of the divine person itself as both unity and trinity. We might say that at that point *oikonomía* gets promoted from simple back-office administration to proper 'knowledge management': rendering the internal management of the Trinitarian structure of divine personhood – when and how the One unfolds into three and folds back into One – accountable and meaningful. The difficulties and mysteriousness that beset the practice of such forms of management allow us now to speak of the economy *as* mystery (Agamben 2008: 42, 54–55). In this new context, multiplicity and heterogeneity (the trinity of divine being) are not to be taken for ontological questions but should properly be regarded as matters of praxis and administration (Agamben 2008: 56–57). The government of the divine is an economic, not an ontological, mystery.

In early Christian thought and medieval theology, the semantic field of the economy therefore performs a dual function: on the one hand, it administrates the internal organization of divine ontology; on the other, it offers a tool for carrying out or dispensing the providential government of the world. It is a *duplex ordo*, as Thomas Aquinas calls it, a mutually co-implicated order of transcendental and immanent goods and beings (Agamben 2008: 100–101), and a placeholder for reconciling the contradictory exigencies of the transcendent and the quotidian. The economy, then, becomes an operator for both ontology and history (Agamben 2008: 67). The point rehearses Keith Hoskin's argument, elaborated upon in Chapter 2, about the reversible nature of bookkeeping practices. We saw then how bookkeeping pre-empted or anticipated the perspectival gaze – the splitting of our representational strategies into ontological and epistemological descriptions of the world. As historians of accounting practices have argued, in a way that befits Agamben's genealogy of *oikonomía,* accounting first developed as a technology for the administration of providence, including 'accounting for sins', 'accounting for the soul', and accounting for the bureaucratic activities of the Church colleges themselves (Quattrone 2004). Working on a ledger, accountants thus simultaneously exercised an ontological and epistemological task: administration of spiritual salvation on the one hand, and of bureaucratic affairs on the other. And as they did so, echoing Hoskin's argument, they cultivated an emerging form of 'double vision': a 'book-keeping mentality' that promoted the rise of a 'viewing self' capable of holding internal and external – debit and credit – accounts of the world (Hoskin 1995: 150, 151). In double-entry bookkeeping we encounter therefore an *agencement* holding together the infrastructural equipment of the economy's *duplex ordo* and the artisanal epistemology of strabismus.

The polysemic and duplicitous character of the economy has sourced all theories of governmentality since, and thereon the nature of the rule of order and power is fraught with the dynamics of a 'bipolar machine' (Agamben 2008: 78). This bipolarity becomes a genealogical fund for future histories of political theology, including the political ontology of modernity. Thus, the development of political theology in medieval thought turns on the development of a theory of the nature of kingship such that the king was said to have two bodies (Kantorowicz 1997 [1957]), a body natural (*oikonomía as* mystery – ontology) and a body politic (*oikonomía of* mystery – administration). In time, the problem of the double nature of kingship gave rise to a coterminous set of polar contrasts between divine and human justice, canon and civil law, or the genealogical and dynastic succession of the king and the biological perpetuity of the body politic. Two natural theories of society emerged: an organic model, where the community was said to be naturally reproduced through the birth of new members; and a corporational model where, it was argued, the body politic reproduced itself through the genealogical integrity of the crown's dynasty. Said differently, the king's body was taken as both an indexical condensation of the will of the people (*vox populi*) and a representation of supreme sovereignty on earth (*vox Dei*). It is this distinction, between government and kingship, that is, between social organization and power, between economic and political ontology, that Agamben's genealogy sources in early Christian theology, and that of course lies at the heart of Foucault's famous distinction between governmentality and sovereignty (Foucault 2007). The distinction further informs, as Agamben also notes, the *vicarious* condition of modern power; that is, the possibility of power being delegated, of effecting a separation between *auctoritas* and *potestas*, the authority of divine kingship and the power of its vicarious modalities of representation, as in, for example, modern democratic societies' separation of powers (2008: 153–154).

The vicariousness of power plays also a crucial role in the classical anthropological literature on kingship and sovereignty. Matei Candea and Giovanni da Col have recently reviewed this literature to make an original argument about the larger relevance of hospitality as a heuristic for social theory (Candea and da Col 2012). Here, the relevant aspect of their argument is their account of the stranger/host relation that informs the literature on divine kingship. The vicariousness of power is here signalled by the fact of *visitation*. As Candea and da Col remind us, anthropological analyses of divine kingship from Hocart to Sahlins have insisted on the external validation of the stranger-king, the cosmic figure whose arrival to a land thereafter is a source of its people's fertility and well-being: 'Vitality and sovereignty always come from "elsewhere" or are in relationship with an "externality"' (Candea and da Col 2012: 7). However, notwithstanding the fact of divine patronage, tension is always immanent in the encounter between the stranger and his hosts, needing therefore to be assuaged through the 'prophylaxis' of hospitality (Candea and da Col 2012: 3). The craft of hospitality, then, parallels the economy of mystery that in Agamben's account is responsible for administering the worldly presencing of the divine. We may say that hospitality is a technique of *oikonomía*: the social form that outsiderness takes when its immanent insiderness is revealed. The question of the co-implicated immanence of the outside-inside relation leads Candea and dal Col to further draw out an analogy between hospitality and the processes of meta-affinity or 'predation' through which Amerindian societies interiorize strangers and enemies (Candea and da Col 2012: 7). The economy's umbra figures thus as a source of social productivity: the threshold where productive relations encounter the tenebrous and mysterious limits of extra-sociality. The images of the stranger-king and Amerindian predation symbolically mark this umbra. Chapters 5 and 6 will explore at greater length the role of market externalities and immaterial or cognitive capital (that is, the labour of knowledge) in the redefinition of the umbrae of global political economy.

In medieval Christian thought, we have seen, the question of the umbrae of the economy – the mystery of divine presencing in worldly affairs – was partly resolved through the figure of the *duplex ordo*. Political theology's assumption of such an architectural framework opened up a space for the emergence of something akin to a politics/society relation at the very heart of social thought. The very process of think-ing about the social required an ontological tension between Politics and Society – between power-as-authority and power-as-administration. The king's two bodies – his corporate, political body, and his organic, bio-sociological one – thus provided the grounding image for the schizo-phrenia of all political sociology thereafter. Hence there emerged the idea of social life as a duplicitous process: at once an object in need of discipline, requiring the imagination of the state as a sovereign power (Schmitt 2005 [1922]) and of sociality as a self-regulated process, an organic and dynamic body of community life. Hobbes's political theory of the Leviathan epitomizes this transformation: a theatrical vision of social life as both political personification and communal process, and the imagination of the political as both a figure of power (as politics) and an index of a community's identity (as *politeia*). It is hardly surprising that the figures of Politics and Society rose as gigantic Leviathans under the umbrella of such a sociological imagination, leaving the actual flow of social life in shadows. This space of shadows, where the bodies of sovereignty and government superpose and press against each other, is therefore also where the unexpected and the consequential suddenly emerge: where social life takes the form of 'collateral damage' (Agamben 2008: 135, 159).

An argument I want to put forward is that such fugitive and im-provisational conception of the social, and such intuition of the politi-cal as an inherently fragile and tensional shadow-movement, are in fact constant and historical characteristics of the modern condition. In an important essay on the relationship between democracy and totalitari-anism, Claude Lefort draws precisely on the work of Ernst Kantorowicz to analyse the sociological imagination that makes political bodies ap-pear as wholes, as total social facts. Building on Kantorowicz's analysis of the homological and symbolic correspondence between the king's body and the body politic, Lefort describes the rise of democratic sensibility in the eighteenth century as a 'disincorporation of individuals' (Lefort 2004a: 253). Society disembowelled itself out into a corporeal multi-plicity of individual forms, a multiplicity that posed 'a direct challenge to the very idea of social substance' (Lefort 2004a: 253). Such multiple and quantitative imagination posed a threat to the stability and ontology of the social order, a 'threat of numbers' that rendered Society into a new, 'accountable' object. As Lefort puts it, 'numbers disaggregate unity, they undo identity' (Lefort 2004a: 253–254).

The dissolution of society's ontological wholeness did not entail, however, the parallel dissolution of the ontological imagination of so-ciety. This was now triggered into existence instead by what Lefort calls the 'phantasmagorical image of the People-as-One' (Lefort 2004a: 255). Said differently, it is the ghostly fiction of the Public, of the People-as-One, that allows today for the temporary experience of ontological robustness. The Public thus moved in to occupy the now vacant space opening up between the household and the wilderness (of political economy). It assumed the properties of a threshold category: a technology and prophylaxis for the exchanges of modern hospitality, that is, of knowledge.

The Public is what Society has turned into when all experiences of social life are mediated through the sensorial and corporeal figurations of political economy. Elsewhere, Lefort describes this ambivalence between political and individual freedom, or the tension and ultimate excess and 'overflowing' that take place between the experiences of political and individual ontology, as 'reversibility' (Lefort 2004b). For Lefort, the experience of reversibility is what characterizes the democratic condition. It is the necessary categorical prophylaxis offering anthropological continuity to the political ontology of modernity.

The image of social life as a ghostly presence – a 'phantasmagorical image', as Lefort called it: visible yet hard to visualize, tangible yet somehow immaterial – is a constant in the history of public-sphere discussions. Not without reason, Walter Lippmann titled his landmark treatise on the condition of the public sphere *The Phantom Public* (Lippmann 1993 [1925]). For Lippmann, '[m]odern society is not visible to anybody, nor intelligible continuously and as a whole' (Lippmann 1993 [1925]: 32). To speak of the public as a proxy for democratic accountability, for the political visibility of governance, was therefore meaningless and ultimately out of joint with reality. But the image is recurrent. Paraphrasing Hamlet's famous sentence 'the time is out of joint', Derrida described this spectral quality of political justice as a form of 'out-of-jointness'. For Derrida, all forms of political life are, existentially, out of sync with themselves. Gift-giving and debt-honouring, for example, are both paradigmatic expressions of the necessary asynchrony of human sociality (Derrida 1995: 40). Derrida's own spectre, Marx, felt a similar compulsion to describe the hollow cadence of historical life, such that when he wrote in the "Eighteenth Brumaire" about the poverty of a history without relational tension (without class struggle) he explicitly stated that '[i]f any episode in history has been coloured grey on grey, this is the one. *Men and events appear as Schlemihls in reverse, as shadows that have lost their bodies*' (Marx 2002 [1852]: 40, emphasis added). Likewise for Kierkegaard, the public operated as a sort of phantasmagorical invocation, a 'ghostly accountant' conjured to disguise the death of social responsibility – that is, of sociological knowledge itself (cited in Hannay 2005: 46).

More recently, Michael Warner has noted the early allegorical 'ghostly body' through which *The Spectator* constituted itself as the paradigm of public-sphere communications in the seventeenth century – and indeed speaks more generally of today's popular imagination of the public as an 'invisible presence' 'that flit around us like large, corporate ghosts' (Warner 2005: 112, 7). *The Spectator* is also among the publications Terry Eagleton singled out in his recent account of the rise of 'sensibility' in eighteenth-century Europe as a moral and socio-economic ideology (Eagleton 2009: 16). Eagleton is intrigued by the contemporary imagination of sensibility and sentimentalism in terms that echo Lacan's description of the work of the imaginary. The 'imaginary', Eagleton reminds us, 'involves what is technically known as transitivism': 'some primitive bond of sympathy', a 'peculiarly graphic instance of sympathetic mimicry' where my 'interiority is somehow 'out there', as one phenomenon among others, while whatever is out there is on intimate terms with me, part of my inner stuff' (Eagleton 2009: 3). Eighteenth-century sensibility works just in such fashion, opening up the soul as a vibratory impulse that remains in continuous communion with the world. 'Bodies, and countenances in particular, are … directly expressive of the moral condition of their possessors, so that in the manner of the imaginary, *interiors and exteriors are easily reversible* and seamlessly continuous' (Eagleton 2009: 17, emphasis added). At one with the universe, the man of feeling is therefore sometimes carried away by his 'lavishness of sensibility' and a 'cavalier carelessness of *proportion*' (Eagleton 2009: 19, emphasis added), an expression of *geometrical adequation* reminiscent of Giordano Bruno's relational fancies. Thus, as a mysterious and magnetic source of moral communion with the world, the public ethic of sensibility is felt as a 'spectral moral sense … a kind of spectral shadowing of our grosser organs of perception' (Eagleton 2009: 22).

The transformation of the public ethic of sensibility into a commodity-world of fragments, ruins and fictitious excitations, for example in the cultural spectacle of a shopping mall or a world exhibition, would later be furiously and critically described by Walter Benjamin as, indeed, 'the phantasmagoria of capitalist culture' (Benjamin 1999: 8 and passim). To name one last occurrence, the idiom returns in Latour, who defines the 'Phantom Public' as 'an impossible feat of metallurgical fiction', a by-product of our mistaking the politics/society relation for an ontologically stable sociological fact in the first place (Latour 2005: 163).

The idea of the liberal public sphere as a critical space for discussing matters of general interest – as the place where communicative rationality takes shape – appears in this new light as the direct product of a dual, ambiguous and fictitious imagination. 'Living with ghosts', says Wendy

Brown, apropos of the place of the spectral and the phantasmagorical in political thought, 'means living with the permanent disruption of the usual opposites that render our world coherent between the material and the ideal, the past and the present, the real and the fictive, the true and the false' (Brown 2000: 32). The still point afforded by rational thought, where a space is opened up for reasoned disagreement and institutional reflection, for the pendular movement between mimesis and distantiation, partakes thus of the original sin of sociological rationality: the positing of an actual *relation* between politics and society, and of the existence of an intermediary, reconciliatory space in the figure of the Public. The Public, that complex invention that attempted to stabilize society's self-image as a political object, is an elusive solution to the impossible problem of political representation. It is the signature of the perennial *duplex ordo* informing the political theology of modernity.

Thus, whatever the public may be, an anthropological account must aim to populate its descriptions with its possible 'doubles', with ghosts and shadows. There is no Public without a ghost. There is no anthropology proper that does not tense the form of description – of any description – with an allusion to its possible phantoms. For all of the above reasons, reversibility – the notion that the relation between knowledge and sociality, between politics and society, always and everywhere requires a particular kind of ontological work to keep it stable, to cancel its inherent tension, its shadow movements – may be seen as the anthropological concept of sociological knowledge.

Notes

1. But the public, historians have long told us, has always been a project in artefactual history –one in which artefacts often spoke to one another. Thus, Colin Jones has described the importance of the *Affiches,* local, provincial newssheets that, he argues, were central in the formation of 'public opinion' in pre-Revolutionary France (Jones 1996). The *Affiches* carried mostly advertisements for professional services (doctors, dentists, lawyers, charlatans) and a spectacular variety of consumer goods: 'Affiches open a window onto an increasingly materialistic, consumerist world, inhabited by increasingly entrepreneurial and publicity-minded professional groupings' (Jones 1996: 34). The materiality of the *Affiches* opened up a space for the emergence of transitorily stable public identities. It provided a residence for the performance of a contingent yet effective political topos.
2. Philip Mirowski is thus developing an analytical programme on the 'political economy of epistemology' (Mirowski 1998: 29). For example, in his recent work on the history of post–World War II philosophy of science, Mirowski explores the writings of certain key figures in American philosophy of science – John Dewey, Hans Reichenbach and Philip Kitcher – and suggests that whilst all three authors envisaged the relation of science to society in terms of 'democracy', not one of them saw

the need to explain their own philosophical production to the actual regime of scientific organization wherein they were located:

> we are concerned to explore how it was that science came to be portrayed by philosophers as a-social, autarkic, and value-free in America in the middle of the 20th century, and then, how it has subsequently become possible for the philosophy profession to come to the conclusion that this portrayal could be easily reversed without deranging their entire project. It so happens that this narrative is intimately intertwined with another strand of discourse, one that tracks attitudes towards the health of "democracy" in America. (Mirowski 2004b: 288)

3. Raymond Geuss writes of what is *analytically* at stake in having to set up political arrangements for providing a community's good:

> If you *have* a state as your form of political organization, and especially if you are living in a world of competitive states, the preservation and flourishing of your state may be thought to give rise to an independent set of reasons for action. If originally 'public' means originally 'pertaining to the concerns of all the people', and offices and magistrates are instituted to take care of these public concerns, then 'public' can come to refer at least as directly to the offices as to the common concerns. 'Public' can, then, come to mean something like 'governmental' ... The public good can then slide from meaning 'the common good of all, *including* the good of the government' ... to meaning 'the good of the government, including the common good of all'. (Geuss 2001: 48).

4. Roy Macleod writes, on the entanglement of scientific knowledge in the imagination of democracy: 'In defining the natural rights of man, the appeal of science to the *imagination and use of space* played a key role in the language of revolution ... science contained all the nouns and verbs needed by what J.C.D. Clark calls the "language of liberty" in the Anglo-American world' (Macleod 1997: 371, emphasis added).

5. Marginalism represented the final and total de-socialization of the 'political economy of free market'. We need remember that although the classical economists certainly liberalized the economy, they did not 'forget' society (O'Brien 1975). Smith, Ricardo, Mill et al. all worked with models of an agrarian society, and in this sense their economics remained sociologically robust in important ways. Marginalism, on the other hand, did away with all this: there is no sociology proper in marginalist economics.

6. Whether the public is elicited by 'injecting' more perspectives (how many?) into social dialogue, or whether it comes into being as the outcome of such a process, is a matter of contention. For Alan Irwin, for example, 'far from being a simple input to decision-making processes, public opinion should more accurately be seen as an *output* from particular institutional frameworks and forms of social construction' (Irwin 2006: 317). James Wilsdon and his colleagues, on the other hand, see the public as something that is already part of social process and needs only to be promoted or elicited: 'Public value provides a route into deliberation about science that avoids the twin pitfalls of determinism and reductionism ... We need therefore to shift from noun to adjective, by asking not only: what is the public value of science? But also, what would *public value science* look like? ... we need to bring out the public *within* the scientist' (Wilsdon, Wynne and Stilgoe 2005: 29, 35).

5

Predation/ Production

Imagine an Amerindian hunter. On a hunting trip he falls sick and returns to the base camp, unable to carry out his hunt. He and his kin start worrying that the original hunting excursion has resulted in a reversed predation: the hunter has been captured by the animals (say, peccaries) he originally set out to kill. As days pass, his condition worsens. His body is in pain, and the spirits of the peccaries haunt him. In a reversed hunt invisible to human eyes, the peccaries prey upon the body of the hunter, tearing it apart, eating his flesh. By feasting on him, the peccaries are inviting the hunter to become party to their own commensality. Through this peccary cannibalism, the death of the hunter's body signals the rebirth of his soul as an animal. The hunter dies, but the peccaries see their own kin increase. He loses his connection to his human relatives but sees himself reborn into a new world of peccary relations.

Carlos Fausto, whose work on Amerindian modes of sociality informs this description of transformative predation (2007), neatly summarizes the relational tension between humans and non-human persons that sustains this reversed hunt as a form of 'oscillation': 'Over the period of illness the patient oscillates, therefore, between the perspective of past relatives [his human kin] and that of future relatives [the peccaries] … However, from the point of view of the nonhuman aggressor, the disease is an act of capture that implies the double movement of cannibal predation and the transformation of another person into kin' (Fausto 2007: 502). Here, humans and non-humans inhabit a meta-relational world where the possibility of moving in and out of the other's condition is always vividly present, a possibility that is made effective through the production of kinship: when the *relation* becomes a *relative*, the hunter is transformed into a peccary. The relationality of relativity (the possibility of relations becoming relatives) oscillates thus in and out of its own condition, tensing its ontological form until it becomes other than itself.

Central to the model of Amazonian sociality, then, is the *productivity* of relations. The transformative tension that animates social organization in the Amerindian context is the *production of kinship*. Predation is what kinship grows on. Eduardo Viveiros de Castro, whose work among the Araweté first introduced the concept of 'predation' as a model for the organization of social relations in Amerindian studies (Viveiros de Castro 1992), has acknowledged he chose the word 'predation' 'for its provocative opposition to the modern complex of "production"' (Viveiros de Castro 2002: 15). More recently, Viveiros de Castro has further described the transformational conditions of anthropology itself (which permit its internal re-theorization from the predatory to the productive) as the 'discursive *anamorphosis* of the ethnoanthropologies of the peoples thus studied' (Viveiros de Castro 2010: 17, emphasis added).

Viveiros de Castro's suggestive turn to anamorphosis echoes James Weiner's call for an anthropological theory of caducity. Both authors resort to the figure of anamorphosis for its powers of analytical distortion: a technique for decentring, or unbundling from within, the terms through which we conceptualize sociological objects. Although there are some notable differences between Viveiros de Castro and Weiner's projects, in this chapter I want to recuperate their joint focus on the anamorphic as a point of view on the point of view (of the social, of anthropological theory, of critique). In particular, I focus on what an anamorphosis of the production of knowledge in the era of cognitive and informational capitalism might look like. The chapter may be read as an attempt to sketch out a trompe l'oeil anthropology from where to apperceive the collapse of the *point of view of social theory* onto the *vanishing point of knowledge production* – where critique and its objects of study are being made to coincide, or in other words, where the ethno/anthropology of affinal capitalism collapses as a self-similar Public.

In what follows, then, I look at two Public forms that in their joint action stand for this moment of collapse. First I examine the rise of a new informational commons and its entanglement in discourses of social robustness and democratic process. The challenge of the new commons speaks to questions of political governance that are familiar to economists grappling with the 'going global' of public goods: how to first disentangle and then delimit the *duplex ordo* of a new social/political relation.

Knowledge, the global public good par excellence, stands as the second of the trompe l'oeil forms I pay attention to. Knowledge, as noted in Chapter 4, is described in contemporary political economy as both a human need and a methodological infrastructure. It plays the role of both insider and outsider, host and stranger to the modern *oikonomía*. It is our main technology of hospitality. The production of knowledge, then, simultaneously fares as production of sociability and production of governmentality. In this context, the chapter takes a closer look at the notion of 'production' (both its labour and its modes of relationality) and subsequently explores the different, complex ways in which social theory is responding to this novel residence of 'knowledge' at the very threshold of the *oikonomía*. I further venture some additional observations on the proliferation of other forms of 'thresholds', such as networks, or affective or cognitive capital. These are all objects whose self-positioning at the threshold is deployed to make them 'see double': half the body inside, the other half outside the modern household of governance. They are objects that aspire to behave like stranger-kings.

Along Viveiros de Castro, then, we may indeed need to ask ourselves about the terms through which social and economic knowledge in contemporary Euro-American society is said to *grow*. Much talk today concerns knowledge as an 'economy', as a productive ensemble. But what do contemporary Euro-American societies *prey on* to make their social organization of knowledge sustainable?

Balances and Thresholds

Liberal political and economic theory has long declared that in the era of globalization, the collapse of statism as the predominant form of political economy has had a massive impact on our theories of political justice, and our imagination of the political is something that appears to be in need of a new 'balance'. A new global ethics, and new global governance institutions, are being called into place to prevent the 'political' and the 'economy' from going their own ways (Nagel 2005; Nussbaum 2006): 'We ride high on a post-cold war triumph,' writes Lawrence Lessig, 'convinced that the ills of communism would be remedied if only they would privatize everything … But there's a competing tradition … not against property, but for a certain balance in property … the strong balance is the *commons*' (Lessig 1999: 2, emphasis in the original). An important corrective mechanism in this gigantic rebalancing exercise, then, has been the call for redefinition and reinvigoration of the 'commons'. A revised and updated extension of the frontier and landholding ideological tropes (the spatial outsides) of the nineteenth-century public domain, the commons has emerged here as a defining signpost of the contours of the new political economy (Dietz, Ostrom and Stern 2003). Now that the regulatory framework of the state has become passé, so the argument goes, only the (ideal of a) commons can stand up to the forces of private interest.

Although discussions of the 'tragedy of the commons' are hardly a recent development (Hardin 1968; Ostrom 1990), the exponential increase in the availability of information brought about by new information and communication technologies (ICTs) has raised serious concerns over an ensuing enclosure of the global knowledge pool (Boyle 2003). An input and outcome of its own production process, 'information' is said to have undergone an important epistemic transformation under the impact of ICTs: its very momentum and velocity of transformation has turned it into a self-defining public good, an object that continually overspills into something greater than what it is, and whose cannibalistic impulses have made it into an expanding externality (Benkler 2006). Knowledge and information, then, are the new political predators at our turn of the century.

Much has been written about the economic, social and technological fundamentals of the new information society. Here I just want to refer to what I see as those elements of a novel political aesthetic of open democracy that often accompany the exaltation of the knowledge economy as an expandable good. Two processes are at stake, rehearsing the ideological tropes of nineteenth- and twentieth-century statist and market political economies of the Public described in Chapter 4: the concealment of the forces that make knowledge *productively* public, and the imagination of a *spatial outside* to society's knowledge of itself.

Even the most sophisticated and subtle of legal and political theorists often conflate the open-source properties of new knowledge with a theory of open society as democratic practice. As Charlotte Hess and Elinor Ostrom have observed, 'In relation to the intellectual public domain, the commons appears to be an idea about democratic processes, freedom of speech, and the free exchange of information' (Hess and Ostrom 2003: 115). Lawrence Lessig, for example, has described the commons in terms of universal, open access: 'The commons: There's a part of our world, here and now, that we all get to enjoy without the permission of any' (Lessig 1999: 2). Likewise, James Boyle, having developed an original analysis of the creative remaking of the public domain by the open-source movement as a process that is parasitic on the complex, modular structure of the Net, goes on to draw an analogy between Popperian social ethics and the ethics of the Net: 'all the mottoes of free software development', he writes, 'have their counterparts in the theory of democracy and open society' (Boyle 2003: 47).[1] The same is true of Yochai Benkler's robust defence of a political economy of creative commons, where the Net's decentralization of production is presented in terms coterminous with the enhancement of individual freedom and social justice (Benkler 2003a, 2003b). And the very same image of an infinitely expandable pool of democratizing knowledge can be found in recent attempts in economic theory to provide a global update to the theory of public goods (Kaul 2003; Kaul, Grunberg and Stern 1999).

A standard operation here is to redefine the notion of publicness by levering and further disaggregating the political. Inge Kaul and Ronald Mendoza, for example, in a work that aims to reinvigorate the field of global public economics, define 'publicness and privateness [as] social constructs' (Kaul and Mendoza 2003: 86). According to Kaul and Mendoza, anything can be a public good today, so long as it has the potential to be so. Thus the standard definition of public goods (whose use is non-rivalrous and non-excludable) is expanded to include both a good's 'special potential for being public' and goods that 'are de facto public' (Kaul and Mendoza 2003: 88). In this context, actuality and potentiality are idioms that summon an image of the political as a globally evanescent field. Such evanescence turns any problem of social choice into a matter of contingent politics (being in the right place at the right time) and makes the definition of public policy verge on the idea of a social movement (cf. Williams 1995), where as long as a good inhabits the public sphere, we are talking of a public good.

The global theory of public goods rests, thus, on a principle of epistemological multiplicity: anything with the potential to be a public good should, de facto, be considered one. Public goods cease to be studied as forms and are reconceptualized instead as forming powers.[2] The problem remains, however, as to where to locate the *public* sphere in a *global* world, where 'public' and 'global' are already meta-sociological distributions. Which is the superordinate category here: the public or the global?

Kaul and Mendoza opt for identifying the location of the global public sphere in the play of three kinds of political processes: (1) the publicness – or participatory nature – of decision making; (2) the publicness – or equity – of the distribution of benefits; and (3) the publicness of consumption (Kaul and Mendoza 2003: 92). However, a closer inspection reveals that these are but reformulations of the political processes that, following Desai, we observed in Chapter 3 were burdening the statist theory of public finance: the problems of *preference revelation, political bargaining* and the identity of the *productive* agency behind public goods (Desai 2003: 64). And, in this order, these are also the sociological fictions – the political aesthetic – that we have seen as burdening the ethical imagination of Euro-American society when it posits itself as a political entity occupying an institutional space *outside* its own productive social-ity: when society is something that stands outside the market or at arm's length of the state, or a value arrived at (internally) through distributive representation. We are back, then, at the Samuelson fiction.

In the Company Of

In truth, it is far from clear that the structural organization of the politi-cal economy of new knowledge is levering the *production* of knowledge in significantly novel ways. Paul David and Dominique Foray recognize that a society rich in knowledge infrastructure still faces the problem of how to organize itself *politically* in order to make its knowledge *produc-tive* (David and Foray 2003: 44). The political visibility of *productivity* is absolutely central here. Grahame Thompson's detailed examination of the configuration of production processes in knowledge-intensive econ-omies has shown, for instance, that most economic growth emanates from industrial bases where clustering and institutional aggregation are predominant, favouring a return to a craft mode of production that Thompson dubs an '"engineer-based" approach to knowledge' (Thomp-son 2004: 571).

Central to Thompson's argument is his contention that, despite all the rhetoric about the importance of networking and the decentralization of production, the e-economy remains alive because of its adherence to old modes of production. His argument is that, contrary to expectations, most of the new business done by networking appears to be a techno-logical extension of business first sanctioned by handshake agreements. In the business-to-business sector – which makes up 85 per cent of total e-business revenues (Thompson 2004: 566) – the complexity in new production designs brought about by ICTs seems to have promoted a parallel increase in face-to-face contact and handshake transactions. ICTs therefore complement, rather than displace, traditional business strategies, which still require 'the continuation of proximity, the cluster-ing of activities where they can be controlled and monitored through handshake transactions ... Networks continue to do their work "locally"' (Thompson 2004: 566). Networking flourishes not on time-space com-pression but on clustering and institutional aggregation. Most signifi-cantly, this involution to clustering and the intensification of knowledge circulation around circumscribed domains would appear to represent, at some level, a return to a craft mode of production. Thompson – contrary to most diagnoses of the knowledge economy, which take a scientific-technological revolution as their organizing paradigm – suggests that networking enables reorganization of production around an engineer-based paradigm, in which tacit knowledge and craftsmanship emerge as all-important (2004: 571). In this mode of production, then, what is recognized as paradigm shifting is not the simple availability of knowledge, but rather engineers' capacity to put knowledge to work.

Thompson's argument has significant implications for the organization of production in universities, which he himself spells out. Against the current of intensified, engineer-based changes in the organization of production, universities seem unique in having embraced the knowledge economy to the letter. Increasingly, universities are networking their operations, moving closer to flexible specialization modes of production (Slaughter and Rhoades 2004). A well-known example is the distinction between teaching and research staff, which often entails the subcontracting of teaching activities to graduate assistants. This is most odd, in Thompson's (2004: 574) view, because in their traditional guild form of organization, universities were best suited to profit from the clustering and intensification of tacit knowledge that the new focus on craftsmanship seems, in fact, to promote. Thus, far from being a precipitate of its expansionary and global reach, the public goodness of knowledge (should we want to call it that) seems therefore to obtain when effort is made to make knowledge *productively public*, which is something that happens in specialized, intensive, craftsmanly ways.

The notion of *production* takes a new lease of life at this stage. I noted above how the ontological tension of transformative predation in Amerindian modes of sociality energizes the *production of kinship* as a mode of both commensality and conviviality. Predation is what kinship grows on, and it does so through the work of ontological ambiguity. At this point, I would like to extend the theoretical point to social theory at large. Building on an original insight by Othmar Spann, Max Scheler proposed as early as 1926 that an axiological condition of social life was the *production* of its own knowledge. This is a central insight that merits restatement.

Scheler distinguished between two main categories of sociological knowledge: a society's 'collective soul' and its 'collective spirit'. These would roughly translate today into 'sociality' and 'culture'. Importantly, for Scheler, both the collective soul and the collective spirit are founded by the action of a fundamental social presence, which he called 'in the company of' (Scheler 1935 [1926]: 50). His argument centred on the notion that 'in the company of' is a socially immanent force that generates, through conviviality, the very conditions of possibility for the sociological understanding of the collective soul and the collective spirit. Social life is always 'in the company of' something else. Crucially, however, knowledge of that 'something else' is ultimately underdetermined. The something else, we might say, is a pure relation of stranger-kinship. The immanence of 'in the company of' therefore ultimately subverts any stabilization of the social and, indeed, of the political; yet it is also what turns the social-cum-convivial into a productive force. The infra-instability of 'in the company of' is in this light reminiscent of the sources of *transformative predation* that inflect the flow of the convivial in the production of Amerindian kinship. 'In the company of' is predatory *and* productive. For this very reason, it is meaningless to speak of an inherent public goodness or goodwill towards the convivial. On the contrary: as we saw in Chapter 4, the modern condition of the social is inflected by a looming historical shadow-force, a limit-figure that keeps every sociological description of the political in tension and potential evanescence. There is no Public without a ghost, we said there, and indeed we should extend the observation to note that there is no social relationship without the company of its shadows.

The point has been brought home most recently by Isabelle Stengers in her *Cosmopolitiques* project, where she has likewise resorted to the idiom of 'in the presence of' to describe the shadowed indeterminacy of social life. For Stengers, 'the political arena is peopled with shadows of that which does not have a political voice, cannot have or does not want to have one' (Stengers 2005: 996). In this light, thinking-with-shadows may be seen as a sort of trap for political correctness, in that it helps to off-sync or interrupt political thought with the presence of emerging possibilities. In a similar register, Marilyn Strathern has suggested a way to describe the ethnographic experience as taking place '*in the presence of others,* because events become interventions, the subjectivity of different persons the issue … there is a sense of holding in one's grasp what cannot be held – of trying to make the body do more than it can do – of making a connection with others in a partial manner' (Strathern 2004 [1991]: 27, emphasis added).

Thinking 'in the company of' works therefore as an analytical figure for the compossibilities of social action, whose potency will always be 'doubled' (by a company of ghosts and shadows). What remains intriguing, then, is the extent to which the contemporary imagination of the 'sociology of knowledge' insists in seeing the generation of knowledge in contributive and relationally expansive terms, as a positive effect or outcome of the ongoing flow of conviviality and social exchange. The predatory intermediation of 'in the company of', however, clearly makes the equation between commensality (cooperation, collaboration, par-

ticipation, tolerance, distributive and social equivalence) and conviviality no longer tenable in social theory. There is no equation that it is not
always already a containment of excess (Bataille 1991 [1967]). Stranger-
kinship is productive, but it is also predatory.

Writing in conversation with the vanguard of new public domain
theorists such as James Boyle or Yochai Benkler, legal scholar Madhavi
Sunder has also brought attention to the perils that the new discourse of
public value holds for on-the-ground processes of knowledge production, especially among indigenous peoples and other holders of 'traditional' knowledge. She calls this the 'romance of the commons: the belief
that because a resource is open to all by force of law, it will indeed be
equally exploited by all' (Sunder 2007: 106). For Sunder, the current
notion of the public domain is a concept put forward and defended
in accordance with a utilitarian metric. It is an economic-legal fiction
that obscures and ignores the intricacies of complex social and political processes (Sunder 2007: 119). More important than the romantic
ideal of an infinite expandable pool of knowledge, argues Sunder, is the
question of

> who makes the goods or whether the goods are fairly distributed to all who
> need them. A broader understanding of intellectual property recognizes the
> importance not just of producing more knowledge goods, but also of partici-
> pating in the process of knowledge creation. Recognizing people's humanity
> requires acknowledging *their production of knowledge of the world*. (Sunder
> 2007: 122, emphasis added)

Producing knowledge of the world as a commons's project, however,
is hardly tantamount to producing the world's knowledge as a commons. Cori Hayden has vividly illustrated this point in her ethnography
of bioprospecting projects in Mexico (Hayden 2003). As she eloquently
documented in her study, the implementation of the UN Convention
on Biological Diversity in 1992 effectively 'enterprised out' Nature by
turning it into a 'biomass for biotech': 'resources once (not unproblem-
atically) characterized as part of the *international* commons – such as
wild plants, microbes, and cultural knowledge – [were redesignated] as
national sovereignty' (Hayden 2003: 29, 63, 64, emphasis in the original). The shift in sovereignty carved out new positions from whence to
lay claims to biodiversity knowledge. Whereas pharmaceutical companies from the global north had previously procured their leads without
reciprocation to source communities, they were now required to enter
into benefit-sharing and compensation agreements with national gov-
ernments and institutions (universities, indigenous communities) from
the biodiversity-rich south. This, in turn, has triggered some innovative

relocations of the source of the public domain for biodiversity knowledge. Today the pharma industry searches for traditional, ethnobotanic knowledge directly in the 'safety of the public domain':

> declaring themselves *daunted* (rather than, we will note, moved to direct representational action) by the prospect of negotiating benefit-sharing contracts with indigenous peoples, many companies, Latin American biodiversity officials, and university researchers have stated a clear preference for screening resources considered 'safely in the public domain' … Microbes on government protected lands and medicinal plants sold in urban markets, weeds on the sides of roads and knowledge published in anthropologists' articles, petri dishes in private university laboratories and vines growing in backyards … What allows researchers to identify this assortment of sites, some of which are indeed private property, as effectively public? Their denomination as such takes shape against what they are not: it's not the private that is other here, but the *ejidal,* the communal, and the indigenous. (Hayden 2003: 45–46)

Hayden's important ethnography details the manifold processes and claims through which 'the public' is activated and brought to life in the complex circuits of an emerging biodiversity economy. She calls these 'processes of "public-ization"' and emphasizes the importance of paying attention to 'how, in the *production* of prospecting's publics, the sectors, accountabilities, and juridical aspects of public-ness mix and mingle' (Hayden 2003: 47, emphasis in the original). It is the *production of the public,* again, that deserves analytical commentary and attention.

In an interesting confrontation with the economists' definition of science as a public good, Michel Callon has similarly paid close attention to the actual organization of *production* in a knowledge environment (Callon 1994). According to Callon, the public goodness of science obtains through the localized dynamics of scientific communities, when these are seen as techno-scientific environments dedicated to reproducing themselves as heterogeneous networks (linking, in classical actor-network fashion, objects, materials, inscriptions, ideas, texts, discourses and people). It is not information, then, and not even knowledge, as economists and legal scholars maintain, that lends the knowledge economy its global political purchase. For Callon, the public value of knowledge is manifest in the radial activities of networks themselves: it is their capacity to proliferate and expand *as networks* that enacts the public element of (scientific) knowledge. Knowledge can be reproduced as a thing only insofar as its very production process can be reproduced too – hence 'the flaw in concentrating on one particular link in the chain of costs, instead of taking them as a whole. Asserting that an isolated copy of a statement has a use value is like saying that a photograph of a cigarette provides as much satisfaction as the cigarette itself!' (Callon 1994: 405).

However, Callon's suggestive take on the conditions under which science becomes productive does not tackle the reasons why science, as an enterprise, should mobilize a political economy deserving of the *public* ethic. 'Science', he writes, 'is a public good when it can make a new set of entities proliferate and reconfigure the existing states of the world' (Callon 1994: 416). But he does not explain why 'proliferation' entails or carries public value – why 'more' objects make for a better world. For Callon, the public value of knowledge is given by a normative political theory, which in his scheme remains unproblematized, as he himself acknowledges (Callon 1994: 418). Thus, whilst he explores how knowledge takes a productive turn, he does not explain why that productivity should assume a public profile too. Publicness is simply seen as an emergent aspect or dimension of the proliferation of networks, where these mirror the expansionary, horizontal qualities of the open society model.

The political rhetoric about the knowledge society remains thus anchored, as Peter Scott has noted, in a 'utopian vision' (2005: 298) of what knowledge can do for people. The utopia of knowledge is meanwhile flawed by the duplicitous value of knowledge as both a commodity and a public good (2005: 299). This is a point recognized by David and Foray, who acknowledge that the new information- and knowledge-rich society is producing 'artificial scarcities – by achieving legally sanctioned monopolies of the use of information [via intellectual property rights] – in fields where abundance naturally prevails, thus giving rise to an enormous amount of waste' (David and Foray 2003: 37). Wastage is the outcome, not of relations of production being ineffective, but of productivity remaining unused. It is the effect of productivity being sourced in the last instance *in a realm of ontological infinity* (as anticipated in Chapter 3). This rehearses a well-known idea in economic theory about the qualities of knowledge as an 'externality': an object unbounded and deterritorialized that cannot properly be kept within market controls (Cornes and Sandler 1996: 6).

Labour Theories of Knowledge

The idea of knowledge as an externality has led economists to point out the similarities between the unstable nature of knowledge as a public good and the precariousness that inflects the imagination of political values in modern theories of global justice, in which the global and the political spill over each other in complex ways, distorting an agent's capabilities to exercise agency over a good (Kaul and Mendoza 2003; Stiglitz 1999). Public knowledge and global justice are both taken as ontological certitudes: they are epistemic objects known to exist whose realization always falls short of itself. I will return to this model of knowledge, which I call Utopia Minus, in Chapter 6. Utopia Minus rehearses classical themes in economic anthropology on the interplay between labour, agency, personhood and value in the make-up and organization of social life (Corsín Jiménez 2003b; Firth 1979; Graeber 2001; Ulin 2002). Two labour theories of knowledge are worth distinguishing in this context.

The first theory is sustained on the idea that knowledge is the relational outcome of people's use of it. The larger the number of people exchanging knowledge, the greater the chances of making the overall stock of knowledge grow. Because of knowledge's inclination to behave as an externality, some economists speak of a 'tragedy of the public knowledge "commons"' (David 2000), in which any attempt at circumscribing and appropriating knowledge – at turning knowledge into property – is seen as a likely subtraction from a future, larger stock of valuable knowledge. The idea participates in what economists call a regime of 'open knowledge' (Dasgupta and David 1994; Foray 2006: 172–179), in which knowledge is rapidly disclosed and freely available: the larger the stock of information 'out there', the greater the chances that people will 'take it in', use it, transform it, add value to it, and return it in the guise of an overall incremental addition. Speaking about Google's metonymic incarnation of the Web, Barbara Cassin draws in this light an analogy with classical Greek categories of holism. Classical Greek distinguishes two modes of holism: *pan,* which designates an open and unbounded whole, and *holon,* which designates a totalizing and bounded whole. According to Cassin,

> when what is at stake is information, the whole we are talking about here must necessarily be a *pan,* connected to the infinite … [Thus,] rather than something bounded by nothingness, what we have is something whose outside is always related to something else. Information + information, *ad infinitum* … an infinite in expansion … The will of information is always a will of further information … Google's vocation is *panic* [from *pan*], akin to the web as an expanding universe. (Cassin 2008: 63, my translation)

It is this model of the incremental exchange and *panic* economy of knowledge that informs what Benkler calls 'the wealth of networks' (2006), whose paradigm is the Internet's 'networked economy of information'.

I call the sociology of knowledge that underpins this vision a 'relational economy of knowledge'.

The second sociological theory of knowledge partakes, too, of the relational imaginary, although it is qualified by what one might call a 'sense of magnitude', an appreciation of the capacity to turn labour into knowledge. In important ways, this mirrors the distinction that Amartya Sen draws between global justice and international equity (1999a), in which what is gauged is neither the amount of knowledge 'out there' nor its velocity of circulation but the capacity of different actors to make knowledge relevant for themselves and others. Indeed, the labour theory of knowledge on which this model is built recognizes the importance of 'open knowledge' but distinguishes between labour and agency in turning knowledge into a political asset. Whereas ease of access to a network economy of knowledge guarantees the availability of knowledge for use (agency), it says nothing of the actor's capability to use it productively (labour). A labour approach requires thus a focus on production, care and sustenance. But at this point, importantly, we may perhaps speak more pertinently of knowledge as a *commons resource* rather than, simply, a public good. As Charlotte Hess and Elinor Ostrom have put it:

> This ability to capture the previously uncapturable creates a fundamental change in the nature of the resource, with the resource being converted from a nonrivalrous, nonexclusionary public good into a common-pool resource that needs to be managed, monitored, and protected, to ensure sustainability and preservation. (Hess and Ostrom 2006: 10)[3]

In fact, with Peter Linebaugh we may go further and prefer to describe the activity of commons-keeping as the labour of *commoning*:

> The activity of commoning is conducted *through* labor *with* other resources; it does not make a division between 'labor' and 'natural resources'. On the contrary, it is labor which creates something as a resource, and it is by resources that the collectivity of labor comes to pass. As an action it is thus best understood as a verb rather than as a 'common pool resource'. (Linebaugh 2010)

After Proliferation

To manage, monitor and protect is to imagine production 'in the company of': to appreciate knowledge's inherent fragility and infra-instability, its partial commonness and its partial elusiveness. Today, this moment of commensality is tensed against a proliferative otherness, a global affinity and ecumenical fellowship epitomized by the politics of networking. This is what leads Callon to speak of the 'contribution of economic markets to the proliferation of the social' (Callon 2007). Thus, although Callon's network is conceptually very different from that of the open society advocates, the two networks share a momentum of horizontal expansiveness and propagation, for it is in the very nature of the network's internal *agencement,* or techno-economic arrangements, that novel modes of framing problems, or modes of problems overflowing their solutions, generate new common wealth and political values – 'markets as networks of innovation' (Callon 2007: 150).

Upon inspection, however, the very organizational form of the network as a globally productive artefact takes on a rather different guise. Anthropological work has shown that the 'imperative to connect' that animates the new network economy is more often than not short-circuited by organizational problems at the local level: the politics of the office outweigh the supra-politics of the network good (Green, Harvey and Knox 2005). Reporting on ethnographic work on the effects of a European Union–funded project to create an 'information city' in Manchester, UK, Green et al. note that in the places they studied, the attempt to use networking to create an 'imagined community' transcending national borders failed – not because people were short-sighted about the long-term benefits of a network economy, but rather because they knew only too well that the political is *not* an evanescent field. Although the networks certainly enabled connections, these connections hardly resembled the uncomplicated business that the network rhetoric imagined. The network was therefore as much an effort in, and a result of, disconnection as it was of 'imagined' – and imperative – connection. Precisely because people were already connected (in various ways), getting the network's 'fantasy of pure connection' to work often proved an insurmountable task (Green et al. 2005: 818).

This brings us to a point that was hinted at before but only now takes on the dimensions of a truly political aesthetic. I refer here to the imagination of 'networked knowledge' as a political artefact itself. One work by Annelise Riles that has already become a classic referent here (Riles 2001) is an ethnography of the political activities of transnational aid and feminist workers, where the network is the primary form of intra- and inter-institutional bureaucratic communication in the world of international development. In Riles's ethnography, transnational aid workers spoke of networks as both social *and* political artefacts. For them, the network was an aesthetic device, one of many ways to represent relationships between bureaucratic actors. Yet they were also keen users of the network and enthusiastically embraced its technological and design possibilities, re-describing existing relationships in network guise and imagining new possible relations through the conditions for networking. It is this recursive aesthetic of the network – now political artefact, now expression of sociality – that, according to Riles, puts the network in its current political predicament.

Riles says that her informants' re-versioning of every social moment in network terms is indicative of a vision where 'sociality is seen twice' (Riles 2001: 23–69). The idiom is of course reminiscent of Malcolm and Schaffer's description of political illusionism. Resuming the vocabulary of seventeenth-century optics, we might say that Riles's informants indulged in another version of dioptric vision: they all knew that they held a perspectival view on 'reality', in other words, that there are other ways (than networking) of looking at things; they also knew that this one perspective they held was an optical trick. What calls for our attention, then, as Riles pointedly insists throughout her study, is the examination of the anamorphic devices – such as the network – that allow this one perspective to come into view, and to rest.[4] The network's strabismus emerges, then, as the aesthetic that transnational NGO activists use to effectively displace their own rhetoric about themselves. This is why networks have become the most extended form of institutionalized liberal rationalism, an ideological aesthetic (both materialist and idealist) that shapes the political organization of bureaucratic work everywhere.

At this juncture, the confluence of the network aesthetic with the theory of global public goods and the political economy of the information commons sets off its own train of political consequences. Caught up between these three discursive formations, 'knowledge' gradually assumes the features of a global political aesthetic: an ethical good of global public proportions. Knowledge becomes a self-proliferating artefact of baroque globality.

Baroque Globality

The extent to which knowledge has been caught up in this triangulation is best apprehended when placed in the context of knowledge's own rise as, in the words of Richard Hull, 'a unit of analysis' (Hull 2000, 2006). Hull has shown how this coming-into-being of knowledge was shaped by the ideological struggles in the first half of the twentieth century that aimed to find a resting place for knowledge *outside society*. In this intellectual battle, fought by the likes of Hayek, the Polanyi brothers, Popper and Mannheim against the alleged totalitarianism of Lukács's sociology, the force of the debate consolidated the opinion that what was at stake was 'how to develop meta-theoretical positions (about science, economics, sociology and philosophy…) which could challenge positivism while retaining the validity of "positive" (in a weak sense) understandings, descriptions and prescriptions for the world' (Hull 2000: 325). The Hayekian view that equated knowledge with individual freedom won the day. Here knowledge stood for individuals' reflexive capacity to bring themselves to action, a view that located knowledge at once inside (tacitly dispersed amongst individuals) and outside society (an outcome of people's choice of action vis-à-vis others), and in so doing effaced the ethical impetus (recognized by Lukács) that comes from knowing one's place in society. This is why, for Hull, the current interest in the place of science (or knowledge) in society is misplaced: the question of the ethics of knowledge is first and foremost a question about the concepts of our social theory (Hull 2000: 326).[5]

Hull describes, for the fields of the sociology of knowledge and science, a shift in epistemic assumptions that echoes some of the changes we have already encountered in the historical development of the theory of public choice, and in its extension to the new networked knowledge economy. Here the economists' old concern about the *intelligence* required to think *collectively* about society developed into a question about the *collection of intelligence*.[6] Whereas in the days of statist intervention society appeared as a residual artefact, the sociological leftover on the margins of an intelligent economic allocation, the rise of knowledge as a unit of analysis gradually made knowledge appear everywhere as a sociologically reflexive datum, and the problem became instead that of identifying the exact location of society.

Nigel Thrift has described this feature of our age as indicative of capitalism's reorganization around 'the whole of the intellect' (Thrift 2006: 296), whereby a new distribution of the sensible as sheer contingent possibility (like the public goods that are now recognized as global social movements) becomes the location of surplus value. There, anything that society knows and values becomes 'knowledge' and 'value', 'making knowledge in to [sic] a direct agent of the technical-artistic transformation of life: knowledge and life become inextricable' (Thrift 2008: 30). In a language that echoes Gabriel Tarde's description of the economy of innovation as 'germ-capital', a mode of production organized around the pure openness and vibration of ideas (Lepinay 2007), Peter Sloterdijk likewise provides an ontological description of our globalized economy as 'a sort of vibrant and hyperactive jelly', where everything collides and has effects on everything else (Sloterdijk 2007 [2005]: 29, my translation). Echoing Riles, we might therefore say that the problem here has become one of figuring out whether society is in the network or the network in society – or perhaps these are both optical illusions and we are witnesses to a baroque formalization: Public knowledge as a social form tripled back upon itself, as economy, polity and society.

We can now start to see why the political imagination of the new knowledge economy as a network economy of global commensality takes a sociological toll. When the idea of public knowledge becomes coextensive with globality – when society is always external to itself, accountable to the productive demands of a global other – the terms 'knowledge' and 'public' emerge as reversibles: they accomplish the dioptric trick of making one 'see double'; they provide, paraphrasing Noel Malcolm, a curious structure of argument, where social ethics and the production of knowledge are conflated, by optical illusion, to the inextricable epistemic regime of a global economy. Public knowledge appears thus as both the aesthetic of a new global capitalism *and* the epiphenomenon of what we may now call an anthropology of political ethics.

Predation and Global Commensality

Disproportionality is a metaphor that does not chime well with philosophical, and managerial, explanations of how science ought to work. As Philip Mirowski has insistently argued throughout his work, the prevalent metaphorical vision of explanation in the philosophy and sociology of science in the twentieth century has been that of geometrical equilibrium. As an aesthetic of structural proportionality, the metaphor of equilibrium has long functioned as 'the primary [locus] for the mathematization' of natural science (Mirowski 2004a: 338), especially in physics, from which it has permeated the scientific aspirations of economics (Mirowski 1989). Classical political economy inherited this mathematical imagination of proportionality as a figure of stability and value, most famously in the development of the laws of supply and demand as integral to the project of neoclassical economics (Mirowski 2004a: 339).

For Mirowski, the new economics of knowledge, of which the globalization of privatized science is the paradigmatic expression, retains the candid vision of a proportional aesthetic. He calls it '"an effortless economy of science" – modern science as a set of self-sufficient and efficient social structures ... patterned upon the neoclassical image of the market' (Mirowski 2004a: 11). The underlying social structure here is a frictionless plane, on which social interventions, whether economic, political or scientific, interact smoothly and efficiently and eventually gravitate towards an equilibrial resting place, obtained through consensus and evidence-based rationality. This is also, of course, the model of the 'open society' (Popper 1945), and of the 'republic of science' (Polanyi 1962), in which the political structures of science are essentially value-free and transparent, and all that is required of scientists and legislators is to provide structures of governance that consolidate and replicate an idea of science as a democratic good in itself. This is also the context in which the metaphorical power of proportionality becomes a sociological surrogate for theories of social democracy and political justice (Corsín Jiménez 2008b), and in which science and scientific knowledge are imagined as political objects that can be 'well-ordered' (Kitcher 2001).

The use of a proportional aesthetic to imagine the rise of the knowledge economy and conceptualize the place of knowledge in sociology has a historical sociology of its own. As Simon Schaffer (1994) has shown, the rise of intelligence as an object of political economy is closely related to the philosophy of machinery that took over the technological imagination of labour at the turn of the eighteenth century. Hand in hand with the ascent of Ricardian political economy arose a debate in which the very location or 'geography of intelligence' was at stake (Schaffer 1994: 223). Whereas philosophers of manufacturing argued that 'the surplus value extracted from the machines was the product of the intelligence of capital made real in the force of steam-driven engines,' socialists held that the factory system 'used, and assumed, the image of the human body as "living machinery"' (Schaffer 1994: 223). In this context, philosophers of machinery provided a rationalistic account of what was otherwise a battle – between the visibility or invisibility of machine versus labour intelligence – whose larger political context was famously re-described by Edward P. Thompson in his account of the conflicts over the Corn Laws and the transition from a 'moral economy of the crowd' to the 'political economy of the free market' (Thompson 1971: 128), as described in Chapter 4.

The image of a balancing of forces between the human and the machine, the visibility and invisibility of intelligence–knowledge, and the conflict between morality and economy provided a set of grounding metaphors for the larger imagination of society in terms of a proportional aesthetic. The implication here is that the analytical categories through which scholars conceive our sociology of knowledge are supplied for us by a sociological imagination in which 'knowledge', 'society', 'public' or 'economy' stand for one another as proportionate objects (Corsín Jiménez 2008a). In the case of Thompson's famous conceptual pair – 'moral economy' and 'political economy' – this is straightforward and manifest in Thompson's own sociological imagination: the larger the slice of 'political economy' in society, the smaller that of 'moral economy'. In the case of the so-called knowledge economy, we have seen, the occasion for this balancing out is the confluence and intersection of the public nature of knowledge and the political economy of science. In all cases, the danger is to mistake 'morality', 'technology' or 'knowledge' for substantive sociological concepts, when all that is at play here is a variant of a geometrically inspired supply-and-demand sociology. The moment this happens, our sociological imagination is seriously compromised: because we can only imagine sociological knowledge through the political philosophy and economy of market value and public choice, our sociology of knowledge becomes, inevitably, a sociology of economic knowledge.

There is perhaps a lesson to be learned here about the relational economy of the new utopianism of knowledge. As Maurizio Lazzarato and Antonio Negri (1991), among others, have argued, the technological qualities of the new knowledge economy contribute to obscuring the collaborative and cumulative nature of labour invested in the production of knowledge, for it is knowledge in all its immaterial dimensions – in its very communicative process – that is now taken as a productive figure (Lazzarato 1996).

However, although the problem of the phantasmagoria of machine intelligence is as old as the philosophy of machinofacture, in a sense hyperlinkages and nonlinearity are making labour disappear in a radically novel way, because it is connectivity–communication that is directly producing the social relation of capital today (Lazzarato 2004). This is no trivial matter, because in the age of network capitalism, the question of the production of knowledge is most often posed in terms of ownership (McSherry 2001). In this context, the question of who owns capital thus appears as a question about the very ownership of social relationality – a capitalist appropriation, anthropologists might say, of the (Melanesian) model of generative, productive knowledge (Strathern 1988).

For this reason, critical legal scholars and public-domain economists rightly argue that in the context of a network economy of information, much is to be gained in keeping the economy open by fostering free access and promoting commons-based peer production (Benkler 2003a; Benkler and Nissenbaum 2006). But a danger lurks here: the notion of 'relational connectivity' often involves conflating the productivity of knowledge with, or mistaking it for the production (i.e., the labour) of knowledge – that is, confusing knowledge with knowledge-work and, accordingly, the demonstration of knowledge (in economy and society) with its socially productive ('in the company of') moments. In this context, some aspects of the nature of knowledge may be better grasped when placed in the context of their own negativity or in the presence of its own shadows. Concerning knowledge, then, we might ask not how it grows or what its conditions of production are, but how it disappears: what contributes to its absences and how it confronts its own sense of diminishment and disproportion. Thus can we hold in view how knowledge transforms its relations into relatives, and bear in mind its productive moments as moments of transformative predation.

Notes

1. Deleuze's evocative description of the rise of pragmatism in late nineteenth-century American society will serve here to exemplify why a sociology of modularity (which he labels *patchwork* or *archipelagian* sociality) should not be mistaken for a sociology of open democratic practice (Deleuze 2005 [1993]). Using Herman Melville's wonderful novel *The Confidence-Man* as an example, Deleuze shows the difference between the genuine 'trust' of archipelagian sociality and the masquerade trust of institutional democratic life. True democratic trust obtains not in open societies but in dispersed and archipelagian ones.

2. As a gesture of political epistemology, the move exudes a certain overstrained self-satisfaction that, with Deleuze, we may call a 'Baroque solution':

    The Baroque solution is the following: we shall multiply principles – we can always slip a new one out from under our cuffs – and in this way we will change their use ... the Baroque represents the ultimate attempt to reconstitute a classical reason by dividing divergences into as many worlds as possible, and by making from incompossibilities as many possible borders between worlds. (Deleuze 1993: 81)

3. Hess and Ostrom's emphasis that work is needed for a common-pool resource to remain resilient is an important point that is often neglected in utopian discussions of the knowledge economy. An example is the arduous work needed to make digital information globally available by investing in the building of trusted digital repositories, which require rules and actions on matters such as 'audibility, security, and communication', 'compliance and conscientiousness', 'reputation' or 'confidence' (Hess and Ostrom 2003: 143–144).

4. Riles extends her analysis of 'networks' to include other bureaucratic artefacts, such as 'documents', 'paperwork', 'newsletters' or 'matrices'. For ease of exposition, I use the term 'network' here to encompass all such devices.

5. Steve Fuller has charted a similar genealogy for the rise of the knowledge society, tracing it, as did Hull, all the way back to 1920s Vienna and also putting Hayek at the top of his list of suspects (Fuller 2001, 2002: 13–16). For both Hull and Fuller the appearance of knowledge as a political object indexes a problem of institutional intelligence: how to divide society up for economic redistribution.

6. Or as Nico Stehr puts it, a historical shift from the 'politics of knowledge' to 'knowledge politics' (Stehr 2003: 643).

6

Exteriority/ Interiority

Walter Lippmann's famous critique of 'the public' as a proxy for democratic accountability (Lippmann 1993 [1925]) makes for uncanny reading in these times of overabundant knowledge. Lippmann's uneasiness with the public derived from his view that democratic robustness was ultimately an 'unattainable ideal', especially if constructed around the 'ideal of the sovereign and omnipotent citizen' (11). For Lippmann, the idea of democracy could not be made to stand on the notion of an absolute and transparent command of all possible knowledge on the part of the citizenry. Therein lay the 'mystical fallacy of democracy', because an average citizen 'cannot know all about everything all the time, and while he is watching one thing a thousand others undergo great changes' (28, 15). In fact, what Lippmann insinuated was that it remains doubtful whether knowledge, politics and the social are indeed correlates or commensurate with each other, for 'the problems of the modern world appear and change faster than any set of teachers can grasp them'. Thus, any attempt at making knowledge into a politically relevant object is 'bound always to be in arrears' (17). The political hopefulness that informs the notion of public knowledge is thus understood as the malaise lying behind all theories of democracy.

Over eighty years have passed since Lippmann published his text, yet it remains intriguing how the terms of his analysis – knowledge, the public and the critical analysis of society – continue to underpin the anthropology of our political imagination. Today, as we have seen in Chapters 4 and 5, the relationship between knowledge and the public continues to inhabit and inform the nature of our political epistemology. Whatever our politics looks like, it is always an expression of some sort of proportional equivalence or balance between knowledge and the public.

The curious equation of knowledge and the public is built on a mathematics of sorts. Take, for instance, mathematics itself. Mathematics, economists argue, is good to think public knowledge with.[1] Once a mathematical theorem is made public, knowledge of it cannot be taken from knowers, no matter how often it is taught.[2] Economists call this property of public knowledge 'non-rivalry': my knowledge of a subject poses no threat or rivalry to someone else's. Meanwhile, once a theorem is published, anyone with the will and skills to learn it can have free access to the theorem. Economists call this property of public knowledge 'non-excludability': knowledge is public when no one is excluded nor discriminated from accessing it.

Note that both non-rivalry and non-excludability define the qualities of public knowledge in terms of epistemic abundance or surplus: knowledge is public if it cannot be depleted by generalized access or consumption. If my holding of knowledge subtracts nothing from what others can have, then what makes knowledge public is also what makes it as 'big' as society: no matter how many people are out there consuming it, knowledge will remain public if its stock remains on a par with, for lack of a better word, Society.

The point is brought home by Clay Shirky, a noted writer on the social and economic effects of Internet technologies, in a recent contribution to the prestigious Internet colloquium space *The Edge*. Here Shirky describes society's potential for self-expression in terms of a 'cognitive surplus' (Shirky 2008). Wikipedia, for instance, 'the whole project – every page, every edit, every line of code, in every language Wikipedia exists in – ', amounts to 'something like the cumulation [sic] of 98 million hours of human thought'. There are good and poor uses of surpluses, however. Watching television, Shirky argues, makes a poor application of social excessiveness and creates social stupor. Playing with Web 2.0 applications, on the other hand, makes for creative social participation. A favourite example of his is a wiki map for crime in Brazil:

> If there's an assault, if there's a burglary, if there's a mugging … you can go and put a push-pin on a Google Map, and you can characterize the assault, and you start to see a map of where these crimes are occurring. Now, this already exists as tacit information. Anybody who knows a town has some sense of, 'Don't go there. That street corner is dangerous. Don't go in this neighborhood. Be careful there after dark.' *But it's something society knows*

without society really knowing it, which is to say there's no public source where you can take advantage of it. (Shirky 2008, emphasis added)

The notion that 'society knows things without really knowing them' complicates the political sociology of public economics in extraordinary ways. For one, the project of having to make knowledge transparent to society remains a daunting one: what sort of *oikonomía*, that is, of household or administrative apparatus, shall be used to intermediate and reconcile the relation between them? Who plays host and who plays guest – knowledge or society – in the house of the global economy? The question of course reminds us of the classical problem in theological economy: the administration of the *duplex ordo* through which the divine made itself present in worldly affairs.

In this final chapter I examine the role that market externalities play in the contemporary *oikonomía* of knowledge-society relations. I explore the economic epistemology through which neo-liberalism internalizes and externalizes its political categories in the global sphere. In doing so, I offer a more general reflection on what may be at stake in making knowledge and society (and their forms of economy and administration, including critique) into correlates of each other. What has enabled the experience of critique to be consistently conceptualized in terms of just such a *différance*? What has made the conceptual imagination of knowledge, economy and the social liable of being separated in the first place, to be magnified or miniaturized, or even made to converge, with one another?

Spillover

In a wonderful passage in Deleuze's lectures on Leibniz's philosophy, he describes the playfulness of concepts. 'Concepts', he writes, 'are always the subject of movements, the movements of thought' (Deleuze 2006 [1980/1986/1987]: 109). To illustrate the variety of playful movements that concepts are capable of, Deleuze resorts to contrasting Leibniz's and Kant's theories of knowledge. Epistemologically, this boils down to the difference between analytical and synthetic models of knowledge. For Leibniz, concepts are intensive movements: to obtain knowledge we must immerse ourselves deep into the nature of the concept. Every concept contains the world within, we just need to probe deep inside it and learn how to disentangle it. This is very different from Kant's epistemology. For Kant, the nature of knowledge resides outside concepts. The trick here lies in learning to say something relevant about a concept:

to look outside the concept for the things that may belong to, or are of interest to the concept. For Kant, as Deleuze puts it, 'to know something is always to spill over the concept' (Deleuze 2006 [1980/1986/1987]: 115).[3]

The idiom of a 'spillover' has recently gained political currency due in part to the redefinition of economic public goods as 'externalities' (Cornes and Sandler 1996). Like Kantian concepts, public goods, economists argue, have a tendency to flow over their market circumscriptions, delivering their 'goodness' beyond their original catchment area. An example is 'knowledge', whose qualities make it the travelling commodity par excellence. As Dominique Foray puts it, knowledge is a 'fluid and portable good' that 'as soon as it is revealed ... slips out of one's grasp' (Foray 2006: 91). The slipperiness of public goods impregnates them with a sociology of horizontality: they radiate and create relations wherever they are deployed. Foray illustrates this radiation eloquently with the example of a musician who provides a positive externality to her neighbour who loves music (Foray 2006: 92). Brett Frischmann and Mark Lemley described this relational effect when defining spillovers as 'uncompensated benefits that one person's activity provides to another' (Frischmann and Lemley 2006: 2). In this sense, although originally coined to provide an idiomatic expression to an economic phenomenon, the notion of spillover may well fare as a sociological theory in its own right, because one may imagine sociality as forever spilling over each and every one of its social moments: my ideas or actions spill over your ideas or actions, which in turn spill over someone else's ideas or actions, and so on. To push the metaphor to its analytical limits, we could even think of society recurrently spilling over itself as a total whole.[4]

The political implications of such a 'spillover sociology' are worth noting. For a start, the image of 'spillover' lends a beautifully excessive trope to our contemporary baroque political. As Chunglin Kwa has noted, among the 'several characteristics of the historic baroque [that may] make the term *baroque* attractive to use for later periods, including the present' is the notion of a 'sensuous materiality' that 'is not confined to, or locked within, a simple individual but flows out in may directions, blurring the distinction between individual and environment' (Kwa 2002: 26). Cuban writer Alejo Carpentier speaks moreover of a 'Baroque dynamism', an 'art in motion, a pulsating art, an art that moves outward and away from the center, that somehow breaks through its own borders' (cited in Kaup 2005: 113). In this light, it does not seem far-fetched to call the externality the *imago* of our neo-baroque political economy.

Second, we may speak of *society as a whole* as a public good, for sociality itself depends on this positive recursive entanglement of people and things over one another (my actions spilling over your actions, spill-ing over other agents' actions, etc.). Utopia Minus is an apposite label for such a sociological image of society because our starting point would be one of wholesale public goodness, from where we piecemeal subtract, one by one, relations and externalities when and if they are not posi-tive, or when and if they must not be divulged. If the walls that separate a musician from her neighbour are too thick, sociality stops short of spilling over itself one more time: we find ourselves one relational ef-fect away from our utopian whole.[5] The 'peculiarity of this utopia', as Sheldon Wolin puts it,

> is that unlike previous utopias, where the blessed land was depicted as the antithesis of the wicked and unjust world 'outside', the realized utopia in-corporates dystopia. Its opposite is 'inside' because this particular utopia cannot be realized without dystopia, without reproducing it; hence utopia never promises to eliminate dystopia, merely to be allowed to recruit from its meritocratic escapees. (Wolin 2000: 18)

Hence the 'Utopia Minus' label: utopia gets subtracted one by one of its externalities, or adds one by one its new recruitments. Not sur-prisingly, it this arithmetic imagination that leads economists to speak of 'internalizing' externalities when the relational effects are unknown or unwelcome. The classic instance of an externality 'internalized' by the market is intellectual property rights. Here the total public good contracts into a private figure: the utopian whole is scaled down and replicated in a partial form.[6]

Marilyn Strathern's recent and insightful analyses of corporate patent-ing and political processes of republican representation provide illustra-tion in this context (Strathern 2002a). According to Strathern, corporate patents are designed to provide society with the benefits of scientific applications; thus, whilst they recognize the fruits of invention, patents also *internalize* the spirit of disclosure of information that guides good practice in science. At the same time, however, patents *externalize* the competitive drive of the market. Patents make explicit and obvious to the research and industrial community that the benefits of scientific dis-covery are reaped by those who innovate first. So an internal movement (patenting) creates its own external domain (a market with predatory compulsions). This is an example of an 'externality' that, by way of an-ticipation, effectively pre-empts its own public: an internal externality (Strathern 2002a: 254).

Her second example looks at the public inquiry carried out by the Canadian Royal Commission on New Reproductive Technologies be-tween 1989 and 1993. The commission was set up to gather information on Canadian society's different opinions on matters of techno-science applied to human reproduction. Strathern observes that the model of Canadian society that the commission worked with implicitly assumed that ethical-cum-political representation was a question of 'balance'. It was assumed that Canadian society would be characterized by a multiplicity of perspectives and interest groups. In this pseudo-republican theory of society, the 'balancing' of this diversity of perspectives became therefore a metonym for a particular ethical model, where ethics is again a reconciliatory space for a number of reversible moments: individuals versus society, or state versus multiple constituent groups. One way or another, the ethical is the space that mediates separation; and this separation is a precipitant of an imagination of society as a (dis)aggregative object. As she puts it: 'In the balancing of the two approaches [individual vs. society, state vs. interest groups], we might ask what value was being given to *balance* itself' (Strathern 2002a: 260, emphasis added). In this light, what is at stake is that the commissioners' latent principles of moral reasoning became another *internal externality*, because in opting for proposing as a model of Canadian society their own vision of how society aggregates into a balanced whole, they chose to leave out those participants in social life whose vision of society did not match the commissioners' parts-to-whole aggregative identity, such as religious minorities. Religious groups were framed off the model of society because they carried their ethics within: they were not willing to make their ethical choices in the space opened up by the balance of consultation (Strathern 2002a: 261). Their ethics was not external to them, hence they became, for modern Canadian society, an externality.

Anticipation

We have seen here and in Chapter 5 the place and role that 'balancing' occupies in contemporary political ethics and economy as a fulcrum used to calibrate the relations between society and economy, knowledge and the public. But as the royal commission's example above shows, the fiction of sociological and ethical equilibrium is obtained at the expense of new bifurcations and incisions, such as religious minorities being cast as ethical pariahs. Balancing, indeed, generates its own spillovers.

In *Public Goods, Private Goods,* philosopher Raymond Geuss offers a genealogical analysis of the public/private distinction, their mutual spilling over and pollution, and how this intermingling and muddling up relates back to the human condition (Geuss 2001). One of the contexts he studies is the notion of the public as a space anyone can have access to, where there is maximal observation of what he calls the principle of 'disattendability', that is, the principle of unobtrusive behaviour towards others in public places. His exemplar is the famous episode of Diogenes of Sinope's masturbation in the marketplace (Geuss 2001: 12–13), where intimacy, privacy and the public collapse shamefully onto one another. The flow of human fluids fuses and confuses the contours of the open plaza and the body. Diogenes's action simultaneously summons the idea of the public and makes it collapse at the heart of its own institutional imagination: rendering the public as something *outside* whose value resides in being *inside*. Both values became visible in Diogenes's body, at once. There is an intriguing sense in which disgust, human vulnerability and the inside/outside of a body map onto the cultural form of the classical western public. The body of Diogenes offers therefore an interesting location for exploring certain prevalent assumptions about the structural characteristics of the modern liberal public. Let us start with disgust.

It is well known in the anthropological literature that certain forms of social relationships, especially those that are inflected by the asymmetry/incommensurability of intimacy or pollution, take residence in particular kinds of spaces. Mary Douglas's famous aphorism, 'Dirt is matter out of place', is a structuralist classic. However, the capacity of relationships to produce effects is also unpredictable and hardly communicable. 'The structure of disgust', for example, 'is like the structure of certain forms of primitive magic. Disgust can render its objects so magically contagious that they infect anything even indirectly or ideationally associated with them' (Geuss 2001: 20). Indeed disgust and shame inflect our relationships towards others:

> In our society, the generation of intimacy is often connected with overcoming the normal boundaries of disgust, so that intimate friends do things in one another's presence without shame (on the one hand) and disgust/offence (on the other) that they would not do in the presence even of good acquaintances ... This can be connected with the notion that an intimate friend becomes, as it were, a 'part' of me, and so I extend my lack of disgust from my own bodily smells, secretions, and so on, to encompass those of the intimate friend. (Geuss 2001: 21)

Who we are in public, then, is an expression of our cultural sense of contagiousness: of whom we surrender the gift of our partial extensions and secretions to. The point echoes Annette Weiner's famous elucidation of the paradox of 'keeping-while-giving', where people enter a gift economy in the expectation of retaining certain valuables (Weiner 1992). The holding and releasing of gift-relationships traces thus the complex, ambiguous and often contradictory lineaments through which people establish the boundaries of their social and personal corporeality. Perhaps for this reason, the western liberal public has largely been imagined as a shameless and perfectly symmetrical object: it is the main place where we are all strangers to one another, and hence where there is no place for disgust. We cannot pollute others in public.[7]

The modern conception of the Public appears tensed, therefore, by a modality of stranger-kinship: it is the outcome of people's negotiation of their intimacy and shame in the threshold of shifting *oikonomías*. The Public is the locus for an administration of contagiousness, where the cultural forms of exteriority and interiority spill over and encroach onto each other.

Perhaps not surprisingly, Bruno Latour and Michel Callon invoke a similar image in their reading of the classic gift-commodity debate in anthropology (Latour and Callon 1997). For Latour and Callon, gift giving and commodity exchange are simply different modalities of 'formatting' similar relational encounters. Whereas a gift-moment is formatted with a view to enhance the relational entanglements between transacting parties, a commodity-moment is construed to liberate instead those parties from the burden of future entanglements. Thus, 'to go from a precapitalist to a capitalist regime, it will suffice to perform two tiny, minuscule deformations; namely, to treat one's near kin and friends like perfect strangers with whom one will call it quits, and to treat remote strangers like intimate friends with whom one will call it quits' (Latour and Callon 1997). Capitalist and non-capitalist economies both spring, then, from a 'paradigm of disinterestedness', into which 'calculation' is strategically inserted and formatted in various degrees to obtain different effects. Calculation and disinterestedness work therefore as cultural ciphers of the administration of contagiousness, in that each has already pre-formatted how and where a relational effect is to be deployed: an intimate, a friend, a stranger. Between the calculative and the disinterested lies administration as a form of (capitalist) *oikonomía*.[8]

Central to Latour and Callon's scheme is the concept of externalities. Externalities, in their argument, are what formatting programs leave out. They are relational entanglements not to be taken into account. In contemporary economic parlance, pollution – industrial and atmospheric pollution, that is – is of course an externality. So is music, we have seen: anyone coming within earshot of a street musician will benefit from exposure. So it would seem that it is some sort of surplus or excessive feature of externalities that lends them their public purchase. Being *outside* society, externalities test the limits of where society should go next. They swell the body of society in anticipation of its future movements.

These movements are in turn fuelled by the pathos of radical contagion, by the perils of radical intimacy and insiderness.

Let me add a third quality to the modern liberal conception of the public (beyond those of shamelessness and excessiveness): the public is a space of horizontal relationality. This follows from the public being conceived as a conceptual meeting point for social relationships unburdened with shame and disgust. To address the public is to relate horizontally: to relate with no effect, bringing shame to no one, disgusting no one, polluting no one. These are relations that do not encroach on or invade people's insides. They aim for the surface. Michael Warner hints at this when noting that in public spaces we encounter 'stranger-relationality in a pure form' (Warner 2005: 75). One can embrace the whole world in a relationship of strangeness, because nothing is at stake except sheer and fleeting connectivity with others. We risk no contamination from strangers. It is for this reason that Warner criticizes those academics who misunderstand the *public* nature of their work and who, 'think[ing] in horizontal terms', make the assumption that a good public intellectual is one 'who seek[s] socially expansive audiences' (Warner 2005: 144).

Shamelessness, excessiveness and horizontal relationality lend the conception of the liberal public a particular social character, at once complex and contradictory and yet ultimately energetic and consequential – that is, contagious. As a liberal political form, the public pre-empts pollution with shamelessness; as an economic agent, on the other hand, its virtue and desirability lie precisely in its capacity to bring about pollution (i.e., to generate positive externalities and spillovers). It would seem, therefore, that pure relationships generate public objects, while public objects irradiate impure relationships. Good music invokes commons values; although 'commons' values sometimes require redress and balance to suit all. The public works thus as an anticipatory machine: generative of its own inside/outside imagination.[9]

The character of the liberal Public intriguingly echoes the elementary political functions of the stranger-king figure. The stranger-king arrives in a land and dethrones the local ruler. He promises benefaction and well-being and marries into the royal family. He exchanges fear of his mysterious wilderness and violence for local patronage. As Marshall Sahlins has put it,

> His violence is then turned outward towards the aggrandisement of the realm, even as his powers deployed inward bring order, justice, security and prosperity, as well as arts of civilisation … of the two sides of the … stranger-king, the terrible and the beneficial, the first is a condition of the possibility of the second … the ability of the king to constitute a new order being *sequitur* to his ability to violate the old. His initial transgressions put him above

and beyond society, alienated even from his own kin; but in so demonstrating that he is stronger than society, he is then able to recreate it ... the social incorporation and distribution of external life powers is the elementary form of the political life. (Sahlins 2008: 183, 184)

There is one difference, though, between the political predicament of the Public and the stranger-king, namely, the location of sovereignty. In the case of the Public, the dynamics of externalities – out, out, out – throw into relief the uncertain threshold of a global economy. The sociological imagination of the global economy aspires to empty all polluting and intimate substances out of the commons's household: in the global public village, remember, we must all be strangers to one another. The economy has no insides and no outsides any more; if anything, ours is a common world of stranger-kings. But who governs this kingdom of kingdoms – who will be host to our externalities? Where to locate sovereignty, when there are no more stranger-kings to come?

Arithmetic

As both an insider and outsider to its own political imagination, the notion of the public belongs to a tradition of political arithmetic whose sociology has gone through some remarkable transformations in the past fifty years. This is the political epistemology of parts and wholes.[10] It was of course Mannheim's larger point in *Ideology and Utopia* that the incommensurable exchange of parts for wholes and wholes for parts characterizes the political culture of democracy in modernity (Mannheim 1952). Charles Turner has neatly re-described Mannheim's argument in terms of this play of excesses of parts and wholes over each other:

> Although the idea of democracy is consistent with the domination of the analytical outlook, in which all parties and groups would be forced to see the political and social world as a structure of elements rather than as an indivisible whole, it is precisely as an indivisible whole ... that both ideological and utopian thinking are wont to view either the society they wish to preserve or the one they wish to see come into being ... For each, a vision of the whole ... obscures insight into current reality which can only be grasped analytically. (Turner 2003: 36)

What is remarkable about Mannheim's imagination of society as a reflux of parts and wholes over each other is that it constitutes the founding moment of the sociology of knowledge as an intellectual project. Although much criticized because it failed to take account of its own moment of political articulation – of its own consciousness as a sociology of knowledge, as Adorno put it (1974) – Mannheim's re-versioning of society into a refraction of parts and wholes set the stage for thinking about society in terms of the political organization of knowledge. Moreover, for Mannheim, the political field wherein knowledge gains currency as an object of sociological consciousness belongs of necessity to the tradition of political utopianism. The sociology of knowledge thus takes its democratic cue from its location in Mannheim's programmatic version of political hope.

A long tradition in Western philosophy and narrative of course senses the sociological import of knowledge as a vehicle of political hope. Russell Jacoby, in a recent book on utopian traditions, cites Aristophanes's play *The Birds* to this effect. He recalls Aristophanes's description of a mathematician's arrival in Cloud Cuckoo Land, the utopian community that figures centrally in the play. The mathematician arrives with the hope of settling there, declaring loudly that his joyful plan is to 'subdivide the air into square acres'. But his programme appeals to no one, and he is advised to leave and 'subdivide somewhere else' (Jacoby 2005: 40). Thus, for the inhabitants of Cloud Cuckoo Land, the subtractions and subdivisions that (mathematical) knowledge is capable of carry no political purchase.

Not so for Mannheim, and certainly not so for some of his most noted generational peers, such as Friedrich Hayek and Karl Popper (Hull 2006: 149), who had no doubts about the place and rank that knowledge ought to occupy in the political organization of society. Popper, for instance, made it clear that there was no point in trying to apprehend society as a total whole, let alone intervene on the basis of such holistic intuitions, which amounted to nothing more than 'utopian engineering' and could only lead to totalitarianism. Knowledge of society resided in the details, in the parts, not the wholes (Popper 1960: 66–67, 78–79). For Hayek, knowledge was also a matter of details, distributed across society as circumstantial evidence, embedded in times and places, so frail and elusive that it is often, especially among the scientifically minded, taken for non-knowledge, 'apparently because in their scheme of things all such knowledge is supposed to be "given"'. (Hayek 1945: 522)

Although Hayek does not employ the language of utopia to describe the arithmetic – the alignment of parts and wholes – of his ideal society, this nonetheless is still imagined in terms of political distribution, a distribution that, in Hayek's vocabulary, is self-evincing: it comes into its own so long as the distributive mechanism is the price system. This political organization is *ideal* because it is *efficient,* capable of signalling its movements and displacements, agile enough to capture its own advances. Hayek develops, then, a model of economic sociology that works, as he puts it, 'as a kind of machinery for registering change, or a system of telecommunications which enables individual producers to watch merely the movement of a few pointers ... in order to adjust their activities to changes of which they may never know more than is reflected in the price movement' (Hayek 1945: 527).

The elegance of Hayek's *formal* solution to the problem of the consciousness of the 'sociology of knowledge' – the problem of having mathematicians around who think society will be better off if we subtract, subdivide or redivide it into different parts and wholes – is that it turns mathematics itself into the tool of consciousness. Society *is* its subtractions and subdivisions, and knowledge *is* the fractions and remainders that are thrown up by every mathematical operation, by every redivision.

I emphasize the word 'formal' above because it is important to distinguish Hayek's institutional economics from his theory of knowledge, a distinction that, as we will see below, has some unexpected baroque inflections. The distinction is worth underscoring because no problem excited Hayek's intensity and preoccupation more than did his theory of knowledge.[11] Indeed, for Hayek the prospects of developing a suitable and adequate economic epistemology were so daunting that when it came to thinking about knowledge (and thinking about how to think about knowledge) Hayek endorsed what Andrew Gamble has called an 'epistemological pessimism' (Gamble 2006: 129).

A remarkable side effect of Hayek's epistemological obsession was his notion that knowledge operates as a social divisor. In his own account, 'the central problem of economics as a social science' can (and should) be reformulated as a 'problem of the *Division of Knowledge* which is quite analogous to, and at least as important as, the problem of the division of labour' (Hayek 1937: 49, emphasis in the original). For Hayek, knowledge of the human condition is so fragmentary, elusive and ultimately opaque that prudence sides with those who acknowledge the limits of reason in human affairs – which is not to say, however, that human affairs cannot be regulated and organized; thence arose Hayek's predilection for market economies.

Although to my knowledge Deleuze never commented on Hayek's solution to the problem of the sociology of knowledge, I think it is fair to say he would in all likelihood have applauded its formal brilliance. Hayek's splendid formalization of the problem of knowledge is paradigmatic of what Deleuze called the 'Baroque solution' to seventeenth-century ontological uncertainty. Hayek develops a concept of society that is at once Leibnizian and Kantian, intensive and extensive, analytical in its efficiency and synthetic in its expansiveness. Hayek's society moves both inwards, holding firmly to the knowledge that it possesses, and outwards, signalling to the places that have knowledge it needs to incorporate. Hayek's brilliance lies in his having developed a socio-logical imagination that aligns society, knowledge and politics in one unified, homological body that responds automatically to its own insuf-ficiencies and internally communicates its external needs – a body that has internalized its externalities. In its double co-presence (internally exterior, externally interior), it assumes the form of what Barbara Cassin has called '*doxa* squared' (*doxa*^{2}) (Cassin 2008: 70): common knowledge twice over.[12]

Reversions

The pulsations or nervous signals that animate Hayek's epistemology recall the work of the sympathetic, the vibratory and the imitative in Renaissance thought. Back in 1588, Giordano Bruno was already strug-gling with a multiplicity of potential dimensions, including aspects such as elusiveness, modifiability, intensionality or inclination, when it came to giving an account of our relational encounters with the world. Not unlike Hayek, in the rhythmic pulsations of knowledge Bruno saw an expression of how the world divided itself up for apperception. One's re-lational dispositions ultimately decanted the rightful or adequate mode of encountering the world – as he put it, relations require 'a degree of size' that elicits the world in its proper form and shape (Bruno 2004 [1588]: 166). In other words, such decantations shape the world's pro-portionality (for us).

However, whilst Bruno's enquiry was directed at the shape and pro-portionality of the world as an infinitesimal process (a journey *into* the shadow), Hayek's formal solution to the problem of the division of knowledge reverts back to the question of scale: how the minutiae of knowledge must *measure up* back to sociological forms. Thus, he imag-ines a homological correspondence or proportional equivalence between knowledge, society and economy. The elegance of Hayek's solution lies ultimately, then, in having disposed of what Bill Maurer has called the problem of 'adequation': the 'action of bringing one's concepts in accord with reality, words with things, mind with matter' (Maurer 2005: xiii). Hayek writes adequation out of the social process. His is a sociology of logo-sociality: common knowledge twice over because it mathematicizes the social as social mathematics. It describes a world that holds itself to-gether through sequences of geometrical correspondences: knowledge *to* society *to* politics – a political ontology of homological society.

Writing about the styles of reasoning used by participants in alternative economies, such as Islamic banking and finance, or the Ithaca-based currency system HOURS, Bill Maurer has observed practitioners' constant reflection on the adequacy of their own practices to the political, empirical and sociological circumstances that nurture and uphold their projects. Far from being held in homological or proportionate correspondence (the way Hayek would have it), knowledge, politics and society must be worked upon to accommodate or be adequated to each other. Adequation is a movement of approximation, a zooming in and out of everyday life and social analysis. The adequate, in sum, functions as an oscillatory balance: the craftsmanship through which the insides of empirical life are carefully mapped on to its more grandiloquent outsides.

Maurer's larger anthropological project is in fact to argue for a mode of analysis that locates itself side by side (as a form of lateral reason) with the very movement of adequation: adequation as both description and analytic, a performance of the empiric. Thus for Maurer, the adequate oscillates around the tension that Islamic financiers or HOURS practitioners find in their practices *and* their own theorization of their practices: between their social forms and their social ontology. For this reason, Maurer's project aims to develop a descriptive language that 'return[s] to adequation its motion, its temporality, its unfoldings and infoldings, its "cyclical reversibility"' (Maurer 2005: xiv, fn. 169). Such reversibility – such oscillation, in Maurer's own terminology – is his methodological recipe for a post-reflexive and post-plural anthropology (Maurer 2005: 75, fn. 175).

In this broader light, the operations of redividing knowledge, of holding knowledge in tension vis-à-vis its inside-outside displacements, may pay off. There may be, I suggest, some rewards in attending to the descriptive potency of *reversibility* as a tool for disentangling the 'infoldings' of knowledge and its forms of economy, including critique – if only because when knowledge as an object of study becomes transparent to sociological critique, critique itself needs to become a project of something else. I would like to digress slightly here to explore the critical purchase of reversibility as, indeed, an (anthropological) concept of the concept: a description of the recursiveness and iterative redivision of knowledge in its encounters with the world. I take as my guide Rane Willerslev's beautiful account of the phenomenology of hunting among the Siberian Yukaghirs (Willerslev 2007).

For the Yukaghirs, social relations' capacity to create relational contexts anew is gauged against the presence/absence of a shadow force they call the *ayibii*. The shadow-movement and shadow-presence of the *ayibii* inflect all social life with a second agency, a latent potency that redoubles the existence of all social forms. An example is the mimetic encounter that brings a Yukaghir hunter face-to-face with a moose. As he confronts the moose, the hunter's skill resides in his capacity to constantly move in and out of his own existential condition, now a human person, now a moose, tricking the animal into believing that it is facing another nonhuman person (another moose). As Willerslev puts it, the hunter makes himself inhabit the fragile ontological space of in-betweenness, where although he is not an animal, he is not *not* an animal either (Willerslev 2007: 94–97). In their encounters with game, then, hunters invest great effort and care in keeping the ontology of human-animal relations deliberately unstable and ambiguous.

More significantly, this ontological ambiguity is held in place by a careful fold of the ontology of all social forms, enabled by the *ayibii*'s complex duplicity. The point echoes the remark made above about the infolding of contemporary knowledge in its forms of economy. In the Yukaghir case, the work of infolding plays itself out as follows: Prior to the hunt, hunters spend time in a sauna to help camouflage (to help make invisible) their human odour. During the hunt itself, the hunter's physical and visible encounter with the moose is mirrored by an invisible sexual encounter that took place in the hunter's dreaming the night before. Finally, after slaying the animal, the hunters leave behind a miniature wooden carving stained with the moose's blood, in the hope that it will help displace and hide (in the eyes of the master spirits) their own agency as predators. Hunters' relationship with nonhuman persons, then, requires them to constantly work on its ontological form: now visible, now invisible; now preying, now preyed upon; now indexing human agency, now instantiating spiritual agency.

This refolding of ontology over itself – moving in and out of the visible and the invisible, indeed, of the condition of social life itself – brings to light the difficulties that beset any attempt to conceptualize the relation between knowledge and social life. An expression of their social relationships with animals, Yukaghir hunting excursions are premised on the presence of this complex ontological tension – the agency of the *ayibii* – that interposes a permanent threat and sense of failure to all knowledge practices. Knowledge of the world requires, first and foremost, knowledge of this tension, of the immanence of such an ontological fold. The Yukaghirs get to know their world, then, 'in the company of' (through the conceptual reversibility of) the *ayibii*.

Public Choice Science

In his extraordinary historical ethnography of Paul C. Zamecnik's project of test-tube synthesis of proteins at Collis P. Huntington Memorial

Hospital in Boston, Hans-Jörg Rheinberger has also made 'reversibility' into a central analytical figure. Rheinberger describes how the layout of a laboratory experimental arrangement rarely if ever accomplishes a 'representation' of nature, or of anything else for that matter (he aims to extend the argument to the production of all 'epistemic things'). Rather, an experimental arrangement aims to make visible and set in motion an ongoing movement of displaceable 'traces', where each inscription or 'grapheme', as he calls them, supplements, suppresses, superposes, reinforces or marginalizes a previous one. It is this dance of traces that, for Rheinberger, constitutes the epistemic as an ontological figuration or grammar. An epistemic thing, says Rheinberger, is not a referential system; it is no model, vicarious, indexical or otherwise. Instead, the making of epistemic things should be approached in the spirit of a choreography of 'material metaphors' (Rheinberger 1997: 105). As he puts it, 'scientists usually do not know which of the possible traces should be depressed and which should be made more prominent. So, at least for shorter spans of time, they have to conduct the game of representation/depresentation *in a reversible manner.* Epistemic things must be *allowed to oscillate between different significations*' (Rheinberger 1997: 112–113, emphasis added).

Rheinberger's description of the nature of epistemic things thus echoes Bill Maurer's description of anthropologists' encounter with forms of empirical reasoning, or indeed Rane Willerslev's ethnographic account of Yukaghirs' description of the ontological company of the *ayibii*. Reversibility, in all three cases, takes the form of a natural language of anthropological description.

At this point, I return to the political economy of public knowledge to make a case for a mode of analysis that attempts to put reversibility to critical use. I turn my attention now to the world of science and its contemporary economy of governance.

Over the past fifteen years, public choice theory (which we encountered in Chapter 4) has arrived in science policy and governance circles. Scientific expertise has been called to account, both politically and economically, and the complex phantasmagoria of the Samuelson fiction – the fiction of sociological and ethical enlightenment in matters of public choice – has crept into the world of science and academia. Perhaps the best known of all accounts of the new politics of public knowledge is the description of the ethical and political requisites for robust science-society encounters provided by Nowotny, Scott and Gibbons (2001). According to Helga Nowotny and her associates, the production of scientific knowledge has recently undergone a paradigmatic, Kuhnian transformation: science's unilateral engagement with society has turned around, and the validation of knowledge as scientifically robust is no longer a matter for scientists to resolve on their own. It has become instead a larger social agenda. Today society decides what makes good science. The question of robustness – of finding out how society decides on these matters – is therefore crucial. New public forums, which Nowotny et al. call *agora,* must be opened up to accommodate the institutional expressions of robustness. (Strathern's analysis of the Canadian Royal Commission's republican consultation is an example.) This is where ethics kicks in. We need, for instance, to trust our scientists; our scientists also need to be responsible (O'Neill 2002a, 2002b). Trust and responsibility emerge as society's new idioms of self-exteriorization – what society comes to look like, and how it comes to 'know' itself (via institutional audits), in the twenty-first century. Like the folding manoeuvres of the *ayibii,* trust and responsibility fold the social within its own reduplicated expressions. But they do so not in a social, but in an institutional form. Sociality thrice folded: as sociality, as trust and as audit. In this scenario, science's new institutionalization fares as society's Public knowledge.

The public relations that institutional audits of trust and responsibility uphold for science today have become paragons of twenty-first-century republican science politics. They are emblems of science's new governance models, developed as an alternative or update to Michael Polanyi's famous (pseudo-) republican theory of a secretive, secluded and authoritative scientific community (Polanyi 1962; see also Fuller 2000). The appeal to the republican analogy is interesting, because it imagines a space for the politics of knowledge-making within the discursive framework of deliberative democracy. It re-situates the question of the governance of knowledge within a political economy of public choice.

The new republicanism hopes to make society politically solvent in science matters by giving science a 'public' profile – although how the public gets to occupy this institutional reflective space remains a contested matter (Irwin 2006; Wilsdon, Wynne, and Stilgoe 2005). What is seldom noted, however, is the sociological value awarded to the Public as a positive (ethical) political location. Much in the way it did in the statist and market versions of the public domain as a fictional aggregative intelligence, the public of 'scientific citizenship' models tends to take the stage as a self-evident reconciliatory collective: an extrinsic ethical good, whose political value derives from adding a 'balance' to competing or disputed knowledge projects. As a functional sociological object, then, 'the public' helps re-establish society's loyalty to, and political symmetry with, scientific experts (Maranta et al. 2003). However, we know from our brief encounter with republican decision-making processes that the 'balancing' of political perspectives does not always entail a fair assessment of what different communities esteem and hold valuable as scientific knowledge. When it comes to making sense of 'knowledge' and deploying it to keep our social world alive, publicity and publicness often mean different things to different people. Rather than something 'added' politically to society, a conception of 'the public' may be something already internal to social life – an existing body or form of knowledge, of which 'science' might be an integral part (or not), defining how people know their place in society. Seen in this light, 'public knowledge' might be better conceptualized as the self-contextualization[13] of an imaginary science-society dialogue.

What would a public that is not chosen for its political value as an external balance – that is not an expression of normative public choice theory – look like? How should one think about such self-contextualized bodies of knowledge? Anthropologists think ethnographic descriptions can be a route to elucidating such bodies of self-contextualized knowledge. Ethnography provides a means for unpacking the knowledge/social reversibility in terms other than those of public choice theory.

I illustrate the point by way of an example. Monica Konrad has described the way people with cases of known hereditary (genetic) diseases in the family (e.g., Huntington's) respond to predictive genetic testing technology by deploying kinship genealogy as bodies of both bio-archival and moral knowledge (Konrad 2003). She reports the case of Rex Kingston, one of six siblings, who is 'lucky' enough to have come away from predictive testing 'clear' of Huntington's disease. He shares this good fortune with two nieces, Mabel and Nelly. The rest of the family has tested positive. Kin members give Rex, Mabel and Nelly's structural position in the family genealogy a new moral description: they have 'got off', escaped the disease; but theirs is too, now, the responsibility of caring for the ill. The body of kinship knowledge elicited by predictive testing technology has transformed the family's internal culture of relatedness: Rex, Mabel and Nelly now feel 'outsiders', 'bonded through exclusion'. A new morality of kinship values has re-articulated family relations through idioms of 'misfortune, regret, and divisiveness' (Konrad 2003: 351). Had these three decided to withhold the results, or to vary the genealogical path by which they were made available to the rest of the family, things might have been different. Thus, genetic and kinship knowledge mutually animate and transform each other, so that '[r]elatedness may recede from view or, conversely, knowledge itself may seem excessive' (Konrad 2003: 353).

Disclosure of genetic information – making knowledge 'go public' – is therefore far from a straight warrant for ethical normativity. Quite the contrary: ethics only *starts* to take shape when people redefine 'disclosure' through various strategies of elicitation, secrecy and concealment: deciding what to tell and what not to tell, to whom, and when. What Konrad calls 'genealogical ethics' takes shape through 'kinship trajectories of conception and [genetically transmitted] secrets': it is the movement and 'life of secrets' (Konrad 2003: 354), within and along familial lines, that shapes 'public knowledge' about the ethics of the new genetics.[14]

Science and Critique: Transformative Predations

Unlike self-contextualizing public knowledge of the sort evinced in Konrad's ethnographic analysis, the call for a public reconciliation between science and society imposes a conception of political governance on bodies of knowledge that have already taken account of each other. The new 'public relations' comes to supplant an existing ethnographic order with a philosophy of public choice that takes pride in the possibility of 'seeing double' – seeing society and science, the state and the market, the collective and the distributive – as parts of the same 'structure of argument'. Under the conditions of this omniscient political economy, only a new Leviathan inhabiting the margins, moving out towards the global – the way an externality works – can sanction our ethics. From this perpetual outside, the new Leviathan holds internal differences together and allows us the illusion of seeing things from within and without, in unified perspective. This ultimate and most magnificent of stranger-kings holds the world to account.

Whereas dioptric anamorphosis was the political aesthetic of Hobbes's Leviathan, I have opted to characterize the new Leviathan as a public philosophy of the Public: an anthropology of political ethics. Such a philosophy is often reminiscent of Hobbes's theory of the state as a duplicitous representation. Like the reduplicative (i.e., representative and representational) structure of Hobbes's theory of theatrical politics, the philosophy of the Public creates the fiction or illusion of a society that knows itself. Knowledge of society comes in the guise of certain surrogate conceptions of a collected and collective supra-intelligence, such as republican decision-making, the pre-emptive market coordination of patenting, networking or public understanding of science programmes. In each case, the possibilities for knowledge are subtly internalized through their very externalization.

We create our ethics by outsourcing our politics: to 'know' science, we need trust and responsibility, properly delivered through audit metrics; politics contributes to society's knowledge of itself through (self-styled) economic information. Thus, in a society that lives under the illusion and spell of the public philosophy of the Public, 'public knowledge' is the knowledge that it takes to make competent use of our political economy. If my description of such a philosophy is anything to go by, it seems that the only sociological location available for describing the ethical landscape of our time is that remaindering space that accrues *after the economy*.

Today the public philosophy of the Public offers a framework and stage for the self-aggrandizement of knowledge as a sociological category. Global commensality has become coterminous with a new utopianism of knowledge. Echoing the analysis of Amerindian forms of sociality with which I opened Chapter 5, we may say that Euro-American sociological imagination has found the source of its transformative predation in the self-expansiveness and anticipatory mechanics of public knowledge. Knowledge 'grows out' of Euro-American society through a mode of predation that reproduces conviviality via the ambiguous relation of critique to political ethics.

Notes

1. For example, Dominique Foray explains the nature of the 'public good problem' (the problem that accrues when the net private gain of producing a good is less than the net social gain of having it available) by asking about the distributive justice of mathematical theories: 'What is the social return of Pythagoras's work and how can it be rewarded "fairly"?' (Foray 2006: 114–15). A similar analogy is drawn by Joseph Stiglitz (1999: 308). My remarks build on their analogies.
2. I know I am not being very sophisticated here, but I hope I am not the only one who does not remember a great deal of the mathematics they were taught at high school. There is a political and cultural history of memory and forgetting that economists do not seem very interested in (see, e.g., Battaglia 1993; Connerton 2009).
3. In *La idea del principio en Leibniz*, Ortega y Gasset makes a similar distinction. He speaks there of the 'two faces of concepts': an 'ad extra' face, which makes concepts look outwards and aim for truthfulness; and an 'ad intra' face, which makes concepts look inwards and captures their logical consistency (Ortega y Gasset 1992 [1958]: 61).
4. Nigel Thrift made a similar observation in noting the shared assumptions of academic and management knowledge: 'a commitment to conceiving the world as *continuously rolling over*, continually on the brink; *a commitment to fantasy* as a vital element of how knowledge is constructed' (Thrift 2005: 97, emphasis added). The commitment to a *rolling-over fantasy* may be alternatively glossed as a commitment to utopia.
5. Aside, we may note two different conceptions of how the public (good) is invoked in this case. For a start, it may be the case that if the walls are too thin, the neighbour's affairs interfere with the musician's concentration as much as the latter's music provides pleasure to the former. In fact, Raymond Geuss draws on this very example to

show how the matter may be seen not as one of public goodness but of *privacy:* of the protective barriers needed to prevent some forms of physical disturbance between people (Geuss 2001: 87). The example provides the cue for the second point, also noted by Geuss, which is that one cannot properly speak of a public or common good if there is no consensus on who is the public in each case. Take the case of three 'persons struggling to stay afloat on a plank that will only bear the weight of one' (Geuss 2001: 94–95). It is unlikely this public will agree on a matter of concern to all. As Geuss argues, it is nonsense to ascribe public goods to a society with no 'shared public conception of the (public) good' in each case (Geuss 2001: 96).

6. But not if one uses a Leibnizian, as opposed to a Kantian, conceptual imagination, where the process of 'spilling over' retains the continuity of (internal) capacities throughout its (external) extension. Elaborating on the impact of Leibniz's philosophy in the larger imaginary of the Baroque, in this case of Baroque art, Deleuze writes:

    If the Baroque establishes a total art or unity of the arts, it does so first of all in extension, each art tending to be prolonged and even to be prolonged into the next art, which exceeds the one before. We have remarked that the Baroque often confines painting to retables, but it does so because the painting exceeds its frame and is realized in polychrome marble sculpture; and sculpture goes beyond itself by being achieved in architecture; and in turn, architecture discovers a frame in the façade, but the frame itself becomes detached from the inside, and establishes relations with the surroundings so as to realize architecture in city planning. From one end of the chain to the other, the painter has become an urban designer. We witness the prodigious development of a continuity in the arts, in breadth or in extension: an interlocking of frames of which each is exceeded by a matter that moves through it. (Deleuze 1993: 123)

7. The etymology of the word, in fact, can be traced back to *pubes* and *pubic:* masculinity, sexuality, power and pollution are central to the western imagination of the public.

8. What is perhaps most intriguing in Latour and Callon's account is that, as differential deformations of the stranger-kinship relationship, the gift and commodity paradigms are in effect 'anamorphoses' (their word) of each other (Latour and Callon 1997). The formatting produces the distortion. They are relationships with a (neo-baroque) form.

9. Steve Fuller has made a similar point of epistemology by noting that when public goods are 'understood as a *collectively* defined product whose use is defined *distributively*… virtually anything can be reclassified as a public good' (Fuller 2001: 191). Elsewhere he re-describes this confusion as an ontological mystification on the part of economists, who have created an asymmetry between their definitions of knowledge *production* (understood as the production of the objects or materials that contain the knowledge – 'the nature of the good itself is specified "objectively"') and knowledge *consumption* (understood as the consumption of the 'knowledge' or ideas contained in the objects – 'the value derived from the good is specified "subjectively"'). The asymmetry contributes to the hiding of the fact that knowledge is always knowledge *for someone* (Fuller 2002: 28).

10. Anthropology has its own history of debate in 'parts and wholes', namely, the formalist versus substantivist debate. The debate echoes too the Leibnizian vs. Kantian epistemological difference, as reported by Deleuze. Scott Cook, an original contributor to the debate, thought for instance to have pinned down the nature of the quarrel when he described the differences between the two camps as precisely one between

analytical (formalists) and synthetic (substantivists) models of knowledge. His own description of this epistemological difference dwelled on the part-to-whole imagery: whilst for formalists the part determines the whole, for substantivists it is the whole that determines the part (Cook 1966).

11. 'His theory of knowledge provides a thread which runs through almost all his work, the organizing idea which he spent fifty years exploring through a variety of intellectual projects ... No other idea is as important for understanding Hayek, his intellectual system, and his mental world. Much of his work is an extended meditation on the problem of knowledge ... At the heart of every Hayek problem is his theory of knowledge, which became the pivot of his thought' (Gamble 2006: 111–112).

12. Hayek's formal solution to the sociology of knowledge echoes Clay Shirky's notion of 'cognitive surplus', with which I opened this chapter: the networking of knowledge such that society 'realizes' all the knowledge that it has. Barbara Cassin has commented on the political epistemology behind such a view in her criticism of Google's self-styled 'democratic' organization of information:

> Hierarchy is not something that is imposed from the outside, the way a Platonic hierarchy would operate, with a philosopher-king deciding on behalf of the mass. Nor is it democratically decided, arrived at through *agón,* that is, a process of open discussion and dissent-consent. Rather, it evinces in a kind of immanence, for 'we' bring it about, in a process that remains nonetheless mechanically and robotically opaque, at once mathematic and systemic. (Cassin 2008: 70, my translation)

13. Nowotny et al. give the name 'contextualization' to the mutual co-invasion of science and society (2001: 50–65 and passim).

14. There is perhaps no better example of the *public insiderness* that all social concepts carry within than Marilyn Strathern's historical and ethnographic insights into the mutual constitution of knowledge/kinship as reversible concepts (2005). For example, Strathern has described the way medical technologies have in certain contexts enabled an analogy between reproductive and intellectual creativity, as when speaking of parents' mental conception (their decision to have a child) taking legal precedence over a surrogate mother's biological inception; the child's relation to his or her legal parents is thus sustained on a conceptual rather than a conceptive relation. Here we see people mobilizing ideas about kinship (what is a relative, what counts as a relation) to rethink ideas about property in bodies and knowledge (the body-to-be of a child as *conceptual,* not *conceptive,* potency). Kinship and knowledge appear thus as reversible epiphenomena of the same epistemic structure: two conceptual orders that can revert to structurally analogous idioms (relatives and relations, concepts and conceptions) to explain their sameness and differences from one another. Ethnographic reversibility allows us to move between 'knowledge' and 'society' without the need to consolidate either as a distinct sociological institution.

At Perpendicular Angles

> To be powerful is to resist comparison.
> To be great is to resist the ladder of sizes.
> —Michel Serres, *Detachment*

> "Scale" is almost never drawn to scale. The kind of
> understanding that insists on magnification, changing the
> scale of things to get the details right, has used the thing
> it needed to see, and "seen" the thing it needed to use.
> —Roy Wagner, *An Anthropology of the Subject*

How 'Social' Is Knowledge?

The 'socialness' of knowledge is of course in many respects a tautological question. As the outcome of particular social relations and energies, knowledge is nothing if not a social project. There is no knowledge that is not always and everywhere social. However, the fact that at some level we can see a point to the question – that it becomes meaningful as an issue of magnitude, in that one may speak of certain modes of producing knowledge as 'more' social than others, and therefore speak of the social/knowledge relation as a relation of sizes or proportions – is, I have tried to argue throughout the book, a mark of the cultural epistemology of our neo-baroque age. We live in a time that makes sense of its place in the world through projects of self-aggrandizement: 'more' knowledge is needed to make sense of extant knowledge.

Thus, for example, legal theorists and information and knowledge economists, prompted by recent developments in intellectual property law, have turned to the Internet to understand the emergence of new distributed and collaborative platforms for the production and consumption of online media. In a sense, the velocity of distribution, circulation, modification and consumption of new media by an expansive community of users imprints the nature of such an exchange economy with a distinctive 'social' dimension (Benkler 2006; Lessig 2008). Here the social is identified with a sense of expansion, velocity and online presence. This is a relational economy of knowledge, where the social is the outcome of people being partners in the exchange of knowledge for mutual benefit of one another. We may push the analogy by saying that where there is no knowledge and no exchange, then, in this economy, there is no sociality – or at least no *productive* sociality (Shirky 2008). It appears that knowledge, economy and the social are therefore conceptualized as certain kinds of substitutes for one another.

Karin Knorr-Cetina and Alex Preda have described this allegedly mutual transparency of knowledge, economy and the social to each other as being founded on (again using an optical metaphor) a 'specular epistemology' (Knorr-Cetina and Preda 2001: 34). The work that the specular performs here is reminiscent of Emmons's rendition of CAD-enabled full-scale architectural drawing, where a computer-generated object is presumed to map transparently, one-to-one, to a future building. Architects work with the model *as if* it were the real edifice. Thus, both the specular and the 'as if' function seem to operate with an underlying principle of substitution that *regardless of the changes in scale* does not neutralize the importance of size. The computer-generated building is scale-free but it is sizeable nonetheless; as Michel Serres said of Thales's accomplishment, it 'expresses the invariance of similar forms over changes of scale' (Serres 1995: 78). Social theory and philosophy thus no longer need scale to deliver impressions of size. We could say that the substitution has effected a sort of proportional equivalence that allows one to stop thinking of size in terms of scale but also retains a sense of dimensionality. In the context of the new economy of knowledge, this is patently obvious: knowledge has a size because the economy has a size – and because society, naturally, has a size too.

This specular epistemology points to a second characteristic of approaches to knowledge that take its sociological condition for granted, as if knowledge were indeed a sociological object per se. Knorr-Cetina distinguishes between 'interiorized' and 'exteriorized' theories of knowledge. The former focus on knowledge as something to be wrought and struggled with, sometimes with care and often with distressing, maybe even painful effects. Knowledge is put together through time, laboriously, and its permanency and stability are often transitory and contingent. Exteriorized theories of knowledge, on the other hand, see knowledge as a ready-made object upon which other forces exert pressure. Knowledge is here imagined as a body of sorts, a commodity or resource to be variously transacted, stored, managed or appropriated.

The idioms of specularity, exteriority and interiority rehearse the qualities of inside:outside and optical transformation that we can now recognize as proper to a baroque epistemology. They render knowledge an effect of strabismic transformations. Thus, the idea that exteriorized knowledge can be put to work alongside other objects of political economy, such as governance, interdisciplinarity or user-centred designs, partakes of a specular epistemology, because insofar as knowledge is treated as a self-contained object it can sit comfortably next to other political bodies. 'Knowledge' and 'governance', for example, are specular to each other because arguments can be made about one *as if* refracted or optically accommodated through the other. They function as proportionate forms for each other. 'More knowledge, better governance', we have seen, is a typical motto and equation of the 'major strategy' (Egginton 2010) of Baroque absolutist politics.

But what about interiorized theories of knowledge, whose attention to craft and laboriousness, even intimacy, bring 'into focus knowledge itself, breaking open and specifying the processes that make [it] up'? (Knorr-Cetina and Preda 2001: 30) In looking for the baroque, what purchase might there be in an approach that focuses on the epistemic intimacy of knowledge?

In her wonderful study of cultures of contemporary science (molecular biology and physics), Knorr-Cetina has further unpacked some of the processes that interiorize knowledge as an epistemic form (Knorr-Cetina 1999). Her focus here is what laboratory work does to scientific knowledge: how objects and human relationships are reconfigured in laboratory settings. According to Knorr-Cetina, what laboratory work accomplishes in essence is the adaptation and reconfiguration of natural processes and objects to suit the spatio-temporal requirements of scientists. Laboratory work can resist an object's natural tendencies and properties in at least three ways: (1) it 'does not need to put up with an object *as it is*, it can substitute transformed and partial versions'; (2) it 'does not need to accommodate the natural object *where it is*, anchored in a natural environment'; and (3) it does not need to 'accommodate an event *when it happens*' but can 'dispense with natural cycles of occurrence and make events happen frequently enough for continuous study' (Knorr-Cetina 1999: 27, emphasis in the original). Under such conditions,

> Laboratories recast objects of investigation by inserting them into new temporal and territorial regimes. They play upon these objects' natural rhythms and developmental possibilities, *bring them together in new numbers, renegoti-*

ate their sizes, and redefine their internal makeup ... In short, they create new configurations of objects that they match with an appropriately altered social order. (Knorr-Cetina 1999: 43–44, emphasis added)

The image of re-combinatorial and re-configurating processes draws of course on a familiar genealogy in science and technology studies. For example, the 'partial versions' substituted for natural objects in laboratory experiments echo the 'partial connections' that relate difference in Donna Haraway's famous cyborg assemblages (Haraway 1986: 37). Manipulation of a laboratory object's internal rhythms and developmental possibilities is not unlike what a cyborg's prosthetic extensions realize by way of supplementary or accelerated capacities. The experimental and the cyborg both operate as scale-shifting devices: they bring about enhancements that are of a different order of magnitude from their original state. 'The one component is of different order from the other, and is not created by what creates that other. They are not built to one another's scale' (Strathern 2004 [1991]: 39). They both create extensions beyond a 1:1 equivalence. Importantly, as Strathern points out, such enhanced capacities work because the partial versions 'are neither proportionate to nor disproportionate from one another' (Strathern 2004 [1991]: 36). They introduce, instead, a form of release or liberation.

This form of liberation – which comes from obtaining release from scale, so that impressions of epistemic consequentiality no longer depend on a proportional imagination – is one of the baroque's greatest epistemological accomplishments. As Richard Sennett put it, it makes a vast Baroque church feel intimate and cosy in scale (Sennett 2008: 85). Largeness ceases to be a function of magnitude, or its magnitude becomes an effect *of something else.*

Release from scale, then, opens up a space for 'something else'. Recounting Diogenes of Sinope's decision to forsake society, Michel Serres observed that

Diogenes is forsaken, in peace. He has forsaken exchange, damage, gift, selling and buying, value ... has forsaken value and scale, forsaken the scale of values, the strong and the weak, the powerful and the miserable. He has left comparison, from which comes all evil of the world. One always detaches oneself only from comparison. (Serres 1989: 68)

Thus he observes, later in the same text, that '[t]o be powerful is to resist comparison. To be great is to resist the ladder of sizes' (1989: 92). Away from scale and the epistemic effects of proportionality, the space of the 'something else' sustains hope in the conditions of possibility of a different type of politics.[1]

I conclude with a comment on what or whom such *politeia* might be 'in the company of'. In his account of Richard Steele's impersonation of the eighteenth-century magazine *The Spectator,* Michael Warner notes how

> The Spectator is a prosthetic person for Steele ... in the sense that it does not reduce to or express the given body. By making him no longer self-identical, it allows him the negativity of debate – not a pure negativity, not simply reason or criticism, but an identification with a disembodied public subject that he can imagine as parallel to his private person. (Warner 2005: 164)

The Spectator's prosthesis enables a displacement, an extra-effect, a something-elseness, we might say. Echoing Deleuze, one might describe it as a 'variation (metamorphosis), or: something = x (anamorphosis)'. The Spectator, then, appears as an anamorphic public: self-removed, skewed, partially negated.[2]

Perhaps the anamorphic public – the political form of the something else – shares also in this context the elementary structures of political life as evinced in stranger-kingship. '[S]ustaining the life of the community through the part-conflictual, part ritual assimilation of the potent enemy: is this not stranger-kingship in another form?' (Sahlins 2008: 185). Partially external and partially internal to a polity, the stranger-king energizes its politics with the fear of destruction and the love of incorporation, rendering it a politics tensed with self-detachment and disproportionality.

The prosthetic/neo-baroque/stranger public offers, too, a grounding image for the embodiment of cyborg politics. As Donna Haraway famously put it, in

> a cyborg world ... people are not afraid of their *joint kinship* with animals and machines, not afraid of permanently *partial identities and contradictory standpoints.* The political struggle is *to see from both perspectives at once* because each reveals both dominations and possibilities unimaginable from the other vantage point. Single vision produces worse illusions than *double vision* or many-headed monsters. (Haraway 1990: 196, emphasis added)

Double vision, partial estrangement, stranger-kinship with animals and machines underpin the cultural epistemology of strabismus. Strabismus becomes the cultural episteme through which the body- and *cogito* polity are made visible as a conduit of dis/proportional configurations.

The architect, the micrographer, the illusionist, the microbiologist, the Spectator, the stranger-king and the cyborg each stand as a genealogical reminder, perhaps, of modernity's strabismic condition.

Notes

1. What kind of politics? Below I offer an analysis of its plausible aesthetics. As for an actual example, let me draw on Marilyn Strathern's description of 'Feminist debate [as] characterized by a compatibility that does not require comparability between the persons who engage in it, bar their engaging in it ... It is almost as though the disproportion were deliberate' (Strathern 2004 [1991]: 35).

2. The Cuban poet and literary critic Severo Sarduy once noted that 'baroque language takes pleasure in the supplement, in the excess, and in the partial loss of its object. Or rather, in the search, by definition frustrated, for the *partial object*' (cited in Kadir 1986: 86).

REFERENCES

Adorno, R. 2001. *Guaman Poma and His Illustrated Chronicle from Colonial Peru: From a Century of Scholarship to a New Era of Reading*. Copenhagen: Det Kongelige Bibliotek.

Adorno, T.W. 1974. 'The Sociology of Knowledge and Its Consciousness', in *Prisms*. London: Verso.

Agamben, G. 2008. *El reino y la gloria. Para una genealogía teológica de la economía y del gobierno. Homo Sacer II, 2*. [Spanish translation of *Il Regno e la Gloria. Per una genealogia teologica dell'economia e del governo*]. Valencia: Pre-Textos.

Alberti, L.B. 1991 [1435]. *On Painting*. London: Penguin Books.

Alpers, S. 1983. *The Art of Describing: Dutch Art in the Seventeenth Century*. Chicago: University of Chicago Press.

Appadurai, A. 2004. 'The Capacity to Aspire: Culture and the Terms of Recognition', in *Culture and Public Action*, edited by V. Rao and M. Walton, pp. 59–84. Stanford, CA: Stanford University Press.

Arendt, H. 1998 [1958]. *The Human Condition*. Chicago: University of Chicago Press.

Arrow, K. 1951. *Social Choice and Individual Values*. New York: Wiley.

Bardhan, P. and I. Ray (eds). 2008. *The Contested Commons: Conversations between Economists and Anthropologists*. New Delhi: Oxford University Press.

Barry, A. 1993. 'The History of Measurement and the Engineers of Space'. *The British Journal for the History of Science* 26: 459–468.

——. 2001. *Political Machines: Governing a Technological Society*. London: The Athlone Press.

——. 2010. 'Tarde's Method: Between Statistics and Experimentation', in *The Social after Gabriel Tarde: Debates and Assessments*, edited by M. Candea, pp. 177–190. London: Routledge.

Barry, A. and N. Thrift. 2007. Gabriel Tarde: Imitation, Invention and Economy. *Economy and Society* 36: 509–525.

Bataille, G. 1991 [1967]. *The Accursed Share*. New York: Zone Books.

Battaglia, D. 1993. At Play in the Fields (and Borders) of the Imaginary: Melanesian Transformations of Forgetting. *Cultural Anthropology* 8: 430–442.

Battistini, A. 2006. 'The Telescope in the Baroque Imagination', in *Reason and Its Others: Italy, Spain, and the New World,* edited by D.R. Castillo and M. Lollini, pp. 3–38. Nashville: Vanderbilt University Press.

Benjamin, W. 1999. *The Arcades Project.* Cambridge, MA, and London: The Belknap Press of Harvard University Press.

Benkler, Y. 2003a. Freedom in the Commons: Towards a Political Economy of Information. *Duke Law Journal* 52: 1245–1276.

———. 2003b. The Political Economy of Commons. *Upgrade* 4: 6–9.

———. 2006. *The Wealth of Networks: How Social Production Transforms Markets and Freedom.* New Haven, CT: Yale University Press.

Benkler, Y. and H. Nissenbaum. 2006. Commons-Based Peer Production and Virtue. *The Journal of Political Philosophy* 14: 394–319.

Borja-Villel, M. 2010. 'Prólogo', in *Principio Potosí. ¿Cómo podemos cantar el canto del Señor en tierra ajena? La economía global y la producción colonial de imágenes,* edited by A. Creischer, M.J. Hinderer and A. Siekmann. Madrid: Museo Nacional Centro de Arte Reina Sofía.

Boudon, P. 1999. 'The Point of View of Measurement in Architectural Conception: From the Question of Scale to Scale as a Question'. *Nordic Journal of Architectural Research* 12: 7–18.

Bowker, G. 1993. 'How to Be Universal: Some Cybernetic Strategies, 1943–70'. *Social Studies of Science* 23: 107–27.

Boyle, J. 2003. 'The Second Enclosure Movement and the Construction of the Public Domain'. *Law and Contemporary Problems* 66: 33–74.

Bredekamp, H. 1995 [1993]. *The Lure of Antiquity and the Cult of the Machine: The Kunstkammer and the Evolution of Nature, Art and Technology.* Princeton, NJ: Markus Wiener Publishers.

Brown, S.D. 2005. 'The Theatre of Measurement: Michel Serres'. *The Sociological Review* 53: 215–227.

Brown, W. 2000. 'Specters and Angels at the End of History', in *Vocations of Political Theory,* edited by J.A. Frank and J. Tamborino, pp. 25–58. Minneapolis: University of Minnesota Press.

Bruno, G. 1995 [1585]. *The Ash Wednesday Supper.* Toronto: University of Toronto Press.

———. 2004 [1588]. 'A General Account of Bonding', in *Cause, Principle and Unity, and Essays on Magic,* edited by R.J. Blackwell and R. De Lucca, pp. 143–176. Cambridge: Cambridge University Press.

Buci-Glucksmann, C. 1986. *La folie du voir: De l'esthétique baroque.* Paris: Editions Galilée.

———. 1994 [1984]. *Baroque Reason: The Aesthetics of Modernity.* London, Thousand Oaks and Delhi: Sage.

Calabrese, O. 1992. *Neo-baroque: A Sign of the Times.* Princeton, NJ: Princeton University Press.

Callon, M. 1986. 'Some Elements of a Sociology of Translation: Domestication of the Scallops and Fishermen of St. Brieuc Bay', in *Power, Action, Belief: A New*

Sociology of Knowledge? edited by J. Law, pp. 196–223. London: Routledge and Kegan Paul.

———. 1994. 'Is Science a Public Good? Fifth Mullins Lecture, Virginia Polytechnic Institute, 23 March 1993'. *Science, Technology, and Human Values* 19: 395–424.

———. 2007. 'An Essay on the Growing Contribution of Economic Markets to the Proliferation of the Social'. *Theory, Culture and Society* 24: 139–163.

Callon, M., C. Meadal and V. Rabeharisoa. 2002. 'The Economy of Qualities'. *Economy and Society* 31: 194–217.

Candea, M. (ed.). 2010. *The Social after Gabriel Tarde: Debates and Assessments*. London: Routledge.

Candea, M. and G. da Col. 2012. The Return to Hospitality. *Journal of the Royal Anthropological Institute* 18: 1–19.

Cassin, B. 2008. *Googléame: la segunda misión de los Estados Unidos*. Buenos Aires: Fondo de Cultura Económica.

Connerton, P. 2009. *How Modernity Forgets*. Cambridge: Cambridge University Press.

Cook, S. 1966. 'The Obsolete "Anti-Market" Mentality: A Critique of the Substantive Approach to Economic Anthropology'. *American Anthropologist* 68: 323–345.

Cornes, R. and T. Sandler. 1996. *The Theory of Externalities, Public Goods, and Club Goods*. 2nd edition. Cambridge: Cambridge University Press.

Corsín Jiménez, A. 2003a. *The Form of the Relation, or Anthropology's Enchantment with the Algebraic Imagination*. manuscript.

———. 2003b. 'Working Out Personhood: Notes on "Labour" and Its Anthropology'. *Anthropology Today* 19: 14–17.

———. 2008a. 'Introduction: Well-Being's Re-Proportioning of Social Thought', in *Culture and Well-Being: Anthropological Approaches to Freedom and Political Ethics*. London: Pluto Press.

———. 2008b. 'Well-being in Anthropological Balance: Remarks on Proportionality as Political Imagination', in *Culture and Well-Being: Anthropological Approaches to Freedom and Political Ethics*. London: Pluto Press.

———. 2010. 'The Height, Length and Width of Social Theory', in *The Social after Gabriel Tarde: Debates and Assessments*, edited by M. Candea, pp. 110–128. London: Routledge.

Creischer, A., M.J. Hinderer and A. Siekmann (eds). 2010. *Principio Potosí. ¿Cómo podemos cantar el canto del Señor en tierra ajena? La economía global y la producción colonial de imágenes*. Madrid: Museo Nacional Centro de Arte Reina Sofía.

Dällenbach, L. 1989. *The Mirror in the Text*. Cambridge: Polity Press.

Damisch, H. 1997 [1987]. *El origen de la perspectiva* [Spanish translation of *L'origene de la perspective*]. Madrid: Alianza Editorial.

Dasgupta, P. and P.A. David. 1994. 'Toward a New Economics of Science'. *Research Policy* 23: 487–521.

Daston, L. and P. Galison. 2007. *Objectivity*. New York: Zone Books.

David, P.A. 1993. 'Knowledge, Property and the System Dynamics of Technological Change'. *World Bank Annual Conference on Development Economics, Washington, DC, 1993*, pp. 215–248. Washington D. C.: World Bank Publications.

————. 2000. *A Tragedy of the Public Knowledge 'Commons'? Global Science, Intellectual Property and the Digital Technology Boomerang.* Stanford, CA: Stanford University Press.

David, P.A. and D. Foray. 2003. 'Economic Fundamentals of the Knowledge Society'. *Policy Futures in Education* 1: 20–49.

Delanty, G. 2001. *Challenging Knowledge: The University in the Knowledge Society.* Buckingham: The Society for Research into Higher Education and Open University Press.

Deleuze, G. 1993. *The Fold: Leibniz and the Baroque.* London: The Athlone Press.

————. 2005 [1993]. *Bartleby o la fórmula.* Valencia: Pre-textos.

————. 2006 [1980/1986/1987]. *Exasperación de la filosofía: el Leibniz de Deleuze.* Serie Clases. Buenos Aires: Cactus.

Deleuze, G. and F. Guattari. 1987 [1980]. *A Thousand Plateaus: Capitalism and Schizophrenia.* Minneapolis: University of Minnesota Press.

Derrida, J. 1995. *Espectros de Marx: el estado de la deuda, el trabajo del duelo y la nueva internacional.* Madrid: Editorial Trotta.

Desai, M. 2003. 'Public Goods: A Historical Perspective', in *Providing Global Public Goods: Managing Globalization,* edited by I. Kaul, pp. 63–77. New York: Oxford University Press. Oxford Scholarship Online. http://dx.doi.org/10.1093/0195157400.001.0001.

Dietz, T., E. Ostrom and P.C. Stern. 2003. The Struggle to Govern the Commons. *Science* 302: 1907–1912.

Durkheim, E. 1974. 'Value Judgments and Judgments of Reality', in *Sociology and Philosophy,* pp. 80–97. New York: The Free Press.

Eagleton, T. 2009. *Trouble with Strangers: A Study of Ethics.* Chichester: Wiley-Blackwell.

Edgerton, Jr., S.Y. 1973. Brunelleschi's First Perspective Picture. *Arte Lombarda* 18: 172–195.

Egginton, W. 2010. *The Theater of Truth: The Ideology of (Neo) Baroque Aesthetics.* Stanford, CA: Stanford University Press.

Elkins, J. 1994. *The Poetics of Perspective.* Ithaca, NY, and London: Cornell University Press.

————. 1996. *The Object Stares Back: On the Nature of Seeing.* San Diego, New York and London: A Harvest Book, Harcourt Inc.

Emmons, P. 2005. 'Size Matters: Virtual Scale and Bodily Imagination in Architecture Drawing'. *arq: Architectural Research Quarterly* 9: 227–235.

Fausto, C. 2007. 'Feasting on People: Eating Animals and Humans in Amazonia'. *Current Anthropology* 48: 497–530.

Featherstone, M. and C. Venn. 2006. 'Problematizing Global Knowledge and the New Encyclopaedia Project'. *Theory, Culture and Society* 23: 1–20.

Firth, R. 1979. 'Work and Value: Reflections on Ideas of Karl Marx', in *Social Anthropology of Work,* edited by S. Wallman, pp. 177–206. London: Academic Press.

Fleischacker, S. 2004. *A Short History of Distributive Justice.* Cambridge, MA: Harvard University Press.

Foray, D. 2006. *The Economics of Knowledge.* Cambridge, MA, and London: MIT Press.

Foucault, M. 1970. *The Order of Things: An Archaeology of the Human Sciences*. New York: Vintage Books.

———. 2007. *Security, Territory, Population: Lectures at the Collège de France 1977–1978*. New York: Palgrave.

Frischmann, B.M. and M.A. Lemley. 2006. 'Spillovers'. Stanford Law and Economics Olin Working Paper no. 321. http://ssrn.com/abstract=898881.

Fuller, S. 2000. *The Governance of Science: Ideology and the Future of the Open Society*. Milton Keynes: Open University Press.

———. 2001. 'A Critical Guide to Knowledge Society Newspeak: Or, How Not to Take the Great Leap Backward'. *Current Sociology* 49: 177–201.

———. 2002. *Knowledge Management Foundations*. Woburn, MA: Knowledge Management Consortium International Press, Butterworth Heinemann.

Galilei, G. 1968. *Opere*. Vol. 11. Florence: Barbèra.

Gamble, A. 2006. 'Hayek on Knowledge, Economics, and Society', in *The Cambridge Companion to Hayek*, edited by E. Feser, pp. 111–131. Cambridge: Cambridge University Press.

Gatti, H. 1999. *Giordano Bruno and Renaissance Science*. Ithaca, NY, and London: Cornell University Press.

Geuss, R. 2001. *Public Goods, Private Goods*. Princeton, NJ: Princeton University Press.

Graeber, D. 2001. *Toward an Anthropological Theory of Value: The False Coin of Our Own Dreams*. New York and Basingstoke: Palgrave.

Green, S., P. Harvey and H. Knox. 2005. 'Scales of Place and Networks: An Ethnography of the Imperative to Connect through Information and Communications Technologies'. *Current Anthropology* 46: 805–826.

Grootenboer, H. 2005. *The Rhetoric of Perspective: Realism and Illusionism in Seventeenth-Century Dutch Still-Life Painting*. Chicago and London: University of Chicago Press.

Habermas, J. 1970. *Towards a Rational Society: Student Protest, Science, and Politics*. Boston: Beacon Press.

———. 1989. *The Structural Transformation of the Public Sphere: An Inquiry into a Category of Bourgeois Society*. Cambridge: Polity Press.

Hannay, A. 2005. *On the Public*. London and New York: Routledge.

Haraway, D. 1986. 'Primatology Is Politics by Other Means', in *Feminist Approaches to Science*, edited by R. Bleier, pp. 77–118. New York: Pergamon Press.

———. 1990. 'A Manifesto for Cyborgs: Science, Technology, and Socialist Feminism in the 1980s', in *Feminism/Postmodernism*, edited by L.J. Nicholson, pp. 190–233. New York and London: Routledge.

Hardin, G. 1968. 'The Tragedy of the Commons'. *Science* 162: 1243–1248.

Harris, J. 1992. 'Political Thought and the Welfare State 1870–1940: An Intellectual Framework for British Social Policy'. *Past and Present* 135: 116–141.

———. 2002. 'From Poor Law to Welfare State? A European Perspective', in *The Political Economy of British Historical Experience*, edited by P. O'Brien and D. Winch, pp. 409–438. Oxford: Oxford University Press.

Hayden, C. 2003. *When Nature Goes Public: The Making and Unmaking of Bioprospecting in Mexico*. Princeton, NJ, and Oxford: Princeton University Press.

Hayek, F.A. 1937. 'Economics and Knowledge'. *Economica* 4: 33–54.

———. 1945. 'The Use of Knowledge in Society'. *American Economic Review* 35: 519–530.

Henare, A., M. Holbraad and S. Wastell (eds). 2007. *Thinking through Things: Theorising Artefacts in Ethnographic Perspective*. London and New York: Routledge.

Hess, C. and E. Ostrom. 2003. 'Ideas, Artifacts, and Facilities: Information as a Common-Pool Resource'. *Law and Contemporary Problems* 66: 111–145.

———. 2006. 'Introduction: An Overview of the Knowledge Commons', in *Understanding Knowledge as a Commons: From Theory to Practice*, edited by C. Hess and E. Ostrom, pp. 3–26. Cambridge, MA: MIT Press.

Holbraad, M. 2005. Expending Multiplicity: Money in Cuban Ifá Cults. *Journal of the Royal Anthropological Institute* 11: 231–254.

Hooke, R. 1665. *Micrographia*. London.

Hoskin, K. 1995. 'The Viewing Self and the World We View: Beyond the Perspectival Illusion'. *Organization* 2: 141–162.

Hull, R. 2000. 'Knowledge and the Economy: Some Critical Comments (Review of *Economics and Utopia* by Geoffrey M. Hodgson)'. *Economy and Society* 29: 316–331.

———. 2006. 'The Great Lie: Markets, Freedom and Knowledge', in *Neoliberal Hegemony: A Global Critique*, edited by D. Plehwe, B. Walpen and G. Neunhöffer, pp. 141–155. London and New York: Routledge.

Huston, J.L. 1998. *Securing the Fruits of Labor: The American Concept of Wealth Distribution 1765–1900*. Baton Rouge, LA.: Louisiana State University Press.

Iglesias, C. 2006. 'América o el paraíso de lo posible en el siglo XVIII', in *Razón, sentimiento y utopía*, pp. 416–446. Barcelona: Galaxia Gutenberg/Círculo de Lectores.

Ihde, D. 2000. Epistemology Engines. *Nature* 406: 21.

Irwin, A. 2006. 'The Politics of Talk: Coming to Terms with the 'New' Scientific Governance'. *Social Studies of Science* 36: 299–320.

Irwin, A. and M. Michael. 2003. *Science, Social Theory and Public Knowledge*. Maidenhead and Philadelphia: Open University Press.

Iversen, M. 2005. 'The Discourse of Perspective in the Twentieth Century: Panofsky, Damisch, Lacan'. *Oxford Art Journal* 28: 191–202.

Jackson, B. 2005. 'The Conceptual History of Social Justice'. *Political Studies Review* 3: 356–373.

Jacoby, R. 2005. *Picture Imperfect: Utopian Thought for an Anti-Utopian Age*. New York: Columbia University Press.

Jay, M. 1988. 'Scopic Regimes of Modernity', in *Vision and Visuality*, edited by H. Foster, pp. 3–23. Seattle: Bay Press.

Jones, C. 1996. 'The Great Chain of Buying: Medical Advertisement, the Bourgeois Public Sphere, and the Origins of the French Revolution'. *American Historical Review* 101: 13–40.

Kadir, D. 1986. *Questing Fictions: Latin America's Family Romance*. Minneapolis: University of Minnesota Press.

Kantorowicz, E.H. 1997 [1957]. *The King's Two Bodies: A Study in Mediaeval Political Theology*. Princeton, NJ: Princeton University Press.

Kaul, I. (ed.). 2003. *Providing Global Public Goods: Managing Globalization.* New York: Oxford University Press. Oxford Scholarship Online. http://dx.doi.org/10.1093/0195157400.001.0001.

Kaul, I., I. Grunberg and M. Stern (eds). 1999. *Global Public Goods: International Co-operation in the 21st Century.* New York: Oxford University Press. Oxford Scholarship Online. http://dx.doi.org/10.1093/0195130529.001.0001.

Kaul, I. and R.U. Mendoza. 2003. 'Advancing the Concept of Public Goods', in *Providing Global Public Goods: Managing Globalization,* edited by I. Kaul, pp. 78–110. New York: Oxford University Press. Oxford Scholarship Online. http://dx.doi.org/10.1093/0195157400.001.0001.

Kaup, M. 2005. 'Becoming-Baroque: Folding European Forms into New World Baroque with Alejo Carpentier'. *The New Centennial Review* 5: 107–149.

———. 2006. 'Neobaroque: Latin America's Alternative Modernity'. *Comparative Literature* 58: 128–152.

Kelty, C.M. 2008. *Two Bits: The Cultural Significance of Free Software.* Durham, NC, and London: Duke University Press.

Kemp, M. 1990. *The Science of Art: Optical Themes in Western Art from Brunelleschi to Seurat.* New Haven, CT, and London: Yale University Press.

Kitcher, P. 2001. *Science, Truth, and Democracy.* New York: Oxford University Press.

Knorr-Cetina, K. 1999. *Epistemic Cultures: How the Sciences Make Knowledge.* Cambridge, MA: Harvard University Press.

Knorr-Cetina, K. and A. Preda. 2001. 'The Epistemization of Economic Transactions'. *Current Sociology* 49: 27–44.

Konrad, M. 2003. 'From Secrets of Life to the Life of Secrets: Tracing Genetic Knowledge as Genealogical Ethics in Biomedical Britain'. *Journal of the Royal Anthropological Institute* 9: 339–358.

Kwa, C. 2002. 'Romantic and Baroque Conceptions of Complex Wholes in the Sciences', in *Complexities: Social Studies of Knowledge Practices,* edited by J. Law and A. Mol, pp. 23–52. Durham, NC, and London: Duke University Press.

Lacan, J. 1979. *The Four Fundamental Concepts of Psycho-Analysis.* Hardmondsworth: Penguin.

Lambert, G. 2008. *On the (New) Baroque.* Aurora, CO: The Davis Group.

Lash, S. 1994. 'Reflexivity and Its Doubles: Structure, Aesthetics, and Community', in *Reflexive Modernization: Politics, Tradition and Aesthetics in the Modern Social Order,* pp. 110–173. Stanford, CA: Stanford University Press.

Latour, B. 1983. 'Give Me a Laboratory and I Will Raise the World', in *Science Observed,* edited by K. Knorr-Cetina and M. Mulkay, pp. 141–140. London: Sage.

———. 1993. *We Have Never Been Modern.* Harlow: Longman.

———. 2002. 'Gabriel Tarde and the End of the Social," in *The Social in Question: New Bearing in History and the Social Sciences,* edited by P. Joyce, pp. 117–133. London: Routledge.

———. 2005. *Reassembling the Social: An Introduction to Actor-Network-Theory.* Oxford: Oxford University Press.

Latour, B. and M. Callon. 1997. '"Thou Shall Not Calculate!" Or How to Symmetricalize Gift and Capital' (Translated into English by Javier Krauel and available online at http://www.bruno-latour.fr/poparticles/poparticle/p071-en.html). *Revue du MAUSS* 9: 45–70.

Law, J. 1999. 'After ANT: Complexity, Naming and Topology', in *Actor Network Theory and After,* edited by J. Law and J. Hassard, pp. 1–14. Oxford: Blackwell Publishers/The Sociological Review.

Law, J. and A. Mol. (eds). 2002. *Complexities: Social Studies of Knowledge Practices.* Durham, NC, and London: Duke University Press.

Lazzarato, M. 1996. 'Immaterial Labor', in *Radical Thought in Italy: A Potential Politics,* edited by P. Virno and M. Hardt, pp. 133–147. Minneapolis: University of Minnesota Press.

———. 2002. *Puissances de l'invention: la psychologie économique de Gabriel Tarde contre l'économie politique.* Paris: Seuil.

———. 2004. 'From Capital-Labour to Capital-Life'. *ephemera* 4: 187–208.

Lazzarato, M. and T. Negri. 1991. 'Travail immaterial and subjectivité'. *Futur Antérieur* 6: 86–89.

Lefort, C. 2004a. 'La imagen del cuerpo y el totalitarismo', in *La incertidumbre democrática: ensayos sobre lo político,* pp. 241–257. Barcelona: Anthropos.

———. 2004b. 'Reversibilidad: libertad política y libertad individual', in *La incertidumbre democrática: ensayos sobre lo político,* pp. 107–129. Barcelona: Anthropos.

Leibniz, G.W. 1991. *Monadology.* Pittsburgh: University of Pittsburgh Press.

Lepinay, V.-A. 2007. 'Economy of the Germ: Capital, Accumulation and Vibration'. *Economy and Society* 36: 526–548.

Lessig, L. 1999. 'Code and the Commons'. Keynote Address at Media Convergence Conference, Fordham University Law School.

———. 2008. *Remix: Making Art and Commerce Thrive in the Hybrid Economy.* New York: The Penguin Press.

Linebaugh, P. 2010. 'All for One and One for All: Some Principles of the Commons', in *Counterpunch.* http://www.counterpunch.org/2010/01/08/some-principles-of-the-commons/

Lippmann, W. 1993 [1925]. *The Phantom Public.* New Brunswick: Transaction Publishers.

Macleod, R. 1997. 'Science and Democracy: Historical Reflections on Present Discontents'. *Minerva* 35: 369–384.

Malcolm, N. 2002. 'The Title-Page of Leviathan, Seen in a Curious Perspective', in *Aspects of Hobbes,* pp. 200–233. Oxford: Oxford University Press.

Mannheim, K. 1952. *Ideology and Utopia: An Introduction to the Sociology of Knowledge.* New York: Harcourt, Brace and Co.

Maranta, A., M. Guggenheim, P. Gisler and C. Pohl. 2003. 'The Reality of Experts and the Imagined Lay Persons'. *Acta Sociologica* 46: 150–165.

Maravall, J.A. 1986. *Culture of the Baroque: Analysis of a Historical Structure.* Minneapolis: University of Minnesota Press.

Marx, K. 2002 [1852]. 'The Eighteenth Brumaire of Louis Bonaparte', in *Marx's Eighteenth Brumaire: (Post)Modern Interpretations,* edited by M. Cowling and J. Martin, pp. 19–109. London: Pluto Press.

Maurer, B. 2005. *Mutual Life, Limited: Islamic Banking, Alternative Currencies, Lateral Reason.* Princeton, NJ, and Oxford: Princeton University Press.

Mauss, M. and H. Hubert. 1964. *Sacrifice: Its Nature and Function*. London: Cohen and West.

McSherry, C. 2001. *Who Owns Academic Work? Battling for Control Of Intellectual Property*. Cambridge, MA, and London: Harvard University Press.

Mirowski, P. 1989. *More Heat than Light: Economics as Social Physics, Physics as Nature's Economics*. New York: Cambridge University Press.

—————. 1998. 'Economics, Science, and Knowledge: Polanyi vs. Hayek'. *Tradition and Discovery: The Polanyi Society Periodical* 25: 29–42.

—————. 2004a. *The Effortless Economy of Science?* Durham, NC, and London: Duke University Press.

—————. 2004b. 'The Scientific Dimensions of Social Knowledge and Their Distant Echoes in 20th-Century Amercan Philosophy of Science'. *Studies in History and Philosophy of Science* 35: 283–326.

Miyazaki, H. 2004. *The Method of Hope: Anthropology, Philosophy, and Fijian Knowledge*. Stanford, CA: Stanford University Press.

Miyazaki, H. and A. Riles. 2005. 'Failure as an Endpoint', in *Global Assemblages: Technology, Politics, and Ethics as Anthropological Problems*, edited by A. Ong and S.J. Collier, pp. 320–331. Malden, MA, Oxford, and Carlton: Blackwell Publishing.

Mol, A. and J. Law. 2002. 'Complexities: An Introduction', in *Complexities: Social Studies of Knowledge Practices*, edited by J. Law and A. Mol, pp. 1–22. Durham, NC, and London: Duke University Press.

Moreiras, A. 2005. 'Mules and Snakes: On the Neo-Baroque Principle of De-Localization', in *Ideologies of Hispanism*, edited by M. Moraña, pp. 201–229. Nashville: Vanderbilt University Press.

—————. 2008. 'Notes on Primitive Imperial Accumulation. Ginés de Sepúlveda, Las Casas, Fernández de Oviedo', in *Revisiting the Colonial Question in Latin America*, edited by M. Moraña and C.A. Jáuregui, pp. 15–38. Madrid: Iberoamericana.

Musgrave, R.A. 1985. 'A Brief History of Fiscal Doctrine', in *Handbook of Public Economics: Volume I*, vol. 4, edited by A.J. Auerbach and M. Feldstein, pp. 1–59. Amsterdam: North-Holland.

Nagel, T. 2005. 'The Problem of Global Justice'. *Philosophy and Public Affairs* 33: 113–147.

Ndalianis, A. 2004. *(Neo)Baroque Aesthetics and Contemporary Entertainment*. Cambridge, MA: MIT Press.

Netz, R. 2004. *The Transformation of Mathematics in the Early Mediterranean World: From Problems to Equations*. Cambridge: Cambridge University Press.

Nowotny, H. 2007. 'Introduction: The Quest for Innovation and Cultures of Technology', in *Cultures of Technology and the Quest for Innovation*, vol. 9, edited by H. Nowotny, pp. 1–23. Oxford: Berghahn.

Nowotny, H., D. Pestre, E. Schmidt-Assmann, H. Schulze-Fielitz and H.-H. Trute. 2005. *The Public Nature of Science under Assault: Politics, Markets, Science and the Law*. Berlin: Springer.

Nowotny, H., P. Scott and M. Gibbons. 2001. *Rethinking Science: Knowledge and the Public in an Age of Uncertainty*. Cambridge: Polity Press.

Nussbaum, M.C. 2006. *Frontiers of Justice: Disability, Nationality, Species Membership. The Tanner Lectures on Human Values.* Cambridge, MA: The Belknap Press of Harvard University Press.

O'Brien, D.P. 1975. *The Classical Economists.* Oxford: Clarendon Press.

O'Neill, O. 2002a. *Autonomy and Trust in Bioethics. The Gifford Lectures, University of Edinburgh 2001.* Cambridge: Cambridge University Press.

———. 2002b. *A Question of Trust. The BBC Reith Lectures 2002.* Cambridge: Cambridge University Press.

Ordine, N. 2008 [2003]. *El umbral de la sombra: literatura, filosofía y pintura en Giordano Bruno* [Spanish translation of *La soglia dell'ombra. Letteratura, filosofia e pittura in Giordano Bruno*]. Madrid: Ediciones Siruela.

Ortega y Gasset, J. 1992 [1958]. *La idea de principio en Leibniz.* Madrid: Revista de Occidente en Alianza Editorial.

———. 1996 [1956]. *En torno a Galileo.* Madrid: Espasa Calpe.

Osborne, T. 2004. 'On Mediators: Intellectuals and the Ideas Trade in the Knowledge Society'. *Economy and Society* 33: 430–447.

Ostrom, E. 1990. *Governing the Commons: The Evolution of Institutions for Collective Action.* New York: Cambridge University Press.

Ostrom, V. and E. Ostrom. 1977. 'Public Goods and Public Choices', in *Alternatives for Delivering Public Services: Toward Improved Performance,* edited by E.S. Savas, pp. 7–49. Boulder, CO: Westview Press.

Panofsky, E. 1993 [1927]. *Perspective as Symbolic Form.* Cambridge, MA: MIT Press.

Patey, D.L. 1991. 'Swift's Satire on "Science" and the Structure of Gulliver's Travels'. *ELH* 58: 809–839.

Picker, R.C. 2009. 'The Google Book Search Settlement: A New Orphans-Work Monopoly?' *John M. Olin Law and Economics Working Papers Series* 462.

Plato. 1977. *Gorgias.* Heinemann: Loeb Classical Library.

Polanyi, M. 1962. 'The Republic of Science: Its Political and Economic Theory'. *Minerva* 1: 54–73.

Popper, K. 1945. *The Open Society and Its Enemies.* New York: Harper and Row.

———. 1960. *The Poverty of Historicism.* New York: Basic Books.

Povinelli, E.A. 2001. 'Radical Worlds: The Anthropology of Incommensurability and Inconceivability'. *Annual Review of Anthropology* 30: 319–334.

Pratt, M.L. 1994. 'Transculturation and Autoethnography: Peru 1615/1980', in *Colonial Discourse / Postcolonial Theory,* edited by F. Barker, P. Hulme and M. Iversen, pp. 24–46. Manchester: Manchester University Press.

Quattrone, P. 2004. 'Accounting for God: Accounting and Accountability Practices in the Society of Jesus (Italy, XVI–XVII Centuries)'. *Accounting, Organizations and Society* 29: 647–683.

Rancière, J. 2009. *Hatred of Democracy.* London: Verso.

Rheinberger, H.-J. 1997. *Toward a History of Epistemic Things: Synthezing Proteins in the Test Tube.* Stanford, CA: Stanford University Press.

Riles, A. 2001. *The Network Inside Out.* Ann Arbor: University of Michigan Press.

Rowland, I.D. 2008. *Giordano Bruno: Philosopher/Heretic.* Chicago and London: University of Chicago Press.

Sahlins, M. 2008. 'The Stranger-King or, the Elementary Forms of the Politics of Life'. *Indonesia and the Malay World* 36: 177–199.

Saiber, A. 2005. *Giordano Bruno and the Geometry of Language*. Aldershot and Burlington, VT: Ashgate.

Samuelson, P. 1954. 'The Pure Theory of Public Expenditure'. *Review of Economics and Statistics* 36: 387–389.

Schaffer, S. 1991. The Eighteenth Brumaire of Bruno Latour. *Studies in History and Philosophy of Science* 22: 174–192.

———. 1994. Babbage's Intelligence: Calculating Engines and the Factory System. *Critical Inquiry* 21: 203–227.

———. 2005. 'Seeing Double: How To Make Up a Phantom Body Politic', in *Making Things Public: Atmospheres of Democracy,* edited by B. Latour and P. Weibel, pp. 196–202. Boston, MA: MIT Press.

Scheler, M. 1935 [1926]. *Sociología del saber* [Spanish translation of *Probleme einer Soziologie des Wissens*]. Madrid: Revista de Occidente.

Schmitt, C. 2005 [1922]. *Political Theology: Four Chapters on the Concept Of Sovereignty.* Chicago and London: University of Chicago Press.

Scott, M.W. 2007. *The Severed Snake: Matrilineages, Making Place, and a Melanesian Christianity in Southeast Solomon Islands.* Durham, NC: Carolina Academic Press.

Scott, P. 2005. 'Universities and the Knowledge Economy'. *Minerva* 43: 297–309.

Sen. A. 1999a. 'Global Justice' in *Global Public Goods: International Cooperation in the 21st Century,* edited by I. Kaul, I. Grunberg and M. Stern, pp. 116–126. New York: Oxford University Press. Oxford Scholarship Online. http://dx.doi.org/10.1093/0195130529.001.0001.

———. 1999b. 'The Possibility of Social Choice.' *American Economic Review* 89, 349-378.

Sennett, R. 2008. *The Craftsman.* London: Penguin Books.

Serres, M. 1982. 'Mathematics and Philosophy: What Thales Saw...' in *Hermes: Literature, Science, Philosophy,* edited by J.V. Harari and D.F. Bell, pp. 84–97. Baltimore, MD: John Hopkins University Press.

———. 1989. *Detachment.* Athens: Ohio University Press.

———. 1995. 'Gnomon: The Beginning of Geometry in Greece', in *A History of Scientific Thought: Elements of a History of Science,* edited by M. Serres, pp. 73–123. Oxford: Blackwell.

Shirky, C. 2008. 'Gin, Television, and Cognitive Surplus: A Talk by Clay Shirky', in *The Edge,* http://www.edge.org/3rd_culture/shirky08/shirky08_index.html

Slaughter, S. and G. Rhoades. 2004. *Academic Capitalism and the New Economy: Markets, State, and Higher Education.* Baltimore, MD, and London: The John Hopkins University Press.

Sloterdijk, P. 2006. *Esferas III: espuma. Biblioteca de ensayo.* Madrid: Ediciones Siruela.

———. 2007 [2005]. *En el mundo interior del capital: para una teoría filosófica de la globalización* [Spanish translation of *Im Weltinnenraum des Kapitals. Für eine philosophische Theorie der Globalisierung*]. Madrid: Siruela.

Smith, P.H. 2004. *The Body of the Artisan: Art and Experience in the Scientific Revolution.* Chicago: University of Chicago Press.

Stehr, N. 2003. 'The Social and Political Control of Knowledge in Modern Societies'. *International Social Science Journal* 55: 643–655.

Stengers, I. 2005. 'The Cosmopolitical Proposal', in *Making Things Public: Atmospheres of Democracy*, edited by B. Latour and P. Weibel, pp. 994–1003. Cambridge, MA, and London: MIT Press.

Stiglitz, J.E. 1999. 'Knowledge as a Global Public Good', in *Global Public Goods: International Cooperation in the 21st Century*, edited by I. Kaul, I. Grunberg and M. Stern, pp. 308–324. New York: Oxford University Press. Oxford Scholarship Online. http://dx.doi.org/10.1093/0195130529.001.0001.

Strathern, M. 1988. *The Gender of the Gift: Problems with Women and Problems with Society in Melanesia*, vol. 6: *Studies in Melanesian Anthropology*. Berkeley and London: University of California Press.

———. 1990. 'Negative Strategies in Melanesia', in *Localizing Strategies: Regional Traditions of Ethnographic Writing*, edited by R. Fardon, pp. 204–216. Edinburgh: Scottish Academic Press.

———. 1992. *After Nature: English Kinship in the Late Twentieth Century. Lewis Henry Morgan Lectures, 1989*. Cambridge: Cambridge University Press.

———. 1995a. 'Afterword: Relocations', in *Shifting Contexts: Transformations in Anthropological Knowledge*, edited by M. Strathern, pp. 177–185. London and New York: Routledge.

———. 1995b. 'Foreword: Shifting Contexts', in *Shifting Contexts: Transformations in Anthropological Knowledge*, edited by M. Strathern, pp. 1–11. London and New York: Routledge.

———. 1996. 'Cutting the Network'. *Journal of the Royal Anthropological Institute* 2: 517–535.

———. 2002a. 'Externalities in Comparative Guise'. *Economy and Society* 31: 250–267.

———. 2002b. 'On Space and Depth', in *Complexities: Social Studies of Knowledge Practices*, edited by J. Law and A. Mol, pp. 88–115. Durham, NC, and London: Duke University Press.

———. 2004 [1991]. *Partial Connections*. Walnut Creek, CA: AltaMira Press.

———. 2005. 'Emergent Properties', in *Kinship, Law and the Unexpected: Relatives Are Always a Surprise*, pp. 50–78. New York: Cambridge University Press.

Sunder, M. 2007. 'The Invention of Traditional Knowledge'. *Law and Contemporary Problems* 70: 97–124.

Swift, J. 2002 [1726]. *Gulliver's Travels*. New York and London: W.W. Norton and Company.

Tarde, G. 2006. *Monadología y sociología* [Spanish translation of *Monadologie et sociologie*]. Buenos Aires: Editorial Cactus.

Taussig, M.T. 1992. *The Nervous System*. New York and London: Routledge.

Taycher, L. 2010. 'Books of the World, Stand Up and Be Counted! All 129,864,880 of You', vol. 2010: Google Books.

Thompson, E.P. 1971. 'The Moral Economy of the English Crowd in the Eighteenth Century'. *Past and Present* 50: 76–136.

Thompson, G. 2004. Getting to Know the Knowledge Economy: ICTs, Networks and Governance. *Economy and Society* 33: 562–581.

Thrift, N. 2005. *Knowing Capitalism*. London: Sage.

———. 2006. 'Re-inventing Invention: New Tendencies in Capitalist Commodification'. *Economy and Society* 35: 279–306.

———. 2008. *Non-representational Theory: Space, Politics, Affect*. London and New York: Routledge.

———. 2012. 'The Insubstantial Pageant: Producing an Untoward Land'. *Cultural Geographies* 19: 141–168.

Toews, D. 2003. 'The New Tarde: Sociology after the End of the Social'. *Theory, Culture and Society* 20: 81–98.

Toobin, J. 2007. 'Google's Moon Shot', *The New Yorker*, http://www.newyorker.com/reporting/2007/02/05/070205fa_fact_toobin

Topper, D. 2000. 'On Anamorphosis: Setting Some Things Straight'. *Leonardo* 33: 115–124.

Trattner, W.I. 1988. 'The Federal Government and Needy Citizens in Nineteenth-Century America'. *Political Science Quarterly* 103: 347–356.

———. 1998. *From Poor Law to Welfare State: A History of Social Welfare in America*. New York: Free Press.

Turnbull, D. 2000. *Masons, Tricksters and Cartographers: Comparative Studies in the Sociology of Scientific and Indigenous Knowledge*. London and New York: Routledge.

Turner, B.S. 1994. 'Introduction', in *Baroque Reason: The Aesthetics of Modernity*, pp. 1–36. London, Thousand Oaks, CA, and Delhi: Sage.

Turner, C. 2003. 'Mannheim's Utopia Today'. *History of the Human Sciences* 16: 27–47.

Turner, F. 2006. *From Counterculture to Cyberculture: Stewart Brand, the Whole Earth Network, and the Rise of Digital Utopianism*. Chicago: University of Chicago Press.

Ulin, R.C. 2002. 'Work as Culture Production: Labour and Self-Identity among Southwest French Wine-Growers'. *Journal of the Royal Anthropological Institute* (N.S.) 8: 691–712.

Vaidhyanathan, S. 2011. *The Googlization of Everything (and Why We Should Worry)*. Berkeley and Los Angeles: University of California Press.

Virno, P. 2004. *A Grammar of the Multitude*. Los Angeles: Semiotext(e).

Viveiros de Castro, E. 1992.

———. 2002. *A inconstância da alma selvagem, e outros ensaios de antropologia*. São Paulo: Cosac Naify.

———. 2003. *And. Manchester Papers in Social Anthropology*, vol. 7. Manchester: Department of Social Anthropology, University of Manchester.

———. 2010. *Metafísicas caníbales. Líneas de antropología postestructural* [Spanish translation of *Métaphysiques cannibales. Lignes d'anthropologie post-structurale*]. Buenos Aires and Madrid: Katz Editores.

Wagner, R. 2001. *An Anthropology of the Subject: Holographic Worldview in New Guinea and its Meaning and Significance for the World of Anthropology*. Berkeley and Los Angeles: University of California Press.

Warner, M. 2005. *Publics and Counterpublics*. London: Zone Books.

Weiner, A.B. 1992. *Inalienable Possessions: The Paradox of Keeping-While-Giving*. Berkeley: University of California Press.

Weiner, J.F. 1995. *The Lost Drum: The Myth of Sexuality in Papua New Guinea and Beyond.* Madison: University of Wisconsin Press.

Willerslev, R. 2007. *Soul Hunters: Hunting, Animism, and Personhood among the Siberian Yukaghirs.* Berkeley and Los Angeles: University of California Press.

Williams, R.H. 1995. 'Constructing the Public Good: Social Movements and Cultural Resources'. *Social Problems* 42: 124–144.

Wilsdon, J., B. Wynne and J. Stilgoe. 2005. *The Public Value of Science: Or How to Ensure That Science Really Matters.* London: Demos.

Wolin, S.S. 2000. 'Political Theory: From Vocation to Invocation', in *Vocations of Political Theory,* edited by J.A. Frank and J. Tamborino, pp. 3–22. Minneapolis: University of Minnesota Press.

Yaneva, A. 2005. 'Scaling Up and Down: Extraction Trials in Architectural Design'. *Social Studies of Science* 35: 867–894.

Yates, F. 2002 [1964]. *Giordano Bruno and the Hermetic Tradition.* Routledge Classics. London and New York: Routledge.

Zamora, L.P. 2009. 'New World Baroque, Neobaroque, Brut Barroco: Latin American Postcolonialisms'. *PMLA* 124: 127–142.

Zamora, L.P. and M. Kaup. 2010. *Baroque New Worlds: Representation, Transculturation, Counterconquest.* Durham, NC: Duke University Press.

Žižek, S. 2006. *The Parallax View.* Cambridge, MA, and London: MIT Press.

INDEX